Hadrian's Wall

Hadrian's Wall

Exploring its Past to Protect its Future

Edited By

Marta Alberti and Katie Mountain

ARCHAEOPRESS ROMAN ARCHAEOLOGY 90

Archaeopress Publishing Ltd
Summertown Pavilion
18-24 Middle Way
Summertown
Oxford OX2 7LG

www.archaeopress.com

ISBN 978-1-80327-274-0
ISBN 978-1-80327-275-7 (e-Pdf)

Cover: © Mark Richards

This book is available direct from Archaeopress or from our website www.archaeopress.com

Contents

List of Figures and Tables

Chapter 5: From academic research to delivery: translating knowledge to deliver accessible and captivating programmes

Chapter 6: The role of collections management in the future of the World Heritage Site

Chapter 7: The many faces of the Wall: interpretation strategies, challenges and innovation on a multifaceted monument

Chapter 8: Ruffenhofen, Bavaria: a new way of visualising and presenting a World Heritage Site

Chapter 13: The next 1900 years: a future for Hadrian's Wall World Heritage Site management

Chapter 14: The future of cultural resource management on the Frontiers of the Roman Empire World Heritage property

Closing image

Preface

Marta Alberti and Katie Mountain

This volume originated from the desire, shared by archaeologists, curators and heritage managers, to mark the 1900th anniversary of Hadrian's visit to his visionary project: Hadrian's Wall.

Much ink has been committed to the page regarding this incredible World Heritage Site and what it means to the many people who have an interest in it. You, the curious reader, are spoilt for choice: there are innumerable academic papers focusing on a particular aspect of the Wall's archaeology, comprehensive volumes on its management, excavation reports, and even fiction set on the Wall.

So why choose this book? In the following pages, you will find a candid discussion of the present of Hadrian's Wall, warts and all: a mirror held to what the Wall is now, rather than what it should be. There will be archaeology, and the ways new challenges, methods and technologies such as 3D scanning and modelling interact with it. There will be objects and collections: they have not yet been formally recognised as part of the World Heritage Site, but fascinate thousands every year. There will be talk of the digital world and how it merges with the physical – from gaming to online learning. Difficult and yet ever more relevant topics like sustainability and inclusivity will be discussed, as well as the place that this beloved national landmark holds in the international context. Contributors to this book operate daily on Hadrian's Wall: it is likely that you, our reader, already know them, or would meet them on a visit to one of the sites. If, by the end of this volume, you feel included in the world of Hadrian's Wall, and entitled to form an opinion on the way it is cared for, interpreted, displayed and experienced, then we have succeeded.

MARC FITCH FUND

It is only by looking at the present (and in the case of the Wall, the past) directly in the face that we can form an opinion and plan our actions for the future. Archaeology and the Wall transcend today: just like this book, they will be here when we are gone. But how the next 1900 years will look for the World Heritage Site is, at least in part, down to all of us.

The editors would like to thank Professor David Breeze, archaeologist, Wall luminary and impressively productive author, as well as Dr. Andrew Birley, CEO and director of excavations of the Vindolanda Trust. This book was first born in their minds, and they offered it to us to raise and shape as a living creature. We would like to thank them for their trust.

With them, we thank our advisory board: Dr. Rob Collins, Professor Rebecca Jones and Dr. Matt Symonds. Together they formed an excellent advisory board, which is a term used to define a cheerleading team equipped with outstanding academic expertise.

Thanks are due to our copyeditor, Amy Baker, and to Kathryn Murphy, who crafted our opening maps. Our gratitude goes also to all the contributors, who summarised years of work in 5000 words or less.

Finally, thanks are due to the following funding bodies: the Society of Antiquaries of Newcastle upon Tyne, the Cumberland and Westmorland Antiquarian and Archaeological Society, the Roman Research Trust and the Marc Fitch Fund.

ROMAN RESEARCH TRUST

SIGILLVM SOCIETATIS ANTIQVARIORVM PONTIS ÆLII MDCCCXIII

SCRIPTA MANENT

Foreword

Jane, Lady Gibson

'Having completely transformed the soldiers, in royal fashion, he made for Britain, where he set many things right and – he was the first to do so – erected a Wall along a length of eighty miles, which was to separate the barbarians and Romans.'

Historia Augusta

Little did the anonymous writers of the *Historia Augusta* know that, 1900 years from Hadrian's visit to his monumental masterpiece, the communities who live along the Wall would be celebrating this anniversary with a year-long festival of music and food, plays and dance pieces, art in the landscape, the knitting of bunting and beards and the baking of Wall-shaped cakes. Such is the magnetic attraction of Hadrian's Wall and the power and significance of World Heritage values in this, the most sparsely populated region of England and the Scottish Borders.

We know so much about Hadrian and his 'insatiable curiosity' and I turn always to Anthony R. Birley's biography '*Hadrian – the Restless Emperor*' to find out snippets of information which fuel my imagination to fill in the gaps about what we don't know. We know Hadrian arrived in northern Britain in June or July, a very good time of the year to visit our Borderlands region, and that he supervised the building of his Wall, which one imagines he had envisioned whilst he was on the move, visiting his armies and his provinces. Noted as having a passion for architecture, I like to believe he had strong views about both the construction and the purpose of the frontier.

Had he, at this point, documented *exactly* what he had in mind, and had such documents survived, I muse on whether the Wall would hold the fascination it does today.

The purpose of this book, made special by its publication in this commemorative year, is to offer contributions to archaeological heritage management of the Wall, and to celebrate the people and the organisations who are still asking questions and presenting knowledge with undimmed passion.

Hadrian's Wall and the wider World Heritage Site offer an extraordinary range of experiences to a seemingly unlimited number of people worldwide. The Wall is a centre of excellence for the latest scientific research, it provides proof of the diversity of people living here two millennia ago, it is a living for countless visitor economy businesses, it inspires people to create music and art, digital experiences and even manga comics. It is a place to look at truly dark skies and it keeps us fit and sets us walking and cycling challenges. It provides endless volunteering opportunities and teaches the painstaking skills of archaeology, geology and visitor guiding. It fuels regeneration programmes and gives a boost to community transport schemes. It delights us with its power in the rural landscape and intrigues us with our quest for knowledge of where it lies beneath our urban streets. It places us on the continuum of human existence; indeed it gives us a starring role, and that pride is felt by all who serve on the Partnership Board.

Jane, Lady Gibson

Chair, Hadrian's Wall World Heritage Site Partnership Board

Foreword

Alessandro Balsamo

The cultural and natural heritage is among the priceless and irreplaceable assets, not only of each nation, but of humanity as a whole. The loss, through deterioration or disappearance, of any of these most prized assets constitutes an impoverishment of the heritage of all the peoples of the world. Parts of this heritage, because of their exceptional qualities, can be considered to be of "Outstanding Universal Value" and as such worthy of special protection against the dangers which increasingly threaten them.

If we substitute the words 'cultural and natural heritage' with 'Hadrian's Wall', it is clear how the underpinning notion of World Heritage in the 1972 Convention fits well for this site. The World Heritage Convention is not intended to ensure the protection of all sites of great interest, importance or value, but only a select list of the most outstanding of these from an international viewpoint. Hadrian's Wall is certainly one of these.

The Frontiers of the Roman Empire form one of the largest individual monuments ever conceived in the history of humanity and Hadrian's Wall is probably the most iconic segment of this gigantic undertaking. This says a lot about the importance of this site, which was planned and partially erected according to a uniform project of construction. Beyond its exceptional role as an engineering feat, over the centuries, the Roman imperial frontiers acquired a powerful symbolic character as a demarcation line, marking the cultural difference between the "classical" and "barbarian" worlds of antiquity, a cultural divide, which lingered on throughout the Middle Ages.

Indeed, the nature of this peculiar cultural asset, its significance in terms of cultural value and the approachability of its archaeological evidence by different typologies of users make the necessity of its sustainable management and protection crucial.

Our precious cultural and natural heritage is continuously under pressure because of its intrinsic fragility, therefore the need to handle different risk factors, having both environmental and anthropic causes, translates into the necessity of adequate management and protection. In addition, the great significance of cultural heritage in terms of social, cultural, and economic value further amplifies this necessity.

Ever since it was adopted in 1972, the World Heritage Convention has continued evolving and the World Heritage List has become a leading reference worldwide of the most extraordinary sites on the planet. As the reach of the Convention has expanded, so has the need for high quality standards for the protection and management of World Heritage sites.

The Convention highlights the "importance, for all the peoples of the world, of safeguarding this unique and irreplaceable property, to whatever people it may belong." An inscription on the World Heritage List therefore must provide the protection of heritage of "outstanding universal value" against the dangers which increasingly threaten while facilitating its passing on to future generations.

But the same reasons for which sites are inscribed on the World Heritage List are also the reasons that naturally attract masses of tourists to visit them, year after year. The notion on which the World Heritage Convention is based, notably that sites belong to everyone and should be preserved for future generations, is quite challenging in itself, thus, the only way to ensure the safekeeping of our world's natural and cultural heritage is to set up a framework of provisions that may ensure that the site is preserved over time. The necessity is to establish a plan which, drawing from the definition of the Outstanding Universal Value of the site, protects it by applying legal, administrative, financial and professional conservation methods and tools and prescribing strategies and specific actions. In this domain, the English long-established tradition for conservation of heritage and their ability to produce effective management plans is recognised worldwide. The renewed provisions concerning the management of Hadrian's Wall are a good testimony to this ability.

1900 years after Emperor Hadrian's decision to erect a wall barring the Britannic peninsula along a distance of 118 kilometers, we welcome the improvements in the management of this outstanding site that this new text is introducing. And, as genuine supporters of heritage conservation, we all wish a successful management for this outstanding site, which may conserve it, as Hadrian would have said it, *in saecula saeculorum*.

Alessandro Balsamo

Head of the Nominations Unit
World Heritage Centre
UNESCO

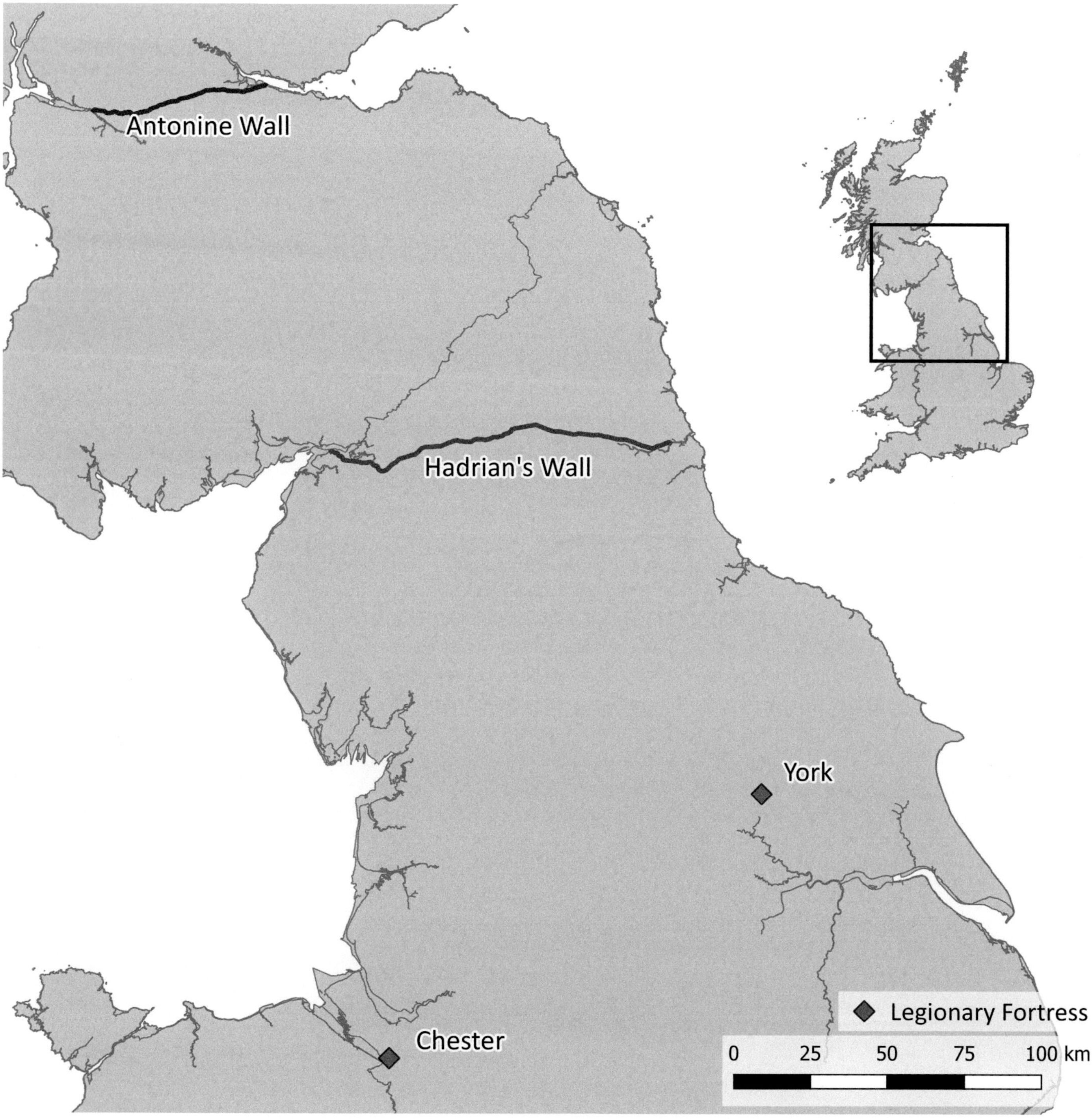

Map 1: A map showing the position of Hadrian's Wall, the Antonine Wall, and the legionary fortresses of York and Chester. Map by Kathryn Murphy.

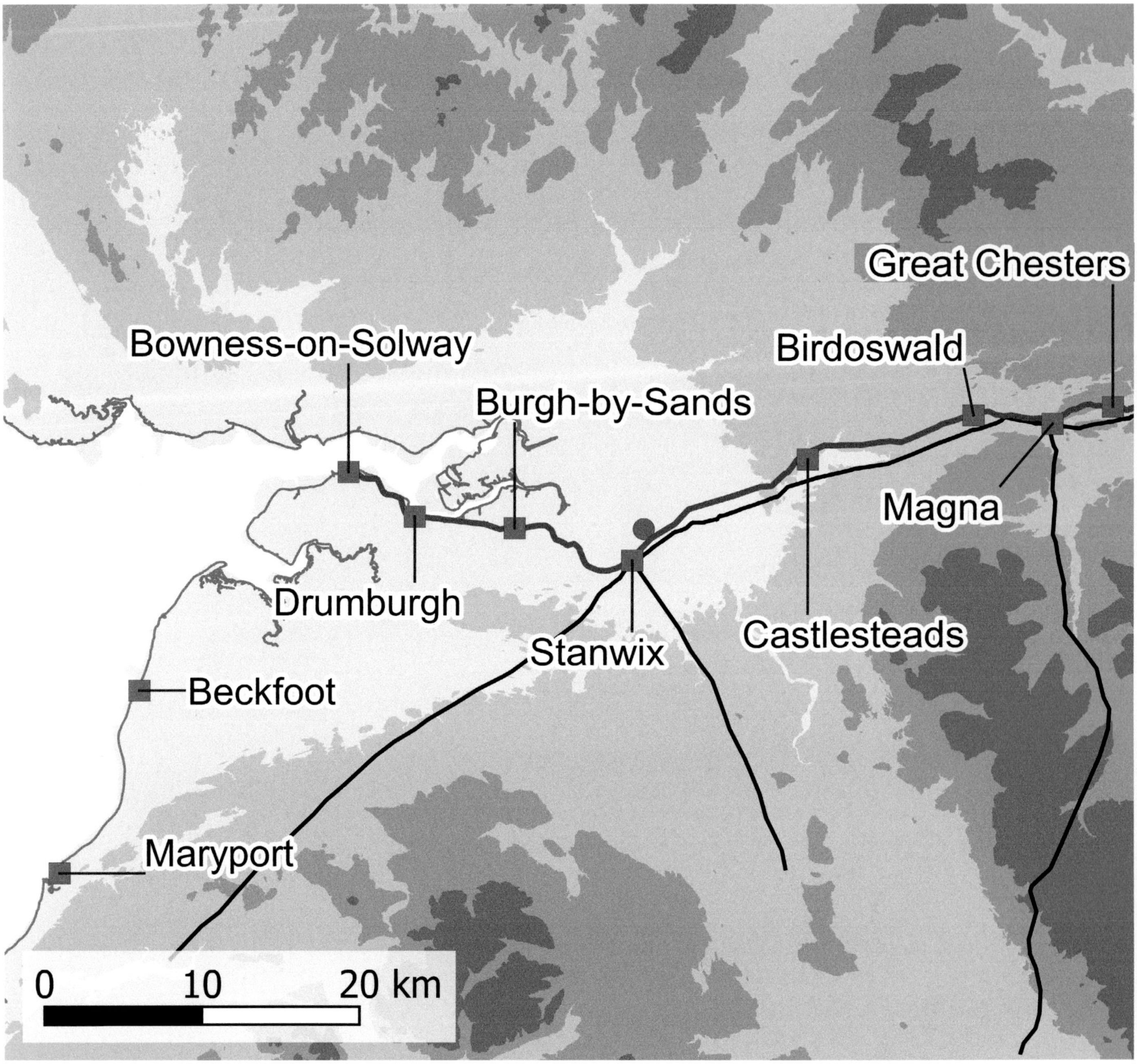

Map 2: A map showing the position of all Hadrian's Wall forts and sites mentioned in this volume. Map by Kathryn Murphy

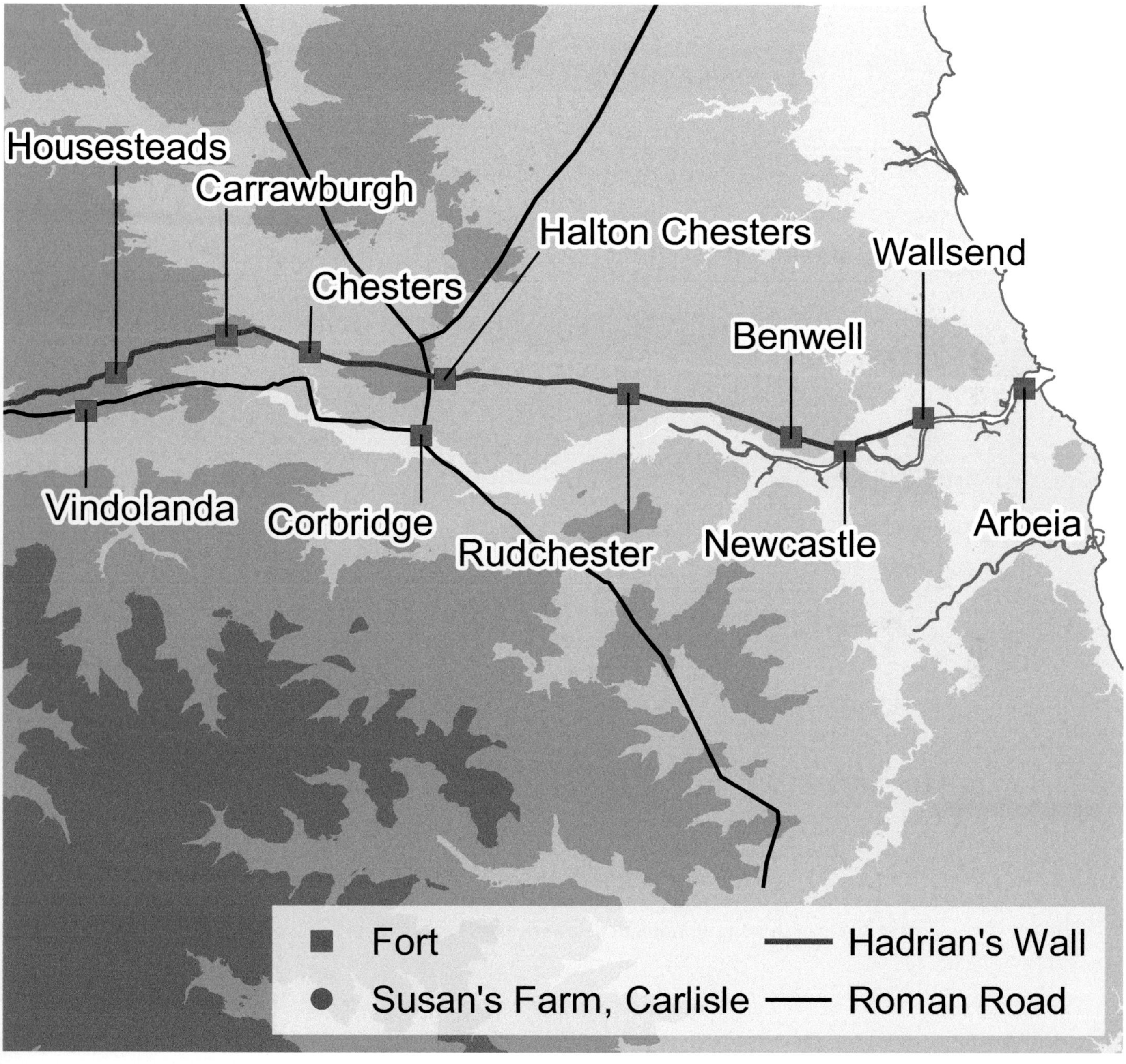

Housesteads
Carrawburgh
Chesters
Halton Chesters
Wallsend
Benwell
Vindolanda
Corbridge
Rudchester
Newcastle
Arbeia
Fort
Susan's Farm, Carlisle
Hadrian's Wall
Roman Road

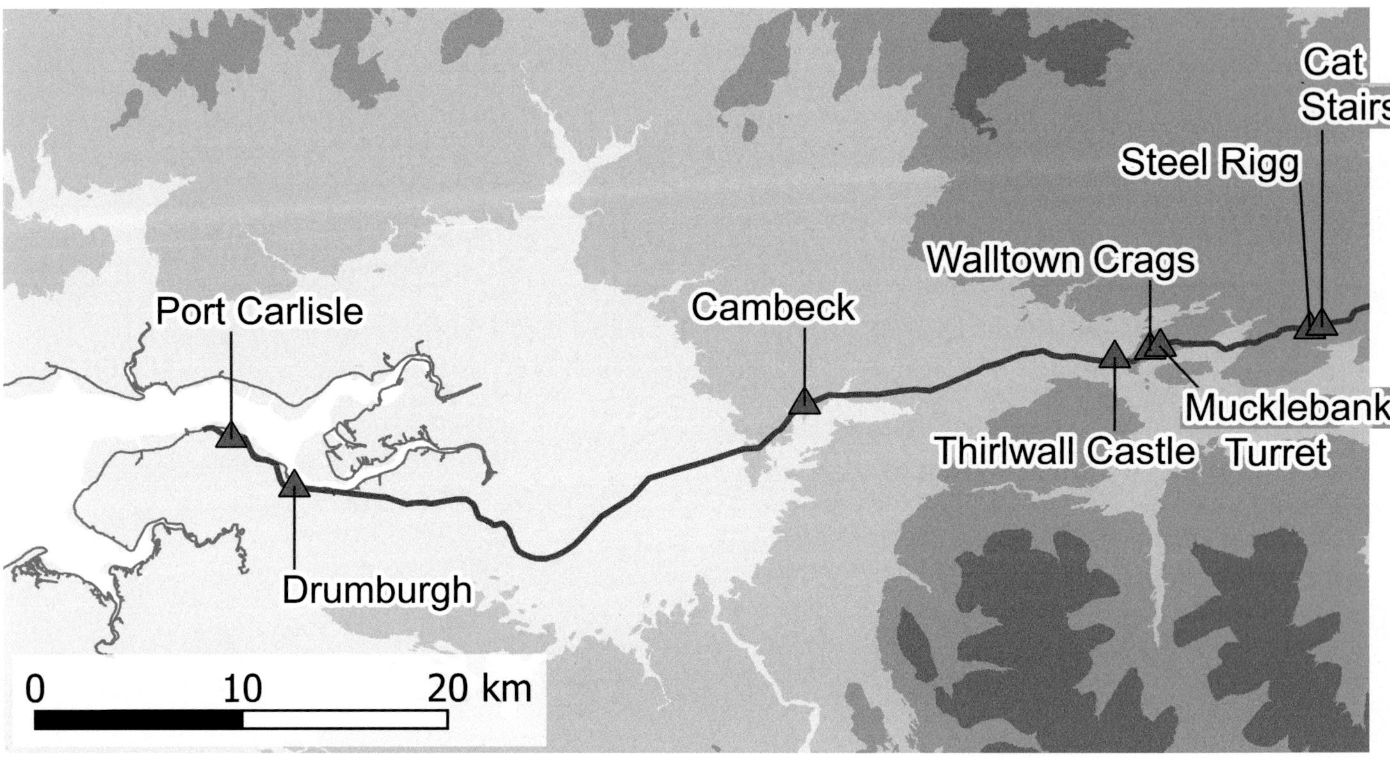

Map 3: A map showing all WallCAP fieldwork sites. Map by Kathryn Murphy

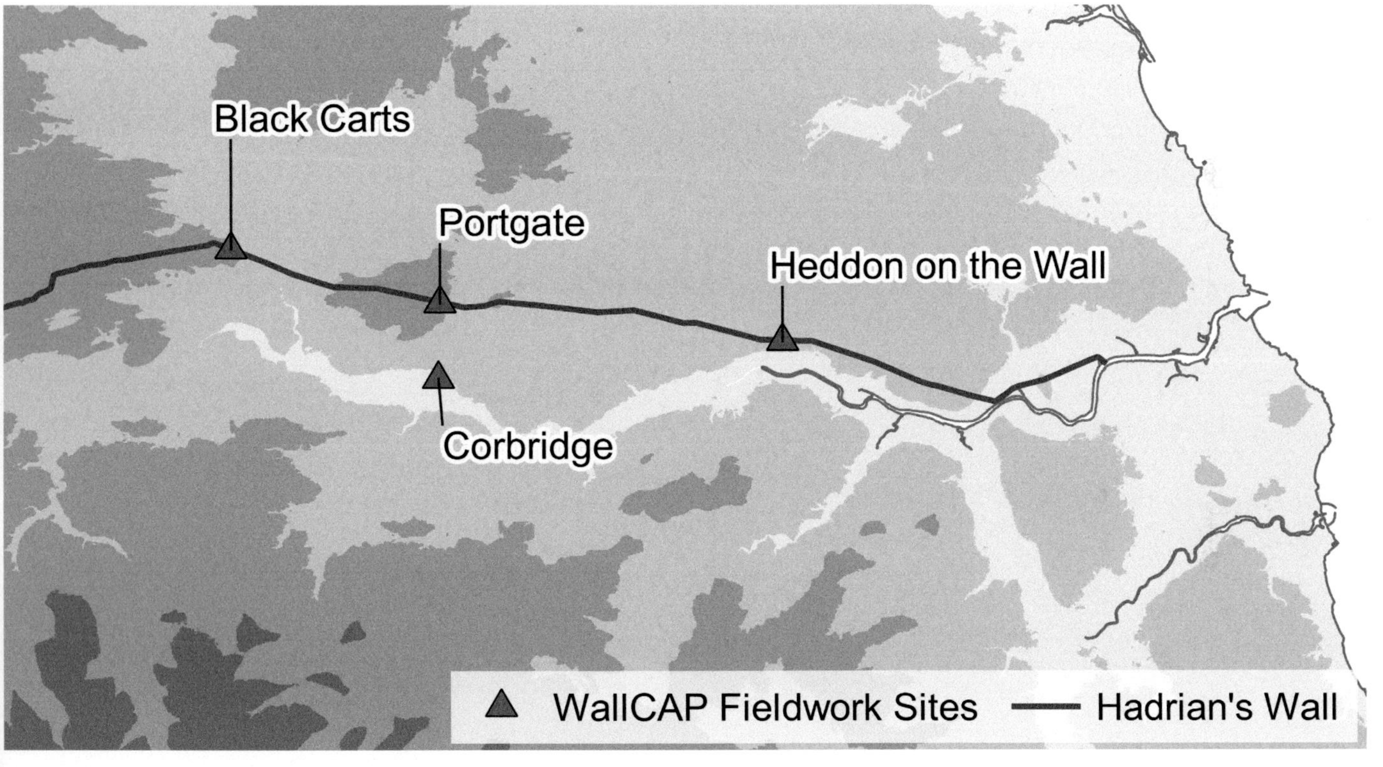
Black Carts
Portgate
Heddon on the Wall
Corbridge
WallCAP Fieldwork Sites
Hadrian's Wall

Hadrian's Wall: an archaeological resource

David J. Breeze

Hadrian's Wall is a complex monument. It is composed of many tangible archaeological remains; some are better understood, and known to the world, than others. It is also composed of intangible elements, such as the many meanings the Wall holds for the institutions who care for it, researchers who study it and people who live alongside it or visit it. But what is the Wall, really? How much do we know about it? Is what we know 'enough'? And is the Wall safe? This chapter explores some of the key questions at the foundation of ensuring the future of Hadrian's Wall.

What is Hadrian's Wall?

This may seem an absurd question, but it is an important one. If we stand back from the line of the Wall, we can see that it sits in an extensive Roman military landscape. To the north, outpost forts reached into the land beyond the Cheviots. To the south, it can be argued that the military landscape's limits were the legionary bases at York and Chester. This was a military zone up to 200km deep, a unique frontier within the Roman Empire, of which Hadrian's Wall was but a part. Even if we reduce our horizons to the area of the Wall, we still have a complex monument. Its primary elements might be considered the linear barrier, consisting of a stone (and turf) wall and ditch, with miscellaneous military installations along its line (towers, milecastles and forts) linked by a road and possibly a track, as well as a great earthwork known from the time of the Venerable Bede as the Vallum to the south (Figure 1).

In addition, there are forts and towers situated close to the south of the Wall, but beyond the Vallum, also linked by a road, the Stanegate. Many of these forts and towers were built before the Wall itself and some continued to be occupied after its abandonment. To the east, there is at least the fort at South Shields, and to the west a series of forts, fortlets and towers continuing down the Cumbrian coast for about 40km.

When defining what Hadrian's Wall is, we also need to consider the ancillary elements such as the civilian settlements, which range in size from individual farmsteads to towns. All these features are embraced by the World Heritage Site (WHS), although, believe it or not, it does not include them all. Another factor we must remember is that beyond the WHS is a much broader buffer zone: an area designated to protect the setting of the archaeological remains. However, to most visitors, the 'Wall' is the linear barrier from Wallsend to Bowness-on-Solway, defined today by the National Trail. Even here we have a discrepancy, for the Trail does not run along the Wall for nearly 20km at its eastern end.

After this discussion, we must now make a choice: what parts of Hadrian's Wall will we be referring to in this volume? The focus, as discussed by the many contributors to this project, will be on Hadrian's Wall as an 'archaeological resource': a combination of tangible and intangible elements connected by the shared thread of archaeology and history. The various chapters in the volume discuss recent and future work on the Wall's linear barrier and the Vallum, and their immediately

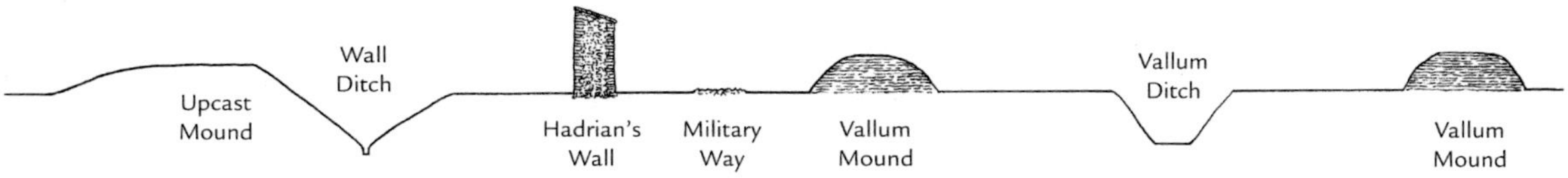

Figure 1: Illustration of components of the Wall and defensive structures. © Mark Richards

associated features (towers, fortlets and forts), together with the Cumbrian coastal installations as far as Maryport to the south-west, with South Shields to the east and the 'Stanegate' sites to the south of the linear barrier. This definition of the Wall's extent does not exactly align with either the WHS boundaries or the National Trail. However, it is meaningful to the archaeologists, curators and researchers, as well as the many audiences who come in contact with the Wall every day: tourists, archaeology enthusiasts, walkers and others.

Before archaeological excavation: inscriptions and literary accounts

We are fortunate on Hadrian's Wall in that several inscriptions survive that record its construction under Hadrian, an occurrence not replicated on every frontier. These record the building of different elements, milecastles and forts on the Wall line and coastal forts to the west. In addition, the Vindolanda writing tablets provide an unparalleled view of life on the northern frontier in the immediate pre-Wall decades.

While stone-carved inscriptions continue to record life on the frontier, literary sources are largely silent on the history of the Wall. We might, for example, be informed of trouble in Britain, but we are not told where it occurred. We are told that a wall is crossed or that a certain enemy lived close to the wall, without it being specified which one. It is stated that Rome's neighbours to the north were belligerent, without any reference to a frontier. Two references stand out. In one, an anonymous commentator, writing about 250 years after the event, stated that in Britain Hadrian was the first to build a wall, eighty miles long, to separate the barbarians and the Romans. This is a succinct statement providing a date, length and purpose. Even so, this statement is not without difficulties: the writer may have been unconsciously offering a view relating to his times rather than those of Hadrian. Other late Roman writers record that the Emperor Septimius Severus ordered the construction of the Wall around AD 200-210, but give its length as 132 or 133 miles. The existence of these late references, six in number, confused later British antiquarians and led them to believe that what we now know to have been Hadrian's Wall was actually built nearly 100 years later.

This is not the place to offer a detailed account of knowledge and understanding of Hadrian's Wall through the Middle Ages and beyond. Suffice to say, it was not lost sight of and was mentioned in written sources and recorded on maps. A leap forward should have taken place as a result of the Renaissance, when study of the Roman and Greek texts was revitalised, and the invention of the printing press made them more readily available. Some perceptive commentators, Polydore Vergil in Italy, Hector Boece in Scotland and Humphrey Lhuyd in Wales, understood what they read and realised that Hadrian's Wall was indeed built by the emperor of that name. However, English xenophobia coupled with a too-heavy reliance on the many late Roman statements that the Wall was built by Severus ensured that the view that this emperor ordered its construction prevailed for another 300 years. As a result, the Vallum was seen as Hadrian's frontier and the Wall called Severus' Wall.

As a deeper understanding of the nature of the remains grew in the 17th century, the attempts to interpret them became more convoluted. It was John Hodgson, in 1840, who finally unravelled the mystery through a careful analysis of the literary references and the inscriptions, and concluded that it was indeed Hadrian who had ordered the construction of 'Severus' Wall'. He also stated that the whole barrier between Wallsend and Bowness, consisting of the Wall and the Vallum with all the forts and towers along its line 'were planned and executed by Hadrian'. It took until the end of the century to persuade the unbelievers, but Hodgson's view was to prevail.

The evidence of archaeology

John Hodgson's pioneering analysis and conclusions coincided with the first excavations on Hadrian's Wall. Anthony Hedley excavated at Vindolanda while Hodgson turned his attention to Housesteads. In 1832, John Clayton, town clerk at Newcastle upon Tyne and powerful political and cultural protagonist of his time, inherited the estate of Chesters on Hadrian's Wall. A decade later he started his archaeological investigations, which continued sporadically along the Wall over the next 50 years. Much was learnt during this early exploration phase, but there was no coherent planning. The main aim was to get down to the 'primary levels' and show the structures as they were under Hadrian. In effect they were creating their own view of Hadrian's Wall. Nowadays, we would leave all the remains *in situ* in spite of their complexity, not least for explaining them to visitors. Unfortunately, past actions resulted in much post-Hadrianic material being thrown away.

This was to change in the 1890s. The new excavators planned their campaigns and did not casually dispose of the post-Hadrianic levels but recorded them and, as for example at Great Chesters, preserved them for later study. J.P. Gibson, later in partnership with F.G. Simpson, sought to understand the structures, while Francis Haverfield examined the earthworks, primarily the Vallum. This was the start of modern excavation. It led, over the next 40 years, to a basic understanding of the building sequence and the chronological history of Hadrian's Wall. Those then working on the Wall, and primarily Ian Richmond, declared that they had solved all of its problems, though of course what they meant was that they had solved the problems that interested them.

As so often is the case with archaeology, it was a new excavation that led to new thinking. In the case of Hadrian's Wall, the excavations of Michael Jarrett at Halton Chesters in the 1950s became the catalyst for change. Jarrett's discoveries did not accord neatly with the accepted history of Hadrian's Wall, which had held the field since the beginning of the century. Gradually, the evidence was re-examined and by the 1970s new interpretations were advanced.

Jarrett had been following a well-travelled path: the investigation of perceived problems in his predecessors' excavations. That approach was to change radically with the advent of rescue excavations – digging and exploration conducted ahead of building and development. In other words, rescue archaeology led to the excavation of many sites that were not on anyone's programme for research on Hadrian's Wall, but were instead excavated because they were threatened by new developments. Rescue excavations led to radical new discoveries, of which perhaps the most significant was the uncovering of pits on the berm of Hadrian's Wall. These were first recognised to the north of the civil settlement at Wallsend in 1991 and might be explained as relating to the defence of that site. However, further discoveries some kilometres to the west in 2000, and then 16km beyond them, forced a radical reappraisal, and a challenge to existing interpretations of the way Hadrian's Wall 'worked'. The argument now lay between those who believed that the existence of the pits (and their original contents, presumably stakes) reinforced the view that Hadrian's Wall was built for military defence, and bore a walkway along its top, and others who suggested that the discovery indicated that there was no wall-walk and therefore Hadrian's Wall was not defended as might be a Roman fort, or a medieval castle. More than any discussion of its implications, the discovery of the pits underlined the possibility that there might be other remains along the Wall which are as yet unknown, and that a potent challenge to our understanding of Hadrian's Wall is only one excavation away.

Rescue excavations, and the gaps in our archaeological forefathers' studies, are enough to show that there are many areas where our knowledge of the Wall and its functioning is woefully inadequate. Our understanding of the western sector of the Wall is very limited. Our appreciation of the later history of most sites is quite simply inadequate. Archaeologists, curators, researchers, visitors, interested parties: we all still find it difficult to determine the function of the Vallum. We argue about how Hadrian's Wall operated and the significance of its various elements. In conclusion, we are still on a steep learning curve when it comes to understanding how Hadrian's Wall was intended to operate within the physical, military, civilian and religious landscapes in which it sat, both when it was originally constructed and in later times.

Is Hadrian's Wall 'safe'?

Today, the archaeology of Hadrian's Wall is well-protected. Its remains, where unencumbered by modern developments, are scheduled as ancient monuments. Many kilometres and many elements are in state care or in the care or ownership of local authorities or trusts. The remains below modern developments are protected under the planning legislations, although, unlike on the Antonine Wall in Scotland, these remains are not part of the WHS. Also not part of the WHS are the artefacts and collections recovered from excavations on Hadrian's Wall and its buffer zone – but despite this, they are well cared for by the many museum authorities operating along the Wall.

International recognition of the importance of the monument is a further element in its protection. However, there will always be what might be regarded as occasional threats to the Wall. These include roads and the traffic they bear. Pipelines can be thrust bored below the archaeological remains. Climate change is also likely to affect them, not least through changes to the hydrology of the area, as discussed in Chapter 2 by Birley and O'Meara. Other challenges include over-visiting, managing responsible tourism and the upkeep of the National Trail, as discussed in Chapter 11 by McGlade, Pickles and Richards, and the dangers posed by metal-detecting.

Most threats to the Wall's 'safety' are related to organised human activities. For example, metal-detectorists often seek 'treasure' in the ground, unaware or unconcerned of the damage thereby created for the surrounding archaeological remains. Tourism is a major factor in the British economy, important to ensuring the economic well-being of the people living in the Wall zone and even, in certain cases, the sustainability of continued research. How do we strike a balance between 'using' and 'exploring' an archaeological resource, and protecting it for future generations? The National Trail is an encouragement for more people to visit the Wall and walk along it but can also be seen as a challenge to the walker (or runner) rather than an exploration of one of the most important Roman frontiers in the world. Along many kilometres of its length, the Trail runs on top of archaeological remains. Erosion by footfall, especially during wetter times of the year, has led in places to the replacement of worn grass by a gravel path- this may seem like a positive intervention, ensuring the safety of the visitor, but it may also be seen as affecting the archaeological levels and/or the look of the monument. All these factors do not just relate to the management of the monument, but are important for the archaeologists, and for you, the reader of this book, as every action has an effect on the archaeological resource, through which we can learn more about life on Hadrian's Wall.

Finally, an important part of an archaeological excavation is its publication: putting archaeological knowledge in writing, in a form that can be understood and discussed at a later date. Without publication, the field work is not fully known, indeed sometimes not known at all, and certainly not available for reconsideration and adaptation to new research. Hadrian's Wall has not always been well served by its excavators: too often finds have remained lurking in museum stores, and its records in archives, as highlighted by McIntosh and Price in Chapter 6. However, over the last 40 to 50 years there has been a concerted and mostly successful drive to publish all available material. Many of the excavation reports and the discussion papers relating to Hadrian's Wall are published in the journals of the two local archaeological societies, the Society of Antiquaries of Newcastle upon Tyne and the Cumberland and Westmorland Antiquarian and Archaeological Society. These societies, and others, have improved access to their published material through its digitisation and uploading online.

As a result of these initiatives, the vast archaeological archive that is Hadrian's Wall has been made more accessible to students and researchers, as well as archaeologists, developers and visitors. This database is now more available for the testing of existing theories as well as for the exploration of new areas of research such as the effects of colonialism on our interpretation of the Wall.

How much information is enough?

The modern era of archaeological excavation on the Wall only began 130 years ago, and archaeologists had to learn how to obtain the most information from the ground. At first, excavations were primitive by modern standards and too often the small size of the area examined led archaeologists to reach the wrong conclusions. That said, some excavations, such as the investigation of MC 48 (Poltross Burn) in 1909 by J.P. Gibson and F.G. Simpson, were exemplary and, in many ways, not surpassed for 60 years. Charles Daniels' near complete excavation of the fort at Wallsend demonstrated how much more could be learnt through large-scale area excavation about the history of the fort and the life of the soldiers within it. That said, only at Vindolanda have archaeologists investigated a fort in its wider setting through the exploration of the civilian community in the shadow of its walls.

Paul Bidwell has emphasised how little excavation has actually taken place on Hadrian's Wall in relation to the whole monument: less than 5% of the whole frontier has been explored. Excavation, however, is expensive because it is labour intensive. This problem has been somewhat ameliorated through modern scientific techniques, including aerial photography and geophysics, the latter discussed in Chapter 3 by Wilmott. Although some work was undertaken before 1939, it was in the late 1940s that aerial photographing techniques took off. Geophysics, from a base set in about 1970, has been able to 'see' under the grass and plot ditches, roads and buildings, but it cannot date them; only excavation will do that. In the last decade or so a new technique is LiDAR, which is short for 'laser imaging, detection, and ranging'. This will allow examination of the landscape under trees and reveal minor changes in the ground surface, but again only excavation can date these discoveries.

Excavation can, and increasingly does, go hand in hand with geophysics and surveying. For example, a detailed survey of Maryport by TimeScape Surveys yielded a plan of the civil settlement outside the fort, far more detailed than that provided by aerial survey. The geophysical survey was extended well beyond the limits of the settlement in order to ensure that our assumptions about its size were correct. This led to the unexpected discovery of a farmstead beyond its boundaries, just a few metres from the Roman urban community. Excavation of a single house and its yard in the civil settlement followed, providing unique information about the life of the soldiers' dependants. We can also learn about communities on the Wall in new ways, such as with isotope analysis, which can provide evidence of where these people – and their animals – originated. Through new technologies, we can come closer than ever before to the people who lived on Hadrian's Wall.

It is sometimes easy to forget that archaeology is an iterative process – it thrives on being done again, and again. New ideas have to be tested against existing knowledge and the sheer size of the Hadrian's Wall database allows that process to be carried out effectively. Furthermore, ideas don't just change on Hadrian's Wall, but also elsewhere. New thoughts and ideas from other fields, and other geographical locations, have to be measured against our collective knowledge of the Wall. The relationships between soldiers and civilians and whether women might live within forts is an example of an issue being discussed across the whole Roman Empire, as is the question of when and why civil settlements outside forts came to an end. The effect of the Roman military presence on the British countryside and its inhabitants also resonates beyond the Channel. Understanding the effectiveness of Hadrian's Wall as a frontier and how it operated in relation to other Roman frontiers relates to discussions about the nature of the Roman Empire. Such areas of discussion rise and fall in archaeological and historical debate and can be blown off course by new discoveries. In short, while the information we already have is certainly 'enough' to build theories and further our knowledge of life on the Wall, in concert with new theories and technologies, the decision to stop unearthing more information is more complex than it looks. What if, by not continuing to explore, we were missing crucial pieces of the puzzle?

The national and international importance of Hadrian's Wall

In 1987 Hadrian's Wall was the first Roman frontier to become a WHS. It was followed by the Upper German and Raetian frontier and the Antonine Wall in Scotland. Many other countries are actively preparing the nominations for their frontiers. The aim is to bring World Heritage status to all the frontiers of the Roman Empire. This would provide a tremendous boost to research across all Roman frontiers, including Hadrian's Wall, and therefore improved understanding of their history and operation. The long and detailed process of seeking to understand Hadrian's Wall, which has now been in progress for several centuries, ensures a key place for this 'first' WHS frontier in its wider context.

There are, of course, challenges in this international project. In some ways these mirror the challenges of working on Hadrian's Wall, not least the fragmentary nature of the management structure and its distance from the centres of power in the UK. Furthermore, World Heritage status is only awarded to monuments; museums are not yet embraced by the concept, despite containing the items which help us understand frontiers. These include the inscriptions which date the monument and inform us about actions performed on its various parts; the pottery and finds which help us understand life on the frontier, not least the relations between soldiers and civilians; and the closing days of frontier life. It would be good to have a more holistic approach to sites and museums, between installations in the field and artefacts in the museum. This is recognised by all archaeologists and cultural managers working on the Wall, and the great database which is Hadrian's Wall allows many of these aspirations to be achieved.

It is not enough, of course, to seek to understand Hadrian's Wall in our time. It has to be protected for future generations and interpreted for its visitors. At the same time, local communities and businesses whose lives and jobs rely on tourism deserve a more participatory and inclusive approach to managing the monument. The long history of protecting the Wall, ensuring the preservation of its archaeological remains and its setting, as well interpreting it from the middle of the 19th century onwards, means that modern cultural resource managers bring to any discussion not only their own considerable knowledge and experience, but also that of those who came before us. The importance of Hadrian's Wall today is indeed multifaceted and complex.

The challenges of managing and monitoring the archaeological deposits of the Wall, with case studies from Vindolanda and Carvoran (Magna)

Andrew R. Birley (Vindolanda Trust) and Don P. O'Meara (Historic England)

The Hadrian's Wall World Heritage Site and its associated buffer zone cross different, interlinked environments. These include areas exposed to coastal and river erosion, floodplains and wetland fringes, exposed rocky uplands, agricultural land, forestry, and changing urban and suburban areas. Though the Wall is present as an upstanding structure and earthworks, much of the significance of the remains lies buried within the landscape. This adds a layer of complexity that other World Heritage Sites do not face.

When it comes to revealing the buried remains of the World Heritage Site, over 50 years of archaeological investigations at the Roman site of Vindolanda have demonstrated the potential of research to continuously shed new light on our understanding of the past. By contrast, the nearby site of Magna, also managed by the Vindolanda Trust, has had very little archaeological investigation to date. Here, a different challenge emerges: qualitative observations of ground conditions have raised concerns for the long-term preservation of buried deposits there. This chapter looks at how environment and archaeology interact at the two sites, and how care for the former is key to the survival of the latter.

Managing Hadrian's Wall

The range of human and environmental impacts on Hadrian's Wall includes erosion and weathering, the maintenance of modern transport, energy, and communication infrastructures, effects from agriculture and forestry, and the management of visitor numbers to the sites and surrounding area. Crucially for heritage management, none of these impacts can be described as affecting Hadrian's Wall consistently along its length. The effects of weather and erosion are heavily contingent on aspect and local weather conditions. Coastal erosion and storm damage are more clearly an issue for the western sector, particularly along the Solway Coast. The impacts of frost and cold-wet winters are prominent issues within the central sector and affect the maintenance of both the upstanding remains, and the Hadrian's Wall Path. Visitor numbers are most intensive around some of the key sites within the central zone of the monument. Impacts from ploughing were at one time most prevalent in the eastern sector of the Wall. However, through many years of engagement, particularly through Country Stewardship Schemes, Historic England has encouraged many landowners to convert their farming practices to maintain areas of the monument as continuous grassland. Forestry impacts are of a very limited extent along the immediate footprint of the Wall route, though recent policies to encourage afforestation in the UK are already leading to the expansion of plantations in Northumberland, and may fundamentally change the current, largely open, landscape of the World Heritage Site (WHS) buffer zone in the coming decades.

An important consideration for the management of all aspects of Hadrian's Wall is that the significance of archaeological remains can change through time. Since the 19th century the intellectual boundaries of Hadrian's Wall have expanded, from being primarily concerned with the physical, tangible, infrastructure of the curtain wall, to a broader appreciation of landscapes, setting, and the preservation of buried archaeological deposits (Breeze 2019: 32-60; Leach and Whitworth 2011). The development of environmental archaeology and material science in the later 20th century has given new significance to remains that may previously have been disregarded (Huntley 2009: 108-118; Huntley 2013). This development is not fixed, and archaeological research into stable isotope analysis, biolipids, sedimentary microbiology and trace element analysis all offer new potential for researching archaeological remains that may previously have been neglected. As well as scientific advances, we should also consider that the definition and understanding of all heritage's significance is a constantly evolving philosophy (Historic England 2019).

At a more local and less philosophical level, continuing archaeological exploration at sites like Vindolanda has highlighted the complexities of managing archaeological sites with variations in preservation conditions, both horizontally and vertically and including interlinking environments of aerobic, anaerobic and waterlogged areas (Taylor *et al.* 2019). The management of such a complex archaeological site can learn from best practice and new techniques, but ultimately must be based on site-specific considerations, backed by both quantitative data as well as professional experience.

Vindolanda and the Vindolanda Trust

The site of Vindolanda lies in south-west Northumberland, centred on the map coordinates of NY 768663, and is individually classified as Scheduled Ancient Monument 1014820. Though this places it within the area of North East England (as defined by the International Territorial Level geocode), it is geographically almost equidistant between the Irish Sea and the North Sea coasts in the district of Tynedale. From the perspective of local government planning policies, the site lies just within the boundary of Northumberland National Park. Vindolanda is a part of the Hadrian's Wall WHS, but is not situated on the Wall itself. Rather, it was originally formed as one of a series of forts, part of the pre-Hadrianic system, known today as the Stanegate. It therefore predated the construction of the linear frontier boundary and remained inhabited after the Wall stopped being a formally occupied position in the early 5th century (Birley and Alberti 2021).

Since 1970, the site has been the location of a series of continuing research excavations administered by the Vindolanda Charitable Trust. The Trust has its own museums, conservation laboratories and full-time archaeological, curatorial, conservation and laboratory staff. Vindolanda annually receives around 100,000 visitors, which the Vindolanda Trust refers to as stakeholders, and the nearby Roman Army Museum (at Magna), also administered by the Vindolanda Trust, receives a further 50,000 visitors each year (Figure 1).

The archaeological site of Vindolanda, and the artefacts it has produced, may be regarded as an iconic public representation of the Roman frontier in Britain – perhaps second only to the image of

Figure 1: An aerial image of Vindolanda

Figure 2: The anaerobically preserved cavalry barracks

Sycamore Gap in the popular imagination. For over 50 years the archaeological remains recovered from the site have been of great significance for both academic research and the popular promotion of Roman archaeology in Britain. This significance has largely been derived from the exceptional preservation of the archaeological layers, which have produced extensive collections of organic artefacts such as leather shoes, worked bone and wooden objects (Birley 2009). However, no object better represents this iconic status than the Vindolanda wooden writing tablets, first discovered in March 1973, with further important caches discovered in the 1980s and early 1990s (Birley 2015).

The Vindolanda tablets are an example of the variability of preservation which might be present in a single archaeological site. This was illustrated by the investigations that took place in 2017. Here the remains of a period IV timber cavalry barracks were discovered (*c.* AD 105-118), well preserved below a later heavy stone and clay foundation in the south-eastern quadrant of the last stone fort, *c.* AD 213+ (Figure 2). The barracks timbers, heather and bracken floors and a range of organic and inorganic finds, copper alloys, leather, textiles and wooden objects (including the delicate 1mm thick wooden writing tablets) were preserved in stable anaerobic conditions. However, just a few metres to the east and west of the barrack rooms, the preservation landscape was uneven and held no trace of anaerobic or organic material. The building's foundations had been situated within a narrow linear depression in the pre-Roman landscape and this extra 40cm of depth below the surrounding clay subsoils was enough to protect the remains of the building from both Roman activities and natural forces (Collins 2018: 342-344).

The Vindolanda writing tablets are also a cautionary reminder of the care which must be taken when monitoring changes in burial environments. With such site-specific variation, a key issue for the Vindolanda Trust is ensuring that all activity on the site, including archaeological investigations, does not inadvertently damage the delicate preservation balance. This issue was addressed previously in 2004, when the Vindolanda Trust combined its resources with the English Heritage Regional Science Advisor for the North East and Hadrian's Wall, Jacqui Huntley, and specialists from wider industry, including Professor Robert Hefford, to examine the impacts of excavation projects on adjacent deposits. On the 4 February 2004, four boreholes were sunk at strategic locations across the site (Figure 3). The cores were analysed before the boreholes were converted into dip wells. The groundwater inside the wells was measured over a two-year period

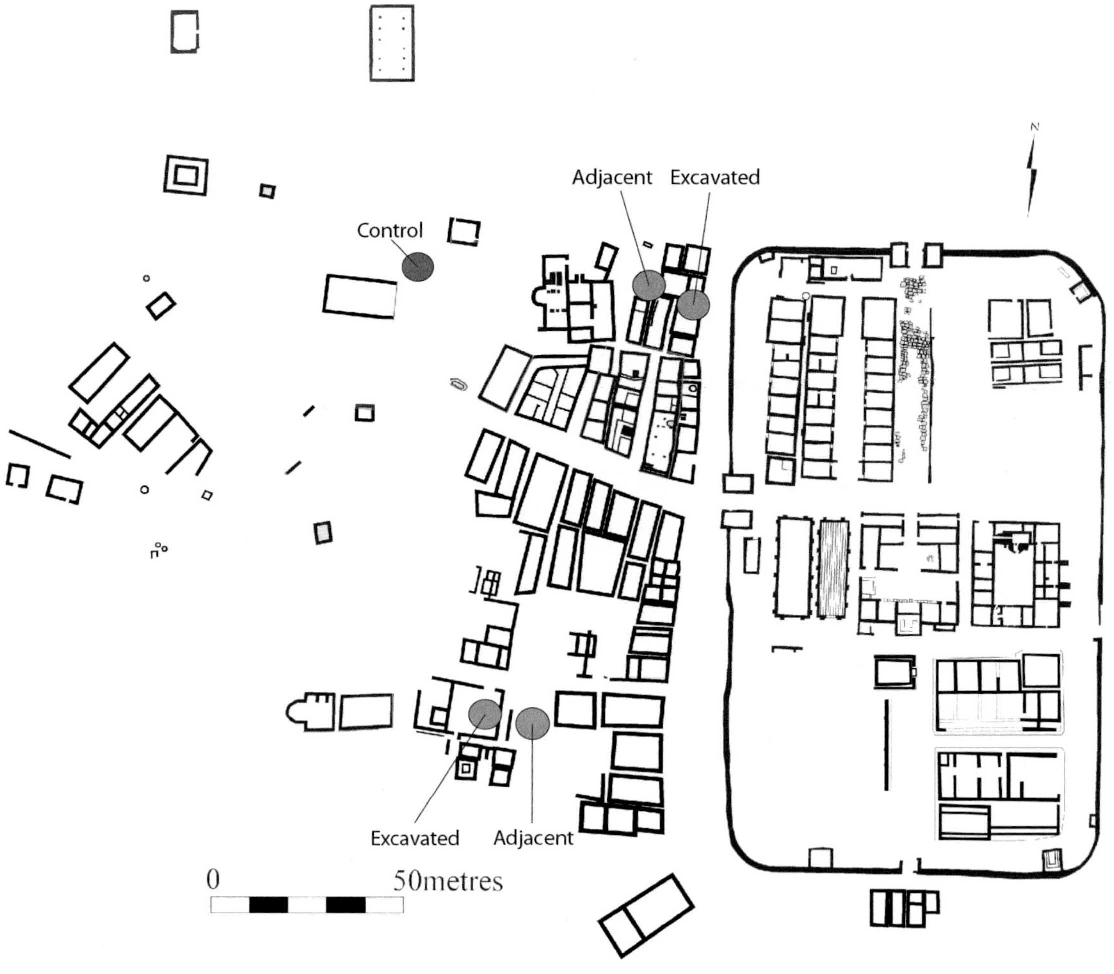

Figure 3: The location of the 2004 boreholes at Vindolanda

for changes in temperature, pH, Specific Conductivity (SC), Dissolved Oxygen (DO), and Oxidation Reducing Potential (ORP) (Hefford 2005: 237-246).

The preliminary results clearly showed, as expected, the negative impact of an excavation on the immediate environment but also indicated how long it took for landscape to recover to previous levels after the archaeological intervention, which was between five and six months. A crucial element for recovery was the method employed for backfilling after the excavation was completed. At Vindolanda the same material that was excavated from the trenches was returned into the ground (minus the artefacts). Although now oxygenated, it retained many of its previous properties, allowing for a rapid re-establishment of the conditions encountered prior to the excavation work taking place.

Magna

The nearby Roman settlement and fort of Magna (NY665656, Scheduled Ancient Monument 1010991) is situated above the village of Greenhead in Northumberland, just over 10km from Vindolanda, and is also owned and administered by the Vindolanda Trust. In many respects Magna is comparable to Vindolanda. Both sit within the same climatic regime and have shared aspects of complexity, such as sensitive organic archaeological material, multiple layers of long occupation, and anaerobic and waterlogged remains in significant parts of their landscape. Historic discoveries through antiquarian excavation, stone-robbing and the building of the military road to the south of the settlement have provided a glimpse of the possible wealth of material at the site (Birley 1998). However, unlike Vindolanda, Magna has not been systematically explored by modern excavation (Birley 2003: 283-294), therefore the extent of subsurface deposits and their condition have remained largely hidden.

In 1999, in collaboration with English Heritage, the Vindolanda Trust commissioned TimeScape Surveys to conduct the first geophysical magnetometer survey of the site. This survey showed that a substantial part of the 3rd and 4th century fort and extramural settlement remained below the fields. Unfortunately, the survey was not able to penetrate the marshy ground to the north of the site, between the Vallum and the northern fort ditches (Biggins & Taylor 2016: 102-133). The comparisons between Magna and Vindolanda have become more significant since that survey was commissioned, as ground-based and aerial observations have suggested that areas of Magna appear to be drying out. This has resulted in previously sunken features such as the fort's ditches becoming more defined (Figure 4) as well as visible changes in surface vegetation and wear on the landscape (Gurney *et al.*, 2021: 1-19).

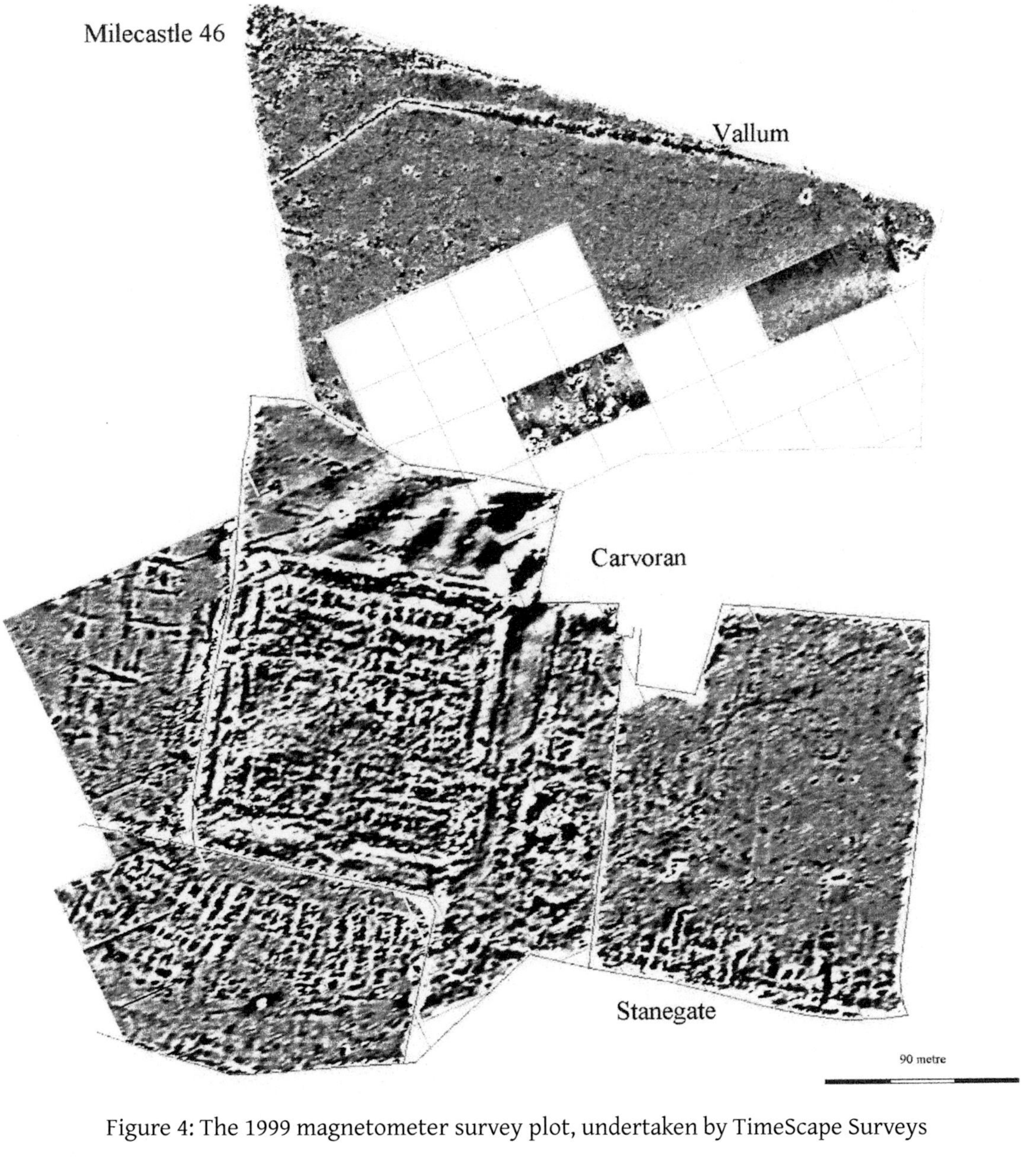

Figure 4: The 1999 magnetometer survey plot, undertaken by TimeScape Surveys

Figure 5: An annotated and rectified aerial image of Magna taken by SUMO in 2019, showing the location of the fort, vallum, bog and Magna boreholes

When considered in the context of what was known from Vindolanda, the Trust became increasingly concerned that they did not fully understand the changes taking place at Magna. With only surface observations to base assumptions on, more work was needed to understand what subsurface changes might be taking place, and whether 'Vindolanda-level' preservation was being threatened by them.

The approach taken for Magna followed Historic England guidance in Preserving Archaeological Remains (Historic England 2016b), and Deposit Modelling and Archaeology (Carey 2018; Historic England 2020). Using this approach, a series of linked questions were posed:

1. What was driving the change in the hydrological regime across the site?
2. What was the nature of the archaeological deposits across this site – vertically and horizontally?
3. How would the drying out of the site affect the archaeological significance of subsurface deposits?

When considering the first point – or, in other words, why the site appeared to be drying – several factors, including climate change, the 19th and 20th century agricultural drainage which crosses the site, and the operation of a nearby quarry, which had been in use until the 1970s (Birley 1998), have been suggested. It is important to understand what might be driving change so that a mitigation strategy can be devised that adequately deals with the root of the problem. The consideration of the hydrological regime is vital to ensure the continued preservation of the site (Gurney *et al.* 2021).

In relation to the second point, it was important to understand the nature of the archaeological deposits across the site, and how their significance might vary both vertically and horizontally. Though it was strongly suggested that Magna may possess comparable deposits to Vindolanda, their state of preservation across the whole site was unclear at the beginning of this project. Understanding this would be key to any mitigation strategy. It would also ensure the time and budget resources of the Vindolanda Trust would be focused most effectively.

A final consideration was to understand how drying may affect the archaeological significance of subsurface deposits. At the early stages of this project, the experience from Vindolanda would be used to consider what sort of loss might be expected from the drying out of waterlogged remains. It could not be stated with certainty whether the two sites were directly comparable; however, with the experience of the Vindolanda conservation facility, the Magna project could begin to formulate a conceptual model of different scenarios for information loss, should it be determined that the preservation conditions on the site were changing. Using this information, the Vindolanda Trust and other stakeholders such as Historic England could begin to consider what course of action might be needed on the site.

To begin this process, in the summer of 2021 five boreholes were placed in different strategic positions across the site, from the Vallum in the north to the southern limit of the scheduled area (Figure 5). Preliminary analysis of the cores provided two significant results. The first was the discovery of a hidden lakebed between the north wall of the fort and the line of the Vallum, concentrated in the area which had the greatest depth of peat formation across the site. Historically this may have been hugely significant, potentially being both a water source for the Roman settlement and a possible reason for the Vallum diversion to the north.

The second discovery was the great depth of anaerobic material to the south of Magna, at over 4.5m deep, and with evidence of organic material, pottery, wood and bone. All the boreholes have now been converted into sealed wells, with the groundwater analysed by piezometers, which will record every hour, between 2021 and 2031, monitoring changes in temperature, atmospheric pressure, conductivity and water levels within those wells. This will enable the Trust to monitor the effects of extreme climatic events on the buried site, such as drought and heavy rainfall, over a longer-term period.

This preliminary work at Magna will form the basis of a water environment assessment (Historic England 2016a), and later a long-term management plan for the site. The strategy of long-term monitoring is becoming increasingly vital in providing the data required to make future decisions about how to manage not only sites like Magna and Vindolanda, but also other sensitive archaeological environments along the Wall. It is also key to consider that monitoring and data collection cannot be divorced from active management of these sites. Monitoring projects are not an end in themselves, but a tool to help informed heritage management of buried remains.

Without the benefits of the information that geoarchaeology can provide, as shown at Vindolanda and Magna, we may be ill-equipped to understand the current and future threats that face this part of the Frontiers of the Roman Empire WHS.

Bibliography

Biggins, J.A. & Taylor D.J.A. 2016. A geophysical survey of the Roman fort at Carvoran, (Magna) Northumberland. *Archaeologia Aeliana* 5 31:102-133

Birley, A. 2003. *The Excavations of 2001-2002, Volume 1.* Vindolanda Research Report 2003, Bardon Mill: Vindolanda Trust

Birley, A. and Alberti, M. 2021. *Sub-Roman to Post-Roman Vindolanda, New Excavations and Research.* Bardon Mill: Vindolanda Trust Publications

Birley R. 1998. *The fort at the Rock: Magna and Carvoran on Hadrian's Wall.* Greenhead: Roman Army Museum Publications

Birley R. 2009. *Vindolanda: A Roman Fort on Hadrian's Wall.* Stroud: Amberley Publishing

Birley, R. 2015. *Vindolanda - Extraordinary records of daily life on the Northern frontier.* Bardon Mill: Vindolanda Trust

Breeze, D.J. 2019. *Hadrian's Wall: A study in archaeological exploration and interpretation.* Oxford: Archaeopress

Carey, C., Howard, A., Knight, D., Corcoran, J. and Heathcote, J. (eds) 2018. *Deposit Modelling and Archaeology*. Exeter: Short Run Press.

Collins R. 2018. England 3. Hadrian's Wall. *Britannia* 49: 342-347

Gurney, R., Santucci, E., Valman, S., Booth, A., Birley, A., Haynes, I., Marsh, S. and Mills, J. 2021. Integration and Analysis of Multi-Modal Geospatial Secondary Data to Inform Management of At-Risk Archaeological Sites. *ISPRS International Journal of Geo-Information* 10 (9): 575

Hefford R. 2005. Some physical chemical measurements on underground water at Vindolanda, in Birley A. 2005. *The Vindolanda Excavations 2003-2004*: 237-246. Bardon Mill: Vindolanda Trust Publications

Historic England 2016a. Preserving Archaeological Remains, Appendix 3 - Water Environment Assessment Techniques. Swindon: Historic England

Historic England 2016b. Preserving Archaeological Remains, Appendix 4 - Water Monitoring for Archaeological Sites. Swindon: Historic England

Historic England 2019. Statement of Heritage Significance: Analysing Significance in Heritage Assets. Historic England Advice Note 12. Swindon: Historic England

Historic England 2020. Deposit Modelling and Archaeology. Guidance for Mapping Buried Deposits. Swindon: Historic England.

Huntley, J. 2009. Landscape and Environment, in Symonds, M.F.A and Mason, D.J.P. (eds) *Frontiers of Knowledge: A research framework for Hadrian's Wall, Part of the Frontiers of the Roman Empire World Heritage Site, Vol. 1 Resource Assessment*: 108–118. Durham: Durham University

Huntley, J. 2013. 'The world is a bundle of hay': Investigating land management for animal fodder around Vindolanda, based on plant remains, in Collins, R. and Symonds M. (eds) *Breaking down Boundaries: Hadrian's Wall in the 21st Century*, JRA Supplementary Series S93: 33-51. Portsmouth, RI: Journal of Roman Archaeology

Leach, S. and Whitworth, A. 2011 *Saving the Wall: The Conservation of Hadrian's Wall 1746-1987.* Stroud: Amberley Publishing

Taylor, G., Hefford, R.J.W., Birley, A. & Huntley, J.P. 2019. Identifying the "blue substance" at the Roman site of Vindolanda, Northumberland. *Journal of Archaeological Science: Reports* 24: 582-587

Aspects of remote sensing in Wall research

Tony Wilmott (Historic England)

Remote sensing in archaeology is the use of instruments which emit, collect and process various signals, which are then further processed and interpreted by technicians with the aim of better understanding what lies below the ground. The results of remote sensing surveys have often been used on Hadrian's Wall to inform archaeological excavation, more so over the last decade. But what has remote sensing accomplished so far? Can it really 'see what is under the ground'? And why are remote sensing techniques an important tool in the management of Hadrian's Wall? This chapter illustrates remote sensing work undertaken on Hadrian's Wall in the last ten years, including the increasing role and new techniques available in aerial photography.

Over recent decades remote sensing has played an increasing role in both research and management on Hadrian's Wall, and the potential of such work was fully acknowledged in the Research Framework for the Wall (Symonds and Mason 2009:43). Geophysical survey, in the shape of resistivity, magnetometry, and, more recently, ground-penetrating radar, has been extensively employed on sites across the zone. The rate at which such survey progressed from innovation to ubiquitous research tool can be measured by reference to the successive Handbooks produced for the last three decennial Pilgrimages of Hadrian's Wall. The Handbook for the 1999 Pilgrimage barely mentions the technique and contains a single survey image – that of Birdoswald (Bidwell 1999: 157-61). Ten years later there were ten reported surveys, mostly on the Wall forts, the outpost forts and their environs (Hodgson 2009: 105, 114, 122, 126, 130-1, 136, 168, 170, 163). In 2019 a further five surveys were reported (Collins and Symonds 2019: 148-51, 179, 202, 214), and a new development in the form of LiDAR (Light Detection And Ranging) survey was reported in these summaries for the first time (Collins and Symonds 2019: 143, 181, 183).

The undoubted pioneers in this work were the late Alan Biggins, David Taylor and their colleagues at TimeScape Surveys, whose work was aimed principally towards the definition of the extramural

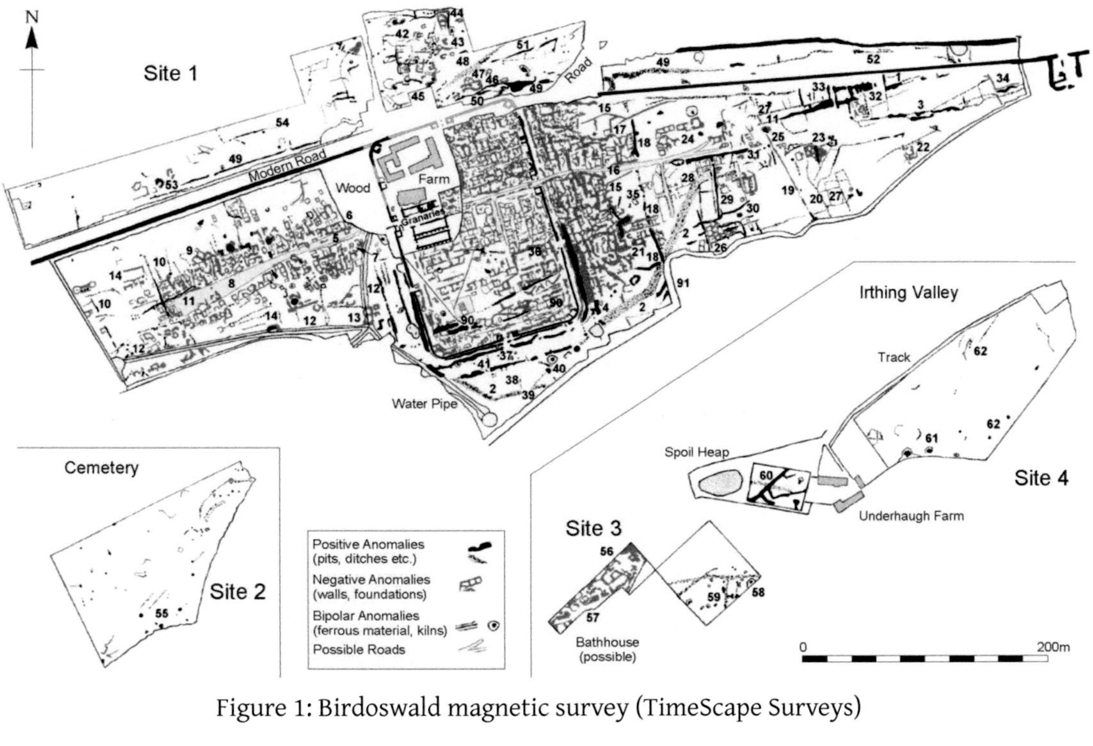

Figure 1: Birdoswald magnetic survey (TimeScape Surveys)

Figure 2: TimeScape Surveys' magnetometry survey of Maryport Roman fort and extramural settlement draped over a Digital Terrain Model (Haynes and Wilmott 2020)

settlements of the Wall forts. Their work demonstrated at a single stroke the size and range of such settlements, which were shown to be much more extensive and complex than had previously been thought. The first such survey was at Birdoswald (Figure 1), where the settlement was shown to cover extensive areas to the west and east of the fort, and even to the north, on the northern side of the linear barrier (Biggins and Taylor 1999, 2004b).

At Maryport the plan of the extramural settlement was revealed in considerable detail through an extensive magnetometer survey (Biggins and Taylor 2004a; Biggins *et al.* 2010), and the survey image has been used in many general publications on the Wall as an exemplar. Figure 2 is a version of this image draped over a digital terrain model in order to combine geophysical and topographical information.

Such surveys are an essential tool for locating, defining the extent of, characterising and managing the archaeological resource. An important use is in prospecting for lost or unknown parts of the Wall landscape, particularly where the course of the frontier or the siting of installations or features is uncertain. One example of such prospection was the search for the location of milecastles to the west of Carlisle. This had mixed results, with Milecastle 73 located (Biggins *et al.* 2004), while a search for Milecastles 69 and 70, the former on two possible sites, proved fruitless. Evaluation trenches excavated on the site of Milecastle 71 indicated the reason: there was virtually nothing left of the stone structure. The stone foundations of the milecastle had been totally robbed, and only a single thin course of turf work remained of its turf predecessor. The same was almost certainly true of 69 and 70 (Wilmott 2009: 177-86) and would render the milecastles invisible to survey.

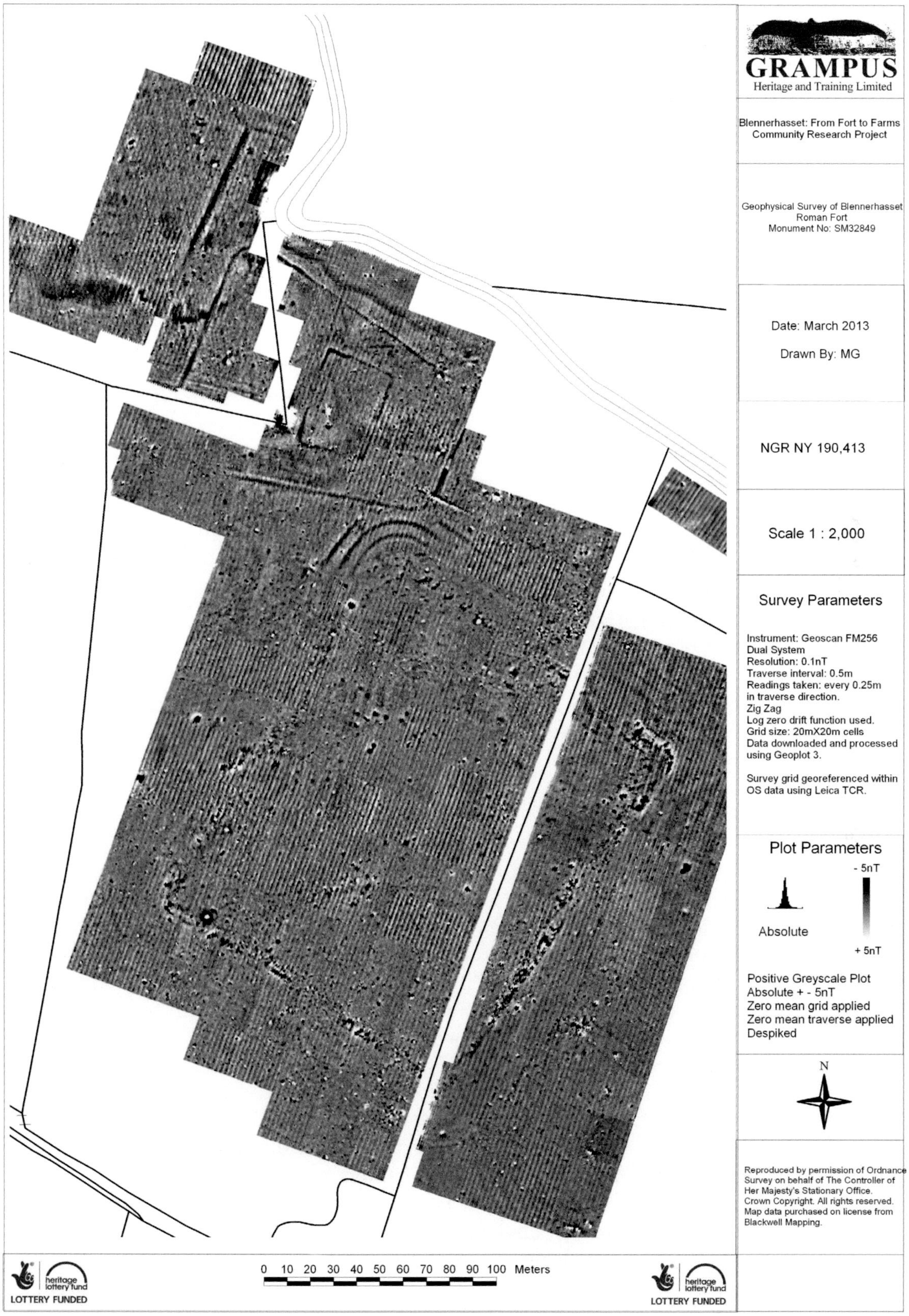

Figure 3: Magnetometer survey of the Flavian fort at Blennerhasset, Cumbria (Grampus Heritage and Training Ltd)

The recent discovery of the so-called obstacle pits on the berm of Hadrian's Wall in Tyneside (Bidwell 2005) has led to the use of geophysics to try to locate such features elsewhere on the Wall line. The magnetometry plot of the berm at Heddon-on-the-Wall in Wall Mile 11 shows a convincing pattern of anomalies, reminiscent of the pattern of known and excavated pits (Collins and Symonds 2019: 140-41), while the pattern suggested from survey in Wall Miles 48 and 49, at Willowford and Birdoswald, was much less clear (AD Archaeology 2019), and the excavation in summer 2021 of a stretch of the berm that had been surveyed to the east of Birdoswald fort demonstrated that here at least the pits were absent.

On smaller installations such as milecastles, single-phase temporary camps, forts such as Flavian Blennerhasset in Cumbria (Figure 3), or on lengths of Hadrian's Wall, the interpretation of survey plots is relatively simple. However, on fort and settlement sites it is difficult and must be used with caution.

These sites were occupied for very long periods of time, and inevitably grew, shrunk and altered over time. Any geophysical survey plot is thus a palimpsest of those parts of the archaeology which are susceptible to survey methods. Frequently excavation strategy is guided by the results of geophysical survey, and results from excavation can test survey interpretation. Two cases where this has recently been the case are at Maryport and Birdoswald.

Two excavation projects took place at Maryport between 2011 and 2015, both guided in large part by the geophysical survey. One of these, conducted by Oxford Archaeology North, was designed to examine a seemingly representative building plot in the heart of the settlement, on the frontage of the main street. Four contiguous building plots on the north-west side of the street were identified from the interpretative plan of the Biggins and Taylor survey, and chosen as the study area. This area was subjected to enhanced survey using ground penetrating radar, a technique which was complementary to the earlier work. This in turn allowed the selection of a single plot within the study area which appeared to have the greatest potential to address the research questions designed for the work.

A key aim of the project was to establish how far the excavated remains were consistent with the interpretation of the geophysical survey results; in other words, ground truthing. In broad terms, the results fully justified the selection of the chosen plot for excavation, and it was possible to closely identify many of the excavated features with anomalies represented in the geophysical survey (Zant 2019: 133-136). Some feature types were not apparent in the survey, such as stone walls that had been totally robbed; however, the area between two such walls contained significantly fewer anomalies, showing that the survey had indicated the shape of the building. Similarly, the survey was not able to distinguish between two walls only 0.4m apart, which thus appeared as a single feature. Despite this, the survey data was a reliable guide to the most promising target for excavation, and the return in terms of new information was considerable.

The second Maryport project, conducted by Newcastle University (Haynes and Wilmott 2020), examined the site of the 1870 discovery of 17 Roman altars buried in pits, and also the site of a pair of cult buildings located in 1880. These excavations were principally guided by knowledge of the work of our antiquarian predecessors, which was augmented by the results of the geophysical surveys. On the 1870 pits' site, the most obvious feature to show on the geophysical survey was a circular ditch, along with other anomalies which also seemed to represent pits. Unfortunately, a large part of the site could not be surveyed, as a broad hedgerow containing metal fencing, which would interfere with magnetic responses, occupied the south-west side of the site. Although the circular ditch was found in its surveyed spot, only seven of the 26 pits excavated within the area surveyed appeared on the survey plot. In the area of the cult buildings the structures themselves were not apparent in the survey data, but a complex of ditched enclosures were accurately

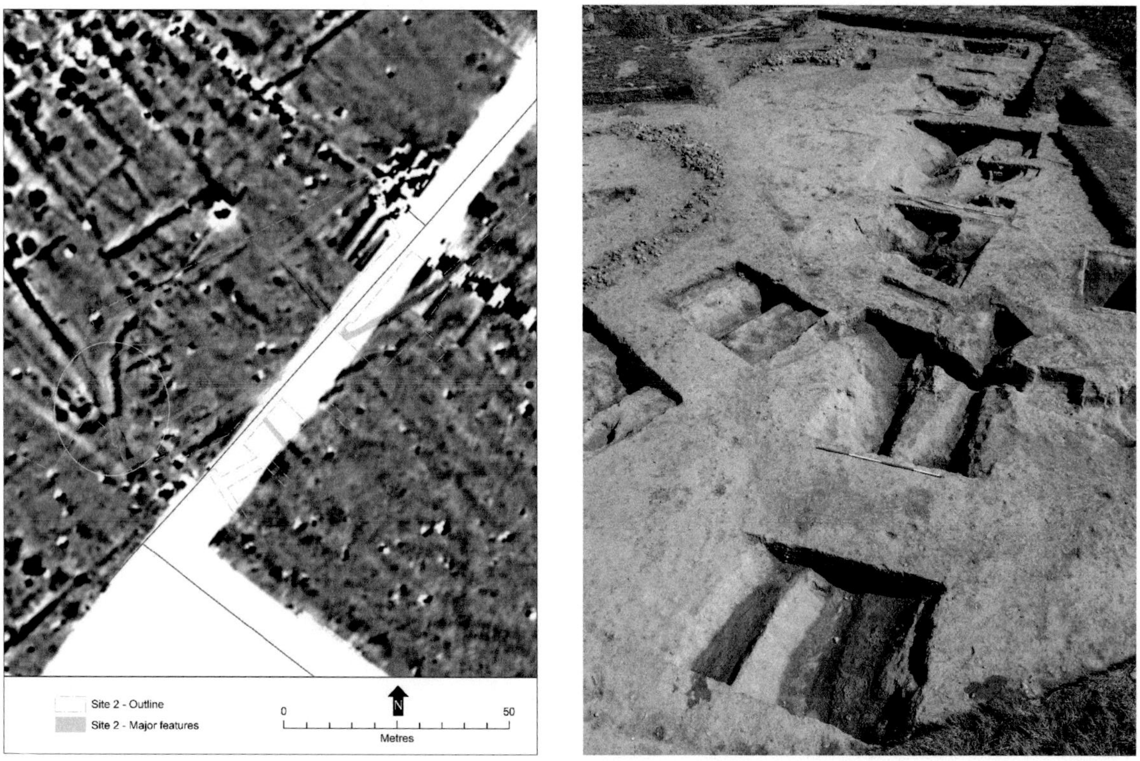

Figure 4: Detail of the Maryport survey with excavated ditches overlain in blue. The multi-phase ditch complex in the photo appears on the survey in the area ringed.
(From Haynes and Wilmott 2020; Newcastle University)

reflected in the survey results. A multi-phase complex of intercutting ditches on the west side of the buildings appeared on the survey as a single broad feature (Figure 4).

The Birdoswald survey has recently guided the selection of areas for excavation in continued efforts to understand aspects of the extramural settlement on the east, west and north sides of the fort. Due to begin in 2020, the first excavation season was cancelled due to the Covid-19 pandemic, and a double excavation season took place in summer 2021. This focused on a portion of the eastern extramural settlement in which previous work had revealed a well-preserved Roman stone building, interpreted by its excavator as a signal tower (Richmond 1931). However, subsequent geophysical survey had shown that the presumed signal tower lay within an extensive complex of buildings.

The survey plot was shown to accurately reflect the plan of the structures excavated (Figure 5), but the team was not prepared for the quality of the survival of the archaeology, of which the survey had, of course, given no indication. Not only was the previously excavated building shown to survive 2m in height, but the walls and floors of a sequence of major stone-built structures were revealed. There were at least three phases of such buildings (Figure 6), one of which was served by a water main which cut through the walls of an earlier structure.

It is now thought likely, on the evidence of the water mains and other finds, that the large complex structure shown on the geophysical plot to the east of the excavated area comprised the fort bathhouse. As at Maryport, further detailed and focused geophysical survey has been undertaken during the project in order to refine the results and better target the excavation.

The Maryport and Birdoswald case studies show the importance of ensuring that the survey and excavation processes are integrated; it is important for geophysicists to observe the excavated reality of areas they have surveyed, and for excavators to ensure that such liaison takes place. This helps geophysicists and excavators alike to understand the potential and limitations of geophysical interpretation.

On a larger scale, aerial photography continues to be an important tool for the detection and recording of sites. In the early 2000s, the Historic England National Mapping Programme (NMP)

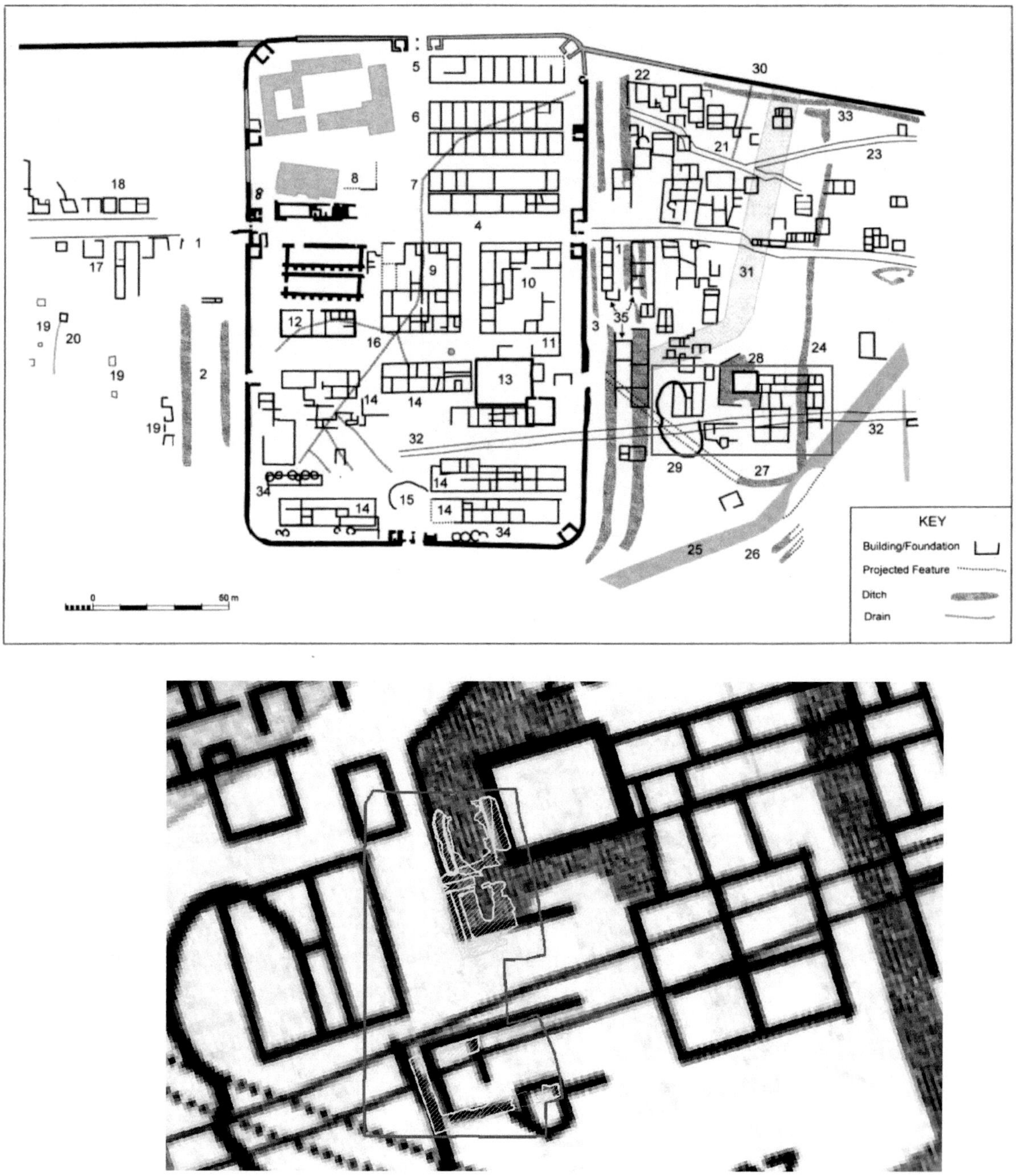

Figure 5: (Above) Interpretive plot of the survey of Birdoswald Roman fort and its immediate environs. The red box defines the area within which excavation took place. (Below) Extract from the survey plan with excavated walls overlain in yellow (Newcastle University and Historic England).

Figure 6: Buildings excavated at Birdoswald in 2021 and highlighted in Figure 5. (Left) 2m high walls of structure to the south. (Right) walls and flooring of structures to the north (Newcastle University and Historic England).

examined over 27,000 aerial photographs to produce an archive of digital mapping and text records. New flying was also carried out as part of the programme. Naturally, the photography revealed archaeological landscape traces from all periods from prehistory to the present, and all of these were mapped. New records were made for 2748 sites, and a further 806 records were enhanced. A good example, combining the enhancement of existing knowledge with new information gained by more recent flying, was at White Moss, Cumbria, where a number of known Roman camps were revealed in more detail, with the addition of three further superimposed camps. Importantly these photographs revealed lines of pits (or possibly ovens) which indicate the internal arrangement of the camps – an aspect about which little is known (Small 2008: 40). The end result of the NMP was a cartographic record which placed the Roman frontier firmly into its broader landscape and chronological context. Not only did it produce a valuable tool for the understanding and management of the monument, but it was also used to produce an accurate archaeological map of the wall to inform researchers, visitors and the interested public.

Even after the completion of the mapping project, Historic England has continued an intensive programme of archaeological flying. The new images that this produces can be compared with older photographs in order to assess the present-day state of preservation, and changes to the monuments through time. This aids in assessing their condition and in identifying potential threats and damage. The photography is also used as illustrative material in a variety of contexts, including academic and general publications, websites and guidebooks.

LiDAR, or airborne laser scanning, is becoming an increasingly useful tool for mapping and prospection. The technology can strip away such surface interference as tree cover to produce imagery of the underlying landform, and of hidden archaeological features that no other technology can see. This technique has been successful in the discovery of new camps and other features within the Hadrian's Wall landscape and has also enhanced knowledge of the landscape of known sites (Figure 7), particularly at Birdoswald where the Roman fort, Wall and Vallum can be seen within a landscape of later, medieval, plough furrows.

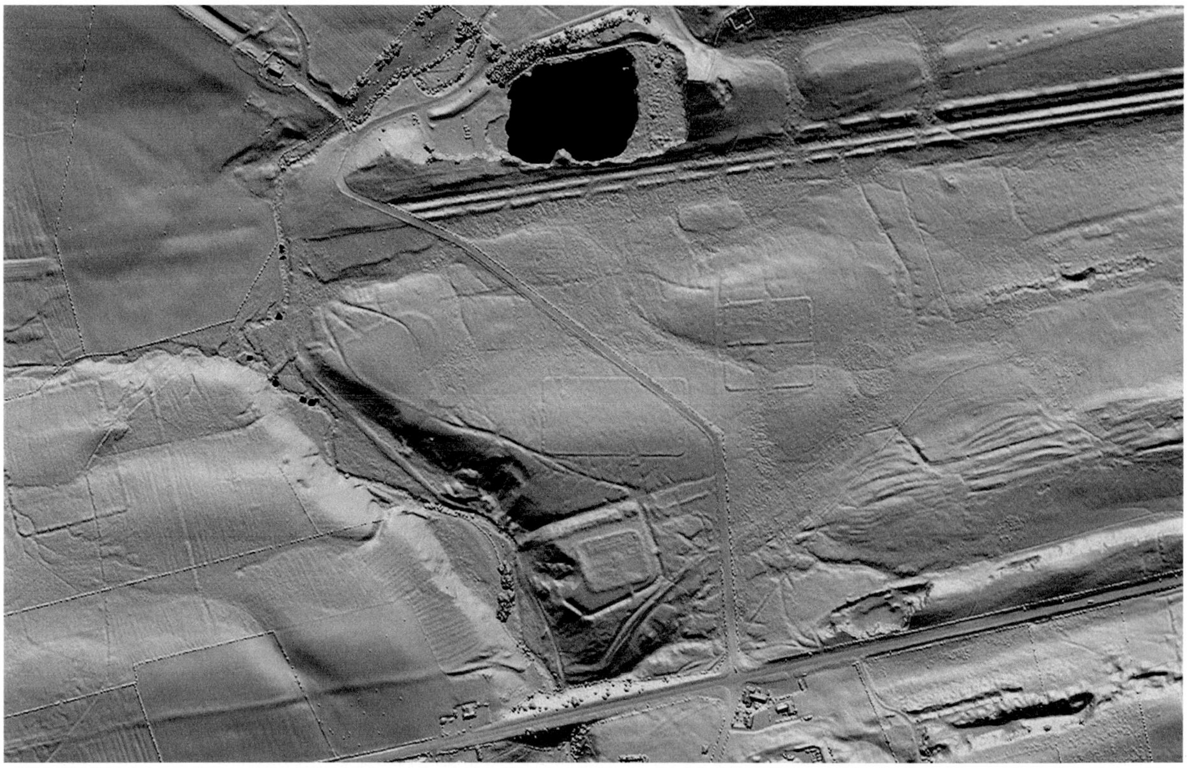

Figure 7: A 16-direction hillshade digital surface model of the Roman camps at Haltwhistle Common derived from 1m resolution airborne laser scanning (LiDAR) data. Tha Stanegate fortlet at Haltwhistle Burn can be seen towards the bottom of the image, and Milecastle 42 (Cawfields) is visible top centre. The Vallum is particularly clear, and several temporary camps are also discernible. © Historic England; source Environment Agency. (Thanks to Matthew Oakey)

In short, LiDAR 'presents great opportunities to identify new archaeological features and reassess those already known' (Collins 2015: 2). The Frontiers of the Roman Empire Digital Humanities Initiative (FREDHI) at Newcastle University has recently undertaken an exercise to assess LiDAR data for the Hadrian's Wall area (Collins 2015). This exercise revealed a number of new camps and 'native' settlements, as well as new information on the course and extent of the Roman road network, an area of study also recently successfully pursued in Cumbria (Ratledge 2020).

A new method of using aerial data is 'structure from motion' – a photogrammetric method which allows the production of accurate 3D data which can be used in a variety of ways. At Birdoswald, a 3D model is now on display within English Heritage's new exhibition (Figure 8). From the first aerial photographs taken along the Wall line, through detailed site survey, to the latest aerial mapping, remote sensing has provided new and exciting insights into the archaeology of Hadrian's Wall. It will continue to do so.

The pace of change in new techniques and technologies over the last three decades has been extraordinary, and we can certainly look forward to the refinement of the existing methods, and the development of new ones. In the meantime, it is necessary to ensure that survey and excavation become a seamless and collaborative process. Survey guides the selection of a site, perhaps, but this should not be the end of it. Re-survey after de-turfing has been proven to tighten up excavation strategy, as shown in the Maryport example, and this should be standard practice. The Time Team television programme made 'geofizz' familiar to its viewers, and stripped away some of the technological mystery, showing that there is great potential to use survey data far more in public outreach, popular publication, and museum display. This is especially true of some

Figure 8: A 3D model of the landscape around Birdoswald Roman fort created using Structure from Motion and derived from around 1000 aerial photographs taken from a light aircraft. © Historic England. (Thanks to Matthew Oakey)

of the new ways of visualising the landscape now and in the past, and something to be considered in museum and site interpretations.

Bibliography

AD Archaeology 2019. Hadrian's Wall Berm East of Willowford Farm and East of Birdoswald Roman Fort, Northumberland: Geophysical Survey

Bidwell, P. 1999. *Hadrian's Wall 1989-1999.* Kendal: Titus Wilson

Bidwell, P. 2005. The systems of obstacles on Hadrian's Wall; their extent, date and purpose. *Arbeia Journal* 8: 2-28

Biggins, J.A., Hall, S. and Taylor, D.J.A. 2004. A geophysical survey of Milecastle 73 and Hadrian`s Wall at Burgh-by-Sands, Cumbria. *Transactions of the Cumberland and Westmorland Antiquarian and Archaeological Society* Series 3, 4: 55-70

Biggins, J.A. and Taylor, D.J.A. 1999. A survey of the Roman fort and settlement at Birdoswald, Cumbria. *Britannia* 35: 91-110

Biggins, J.A. and Taylor, D.J.A. 2004a. The Roman fort and vicus at Maryport, geophysical survey 2000-2004, in R.J.A. Wilson and Caruana, I. (eds). *Romans on the Solway: Essays in Honour of Richard Bellhouse.* Kendal: Titus Wilson: 102-133.

Biggins, J.A. and Taylor, D.J.A. 2004b. Geophysical survey of the vicus at Birdoswald Roman fort, Cumbria. *Britannia* 35: 159-77

Biggins, J.A., Taylor, D.J.A. and Strutt, K. 2010. Detailed mapping of the extra-mural settlement at Maryport: an integrated approach to geophysical survey, July-August. Senhouse Museum, Maryport (unpublished report)

Collins, R. 2015. *Hadrian's Wall and LiDAR; New features in an ancient frontier landscape.* FREDHI Report 1. Newcastle upon Tyne: Newcastle University

Collins, R. and Symonds, M. 2019. *Hadrian's Wall 2009-2019.* Kendal: Titus Wilson

Haynes, I. and Wilmott, T. 2020. *A Cult Centre on Rome's North West Frontier; Excavations at Maryport, Cumbria, 1870-2015,* Cumberland and Westmorland Antiquarian and Archaeological Society Research Series 15. Kendal: Titus Wilson

Hodgson, N. 2009. *Hadrian's Wall 1999-2009.* Kendal: Titus Wilson

Ratledge, D. 2020. Cumbria's Roman Roads – a Second LiDAR Update. *Transactions of the Cumberland and Westmorland Antiquarian and Archaeological Society* Series 3, 20: 37-64

Richmond, I. A. 1931. Excavations on Hadrian's Wall in the Birdoswald-Pike Hill Sector, 1930. *Transactions of the Cumberland and Westmorland Antiquarian and Archaeological Society* Series 2, 31: 122–34

Small, F. 2008. Hadrian's Wall NMP Project, Brampton to Birdoswald: National Mapping Project Report. English Heritage Research Dept. Report Series 69-2008. Swindon: English Heritage

Symonds, M. F. A. and Mason, D. J. P. 2009. *Frontiers of Knowledge: a research framework for Hadrian's Wall - part of the Frontiers of the Roman Empire World Heritage Site; Vol. II, Agenda and Strategy.* Durham: Durham University

Wilmott, T. 2009. The Hadrian's Wall Milecastles Project, 1999-2000, in T. Wilmott (ed) *Hadrian's Wall: Archaeological Research by English Heritage, 1976 - 2000*: 137-202. Swindon: English Heritage

Zant, J. 2019. *The Maryport Roman Settlement Project: Excavations 2013-14*, Lancaster Imprints 27. Lancaster: Oxford Archaeology North

3D scanning of Vindolanda's collection – successes and challenges

Anneke-Susan Hackenbroich (Vindolanda Trust)
and Rhys Williams (Teesside University)

The idea of being able to research and handle an archaeological find from anywhere in the world, without removing it from its museum case, seemed futuristic to most only ten years ago. Technological advancement, and cooperation between sites and museums – who hold the finds – and research institutions – who hold the technical equipment and 'know-how' – have made the 3D scanning of collections a reality on Hadrian's Wall. This chapter talks about the 3D scanning of some of Vindolanda's collections. The authors use this process as a gateway to explore some important questions: where should digital artefacts be displayed? Who is responsible for the care of online collections? What happens when digital artefacts are manipulated by digital users, who may not be archaeologists or researchers? Who do these scanned artefacts, original or modified, end up belonging to? And finally, is there any risk that digital artefacts will come to replace their analogue counterparts?

Background

Archaeology has experienced increased pressure to digitise collections and make artefacts available to a wider audience (Frieman and Janz 2018; Frieman and Wilkin 2016). 3D imaging as a means of digitising artefacts is not a new technique, but it has seen rapid development and publicised use in recent years. This has been particularly true during the COVID-19 public health crisis that struck the world between 2019 and 2022, and forced many museums to find new ways to engage with their audiences. Even before world events brought it to centre stage, 3D imaging was recognised as a useful technique to effectively support conservation, documentation, project planning and public engagement. Using 3D imaging technology to produce digital 3D models of artefacts allows the visitor to explore them in as much detail as their curiosity and abilities allow. 3D models also provide physical interactions and responses, which are critical to effective learning from science exhibits (Allen 2004; Maxwell and Evans 2015; Richards and Menninger 1993). These 3D models can be supplemented with scientific information and displayed to the public or shared with external researchers without risking the preservation or contamination of the original artefact (Frieman and Janz 2018; Kuzminsky and Gardiner 2012).

Online resources enable museums to develop virtual display spaces and showcase artefacts which are not physically on display, and thus expand accessibility to wider and differing audiences. A digitised artefact is not bound to a place but globally available (Bayne *et al.* 2009: 4). This raises many questions not only about ownership, copyright and ethics, but also about what impact 3D modelling has on the authenticity of an artefact. Can 3D models be manipulated? Does digitisation diminish the role of museums? How do people engage with museums' collections online? Do we need to redefine the role of the museum curator? And how do we take care of artefacts which are on display 24 hours a day? This chapter discusses 3D imaging at Vindolanda, and provides possible points for consideration, principles and guidelines to answer some of these questions. The aim is to open a discussion, rather than set those answers in stone.

3D imaging at Vindolanda: a case study

The journey of 3D scanning at the Vindolanda Museum started during a research trip in 2018, where the Teesside University BioArchaeology (TUBArch) group were studying the site and the potential mechanisms in the formation of vivianite (all the 'blue stuff', Taylor *et al.* 2019). Walking through the Vindolanda Museum, the TUBArch group came across the 'Vindolanda bone evidence room', with a range of animal skulls on display, some covered with little perforations from target practice. TUBArch then took advantage of the robust 3D scanning capabilities and research profile at Teesside University to image one bovine cranium used in target practice (Williams *et al.* 2019) as a successful proof of concept. Where scanning the bovine cranium allowed enhanced research capabilities, scanning a human cranium, also on display at Vindolanda, allowed public interaction while protecting the original, fragile, bones.

Following this, TUBArch and Vindolanda began a fruitful cooperation, greatly expanding their 3D scanning output by including 3D printing and public engagement events across a wide range of different artefacts and materials on display in the museum, and leading to the *Digging up Memories* online exhibition project (<https://www.vindolanda.com/Listing/Category/digging-up-memories>). For this project, researchers scanned all the wooden artefacts that the Vindolanda team had chosen as their favourites; these scans were later 3D printed for public engagement on site.

Capturing 3D scans and 3D printing

Whilst several 3D scanning technologies are available for different applications, 3D artefact scanning at Vindolanda has focused on the use of Structured Light Scanning (SLS) technology, using a HP 3D Structured Light Scanner Pro S3 with a single camera in *Quality* mode. Preliminary scanning procedures developed by Williams *et al.* (2019) were used. To summarise, scans were captured indoors with dim, diffused lighting to ensure that texture capture was not affected by external lighting. The shutter speed, aperture size and projector brightness that captured the material texture most accurately without blanching were established for individual artefacts. The projector and camera were calibrated to 240mm or 120mm depending on the artefact size to ensure that maximum accuracy was achieved for each one. The background was captured and automatically removed from all scans. Artefacts were rotated between scans until all visible surfaces were recorded.

Scans were processed by aligning with *pairwise registration*. *Global fine registration* was processed after every five to ten scans to ensure consistent alignment across the model. Scans were manually cleaned of noise and optimised, then fused together to produce a composite 3D model with accompanying textures. All 3D models were imported into MeshLab (Callieri *et al.* 2013) for additional cleaning and simplification to reduce the unwieldly file sizes. All models at this point were prepared for online hosting and viewing, while 3D printing required additional processing steps. Artefacts with perforations and holes in their topography underwent a bespoke manual thickening process in Geomagic Studio to provide a sufficiently thick surface to print whilst preserving the damage. Attempts were made to print all 3D models at 1:1 scale but some models, such as the ox cranium and Atto's workbench, were downscaled to fit the printer bed. Models were printed in ABS filament in successive layers, building up until the full model was printed. Finally, 3D printed models were cleaned and delivered to the Vindolanda Museum ready for public handling.

3D artefacts from the Vindolanda Museum online

The unique levels of preservation at Vindolanda have provided an extensive collection of precious artefacts to select for 3D imaging. Digitised artefacts from Vindolanda's Museum were stored together in online collections that allowed the public and researchers worldwide to access the delicate finds, regardless of distance and overcoming any preservation risk. Sketchfab, an online portal for uploading, viewing and modelling 3D imagery and Virtual Reality (VR), provides view counts and the opportunity to comment on models, offering useful metrics and a means to allow distanced interactions between all users, may they be curious viewers or academic researchers. Based on Sketchfab metrics, the most popular online models at the time of writing include the human cranium, one of the thirteen ox crania used in target practice (interpreted and discussed by Williams *et al.* 2019), a wooden toilet seat, a toy sword, and a lid with engraved peacock decoration (Figure 1).

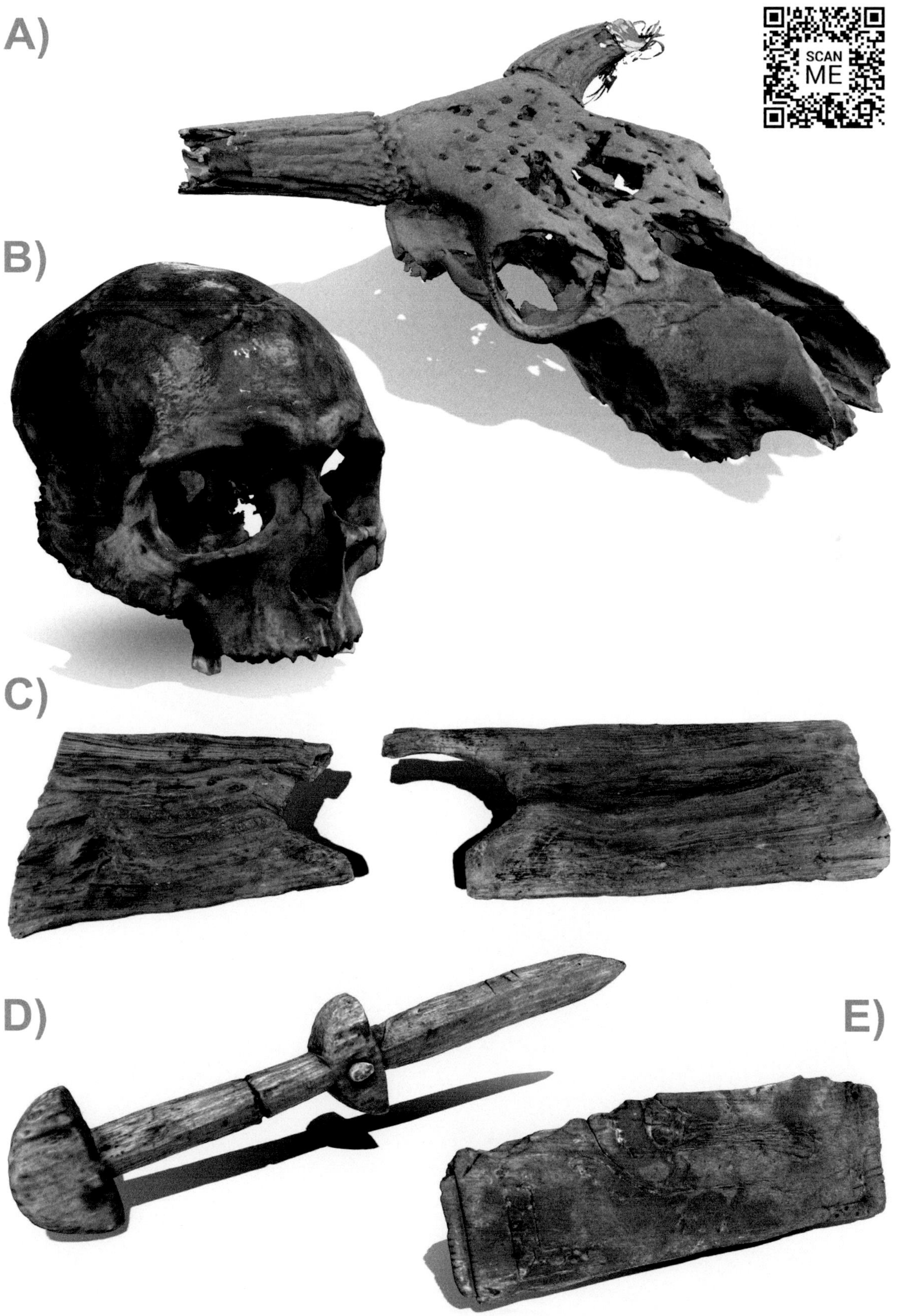

Figure 1: Most-viewed 3D models of artefacts at Vindolanda. A: bovine cranium, B: human cranium, C: toilet seat, D: toy sword, E: peacock decoration. All models can be viewed at sketchfab.com or by scanning the QR code.

Compressed versions of 3D models can be freely viewed online at <https://sketchfab.com/williamsrhy/collections> while researchers may request full-sized formats for academic purposes. The most popular 3D printed models include the decorative turned object, wooden shoes and bath clogs, and Atto's workbench (Figure 2).

Sketchfab data can also help with artefact selection for navigating topics and producing further displays for online and museum viewing. Leaving aside supportive social media posts and the wooden artefacts being part of an online exhibition, the four most popular 3D models from Vindolanda also support Freeman Tilden's principles of heritage interpretation. Tilden states that we are fascinated by artefacts which provoke us, relate to us, or reveal something new to us (Tilden 2007: 161–195). Tilden's principles were reinforced by a research project undertaken by the University of Education (Schwäbisch Gmünd) and the Haus der Geschichte museum (Stuttgart), which identified three criteria of strong museums artefacts: emotional connection, aesthetics, and an obvious narrative (Hackenbroich 2011). Applying these criteria to the 3D artefacts from

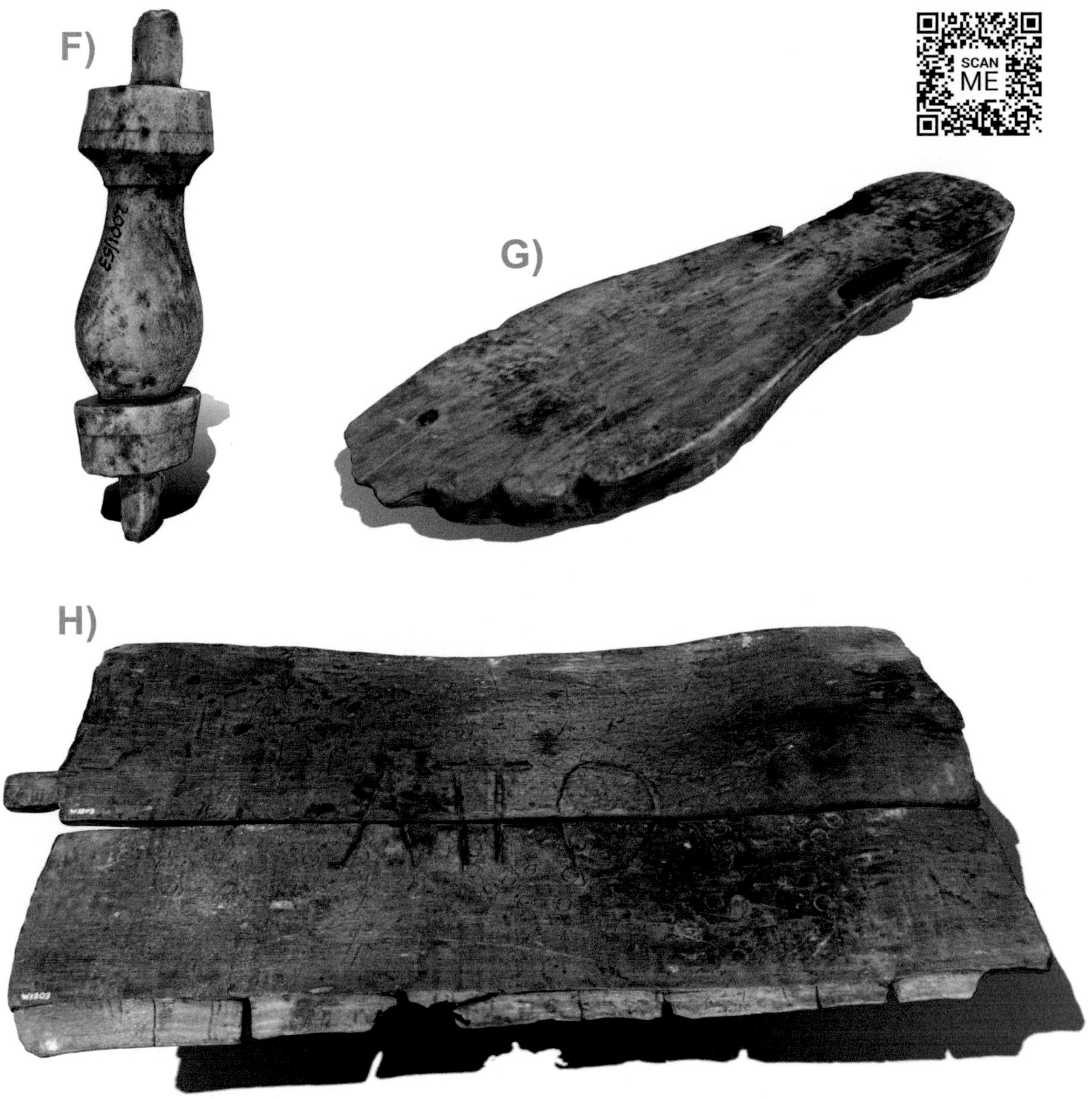

Figure 2: 3D models of the artefacts that receive the most attention when handling 3D prints. F: turned decorative object, G: bath clogs with decorative engraving of toes, H: Atto's workbench with hammer impressions. All models can be viewed at sketchfab.com or by scanning the QR code.

Vindolanda (Figure 1), it becomes clear why they attract attention: the target-practice skull (Figure 1A) and human skull (Figure 1B) with head injury offer obvious storylines, inviting further investigation; the toilet seat (Figure 1C) and toy sword (Figure 1D) are easy to connect with and offer clear narratives; and the peacock lid (Figure 1E) attracts attention through its delicate detail. This demonstrates that online displays follow the same rules as museum displays and that therefore the principles of museum interpretation and ethics apply equally to online displays, and that responsibility for care of the online collection rests with the collection management.

Museums ethics and online displays

A digital artefact is different from its real counterpart: the digital artefact can be duplicated, preserved indefinitely and viewed unrestricted, whereas the real artefact remains immobile in the display cabinet for protection from excessive handling. The evaluation of a National Museum of Scotland online project (Bayne *et al.* 2009) addressed the risk of losing the educational value of the real artefact when making it accessible on an online platform. Bayne *et al.* (2009) provided the following example: the Mona Lisa, as a digital image, can become a Mona Lisa Santa, a Mona Lisa alien, etc. It can be used playfully without any reference to the original intention; the user takes control of the object (Bayne *et al.* 2009: 4). It could be argued that the viewer is engaging with the artefact rather than just looking at it. A Roman altar could be coloured in; Vindolanda's turned wooden object (Figure 2F), which shows remains of red pigment, could be virtually restored. Artistic and expressive ways of visitor engagement are possible and numerous. Is this the way forward for online collections? And what are the ethical implications of this?

Examples of the complex ethical implications of 3D modelling, printing and manipulation include the skull of a murder victim, or the skeleton of the 11-year-old girl found in the barrack blocks at Vindolanda. 3D modelling and digital sharing of such human remains could be seen to leave them open to manipulation and disrespectful display. Does the buffer of time allow for the manipulation of such artefacts, or is it abuse?

Being able to display human remains online opens a discussion of how – or, indeed, if – this should be done (Errickson and Thompson 2020: 229). Relatively little attention has been paid so far to the ethical consequences of 3D imaging and printing (Jones 2020: 86). These techniques allow researchers and professionals to share objects and interact with the wider public within a museum setting, but what is lacking is guidance on how professionals can do that in an ethically correct and meaningful way (Errickson and Thompson 2020). The consensus seems to be that justification and contextualisation is key. Additionally, 3D models and prints should only be used for educational purposes, and visitors need to be made aware of the difference between casts and genuine artefacts (Biers 2020: 253; Bonney *et al.* 2020: 228; Smith and Hirst 2020).

The example of digital human remains shows that online collections need interpretation to ensure meaningful engagement (Museums Association 2015). But how can museum professionals ensure that a robust interpretation always accompanies a digital artefact when the latter is released 'in the wild'? As it stands, Sketchfab is a viewing platform for 3D models without any interpretation, although these can be added *post hoc*. This leads to the wider question of which guidelines, policies and procedures should be followed for online collections, bearing in mind that control may be lost in the public domain (Errickson and Thompson 2020).

Guidelines and examples in 3D modelling on the Wall

It is important to distinguish between online exhibitions, viewing platforms such as Sketchfab, and museum databases uploaded online. Museum databases have an archival function and are embedded in the museum's context, often offering limited and controlled public access. An early example of controlled public access to 3D modelled artefacts on Hadrian's Wall can be found in the

FREDHI (Frontiers of the Roman Empire Digital Humanities Initiative) project. In 2014, small finds and stone monuments from the Hadrian's Wall collection of the Great North Museum: Hancock were scanned with an Artec EVA. The primary aim was to identify the appropriate capture method for objects in a range of sizes and materials. After processing, the scans were manipulated and printed (Dolfini and Collins 2018: 36), and both digital and physical copies have remained in the possession of the Great North Museum and Newcastle University.

Sketchfab is a good example of a viewing platform for 3D models, presenting artefacts without museum context, isolated from their wider meaning and significance. However, online collections are useful resources, and museums must consider how their artefacts can be displayed meaningfully on the platform rather than appearing as if randomly uploaded.

This leads to the third form of display: a structured online exhibition. There are different degrees of structure to an online exhibition featuring 3D models of objects. In the Clayton Trustee's 'Virtual Museum', <http://www.claytonromantrust.online/virtual_museum/index.html>, the viewer can explore the structure of Coventina's Well through the ages, as well as 'zoom in' on the artefacts found during the well's excavations. The artefacts can be rotated and observed from all angles and are positioned where they were found in the well. Each find is accompanied by two levels of information: 'info' and 'technical', the latter offering a bibliography and more academic detail. While the Clayton Trustee's virtual museum does display 3D models of artefacts and structures, it is an online exhibition created by professionals for the benefit of the viewer. On the other end of the spectrum, the structured online exhibition *Digging up Memories,* hosted on the Vindolanda website, is developed for, and with the contribution of, the viewer. To develop the exhibition, the Vindolanda team and volunteers were asked about their favourite wooden artefacts, and the online display presents their responses through creative writing, voice recordings, and short film clips. In addition, the exhibition offers details on the chosen artefacts and 3D models embedded from Sketchfab.

The guidelines below are based on research and recent experience gained during this project, and can be seen as an attempt to raise awareness when looking at online displays, and as thoughts on exhibition planning.

Purpose

A common criticism levelled at digital exhibitions is that digitisation can often be seen as the main point, with educational purpose and thoughts on how to engage with the audience coming later. However, digitisation should be a support tool to help the museum better achieve these aims. It is therefore important to formulate clear objectives which go further than the process of digitisation, and to undertake the scanning with those active objectives constantly in mind. A further point raised is that education often comes after the main work has been done – is retrofitted – whereas it should be the other way round; if something is digital, it doesn't automatically mean it is good (Holt 2014). A project needs to focus on telling the stories of the artefacts; the 'why' should come well before the 'how' in our thinking. 3D models need a purpose, such as adding to research, being part of a wider story, or forming part of online exhibitions. These are the principles of basic exhibition design but are often overlooked in the rush to use a new technology (Holt 2014).

For *Digging up Memories*, interpretation was at the core of 3D scanning efforts, with artefacts being purposefully selected beforehand. 3D scanning was used to enhance the content and give the visitor a chance to see a digital close-up of the artefact and explore details not visible behind glass. A good example is the wooden bath clog (Figure 2G), with visitors to the online exhibition being able to rotate and zoom in on the 3D model. The wedges underneath the clog demonstrate signs of use, suggesting that the wearer might have felt attached to the shoe; even a small piece of the leather strap is preserved. These details are invisible on the static artefact on display in the museum, so 3D scanning adds value and supports the artefact's story. Zooming in and out also allows the visitor to look at the delicate details of the peacock wooden lid (Figure 1E), and investigate the punch marks and letters carved on Atto's work bench (Figure 2H). The artefact itself is key, rather than the fact that it has been scanned.

Embedding artefacts into a narrative

In the past, museums narrated history through artefacts. Through the help of modern digital media, museums can become accessible archives, registering artefacts for people to explore, but they may omit the narrative element of artefacts, which appear in isolation. In effect, the 'show' has lost its 'tell', and the techniques have become the attraction (van Boxtel *et al.* 2016).

A notable example of combining artefacts with a strong narrative is the Rijksmuseum in Amsterdam. The website (<https://www.rijksmuseum.nl>) presents paintings on display and those in storage. The online archive is arranged in themes and provides background information about artist and subject. The digital database of the Rijksmuseum demonstrates clearly which artefacts and paintings are on display. The museum also offers an app to plan in advance a self-led guided tour through the museum, and allows the exploration of paintings that are in storage. The Rijksmuseum was used as the model for *Digging up Memories*. Vindolanda's online exhibition offers different 'galleries' or topics the visitor can explore, such as 'on the move', 'waterways', and 'soldier's paraphernalia'. Voice recordings and videos were used to show the Vindolanda team members' personal connections to the artefacts.

A path to the original

Despite the promises of digitisation and virtualisation in our modern world, there seems to be a longing for tangible heritage as well. Educators argue that participants value the sensory experience of handling a historical artefact, so that the artefact functions as mediator between the past and the visitor (van Boxtel *et al.* 2016). Most teachers will recognise that historical objects can easily trigger people's curiosity, and that it is therefore important to offer a digital path that leads to the real artefacts. 3D scans help to protect the originals, and the scans themselves are not degradable or at risk of damage. Nevertheless, genuine artefacts have a context and presence because they are the real 2000-year-old objects. Therefore, there should be an opportunity for visitors to see the original artefacts in some capacity.

Most of the artefacts showcased in *Digging up Memories* are on display at Vindolanda or the Roman Army Museum, and the exhibition aimed to motivate people who have viewed the artefacts online to go into the museums. Additionally, an online lecture series was provided, as well as artefact-handling days on site. A substantial selection of digital artefacts were 3D printed for public handling (Figure 3). The 3D prints worked amazingly well at embedding narratives within digitised and original artefacts, where the public enjoyed spotting the details and became curious to find the originals in the museum. Furthermore, 3D prints offer opportunities for working with visually impaired groups, even though the material is not authentic. The 3D models from these projects had achieved over 14,000 online views worldwide by the start of 2022, exemplifying the reach and interest in self-directed viewing of archaeological material.

Conclusion

Utilising 3D scanning technology to produce digital and printable models of artefacts at Vindolanda Museum proved to be a valuable public archaeology tool with excellent pedagogical potential whilst maintaining the preservation of the original artefacts. Archives of the digital models also facilitated access for further analysis by researchers around the world. Collating and viewing these models with comparisons against observations in experimental research can uncover hidden knowledge

Figure 3: 3D printed shoe (left) beside the original wooden shoe (right). The 3D print is available for public handling at Vindolanda Museum.

on activities at Vindolanda. However, digital techniques *must* enhance the learning experience beyond the capabilities of existing approaches, with manageable logistics and costs (Kidd *et al.* 2011). As with all interpretive or educational projects, digitisation and online displays need a clear purpose and to be embedded within a narrative. These modern techniques should celebrate the genuine artefacts rather than the techniques themselves. Online displays must follow the same rules of interpretation and code of ethics as museums' exhibitions. It is the responsibility of the collection management to take ownership of and responsibility for how artefacts are showcased on the internet, yet it is a powerful new media technique that we should embrace as it has undoubted benefits. Similar discussions will certainly have taken place during the adoption of photography and video, and likewise, 3D scans will gradually become part of a museum's toolkit, taken for granted in the quest to explore the genuine artefacts.

This journey into the digital version of Hadrian's Wall has already begun. 3D scanning projects at Vindolanda Museum and beyond have been incorporated within several public engagement events. The *Digging up Memories* exhibit in particular has demonstrated how a robust narrative element can still be provided without requiring any access to the museum environment.

Bibliography

Allen, S. 2004. Designs for learning: Studying science museum exhibits that do more than entertain. *Science Education* 88 (S1): S17-S33

Bayne, S., Ross, J. and Williamson, Z. 2009. Objects, subjects, bits and bytes: learning from the digital collections of the National Museums, *Museum and Society* 7(2): 110-124

Biers, T. 2020. Rethinking Purpose, Protocol, and Popularity in Displaying the Dead in Museums, in Squires, K., Errickson, D. and Márquez-Grant, N. (eds) *Ethical Approaches to Human Remains*: 239-263. Switzerland: Springer Nature

Bonney, H., Bekvalac, J. and Phillips, C. 2020. Human Remains in Museum Collections in the United Kingdom, in Squires, K., Errickson, D. and Márquez-Grant, N. (eds) *Ethical Approaches to Human Remains*: 211-237. Switzerland: Springer Nature

Callieri, M., Ranzuglia, G., Dellepaine, M., Cignoni, P., and Scopigno, R. 2013. Meshlab as a complete open tool for the integration of photos and colour with high-resolution 3D geometry data, in Graeme, E., Sly, T., Chrysanthi, A., Murrieta-Flores, P., Papadopoulos, C., Romanowska, I., and Wheatley, D. (eds) *Archaeology in the Digital Era, Volume II. e-Papers from the 40th Annual Conference of Computer Applications and Quantitative Methods in Archaeology (CAA), Southampton, 26-29 March 2012*: 406-416. Amsterdam: Amsterdam University Press

Dolfini, A. and Collins, R. 2018. Modelling Physical and Digital Replication: Bridging the Gap Between Experimentation and Experience. *Open Archaeology* 4(1): 36-49

Errickson, D. and Thompson, T. J. U. 2020. Sharing Is Not Always Caring: Social Media and the Dead, in Squires, K., Errickson, D. and Márquez-Grant, N. (eds) *Ethical Approaches to Human Remains*: 299-313. Switzerland: Springer Nature

Frieman, C. J. and Janz, L. 2018. A Very Remote Storage Box Indeed: The Importance of Doing Archaeology with Old Museum Collections. *Journal of Field Archaeology*, 43(4): 257-268

Frieman, C. J. and Wilkin, N. 2016. "The Changing of the Guards"?: British Prehistoric Collections and Archaeology in the Museums of the Future. *Museum Worlds*, 4(1): 33-50

Hackenbroich, A. 2011. *Schülerinnen und Schüler forschen an authentischen Objekten*, Schwäbisch Gmünd: University of Education

Holt, J. 2014 The digital expert. *Museums Journal*: 24-27. Accessed 2 March 2022 <https://www.museumsassociation.org/museums-journal/features/2014/02/01022014-digital-experts/>

Jones, D. G. 2020. The Ethical Awakening of Human Anatomy: Reassessing the Past and Envisioning a More Ethical Future, in Squires, K., Errickson, D. and Márquez-Grant, N. (eds) *Ethical Approaches to Human Remains*: 73-94. Switzerland: Springer Nature

Kidd, J., Ntalla, I. and Lyons, W. 2011. Multi-touch interfaces in museum spaces: Reporting preliminary findings on the nature of interaction, in Ciolfi, L., Scott, K., and Barbieri, S. (eds) *Proceedings of the International Conference Re-Thinking Technology in Museums: Emerging Experiences*: 5-12. Limerick: University of Limerick

Kuzminsky, S. C. and Gardiner, M. S. 2012. Three-dimensional laser scanning: Potential uses for museum conservation and scientific research, *Journal of Archaeological Science*, 39(8): 2744-2751

Maxwell, L. E. and Evans, G. W. 2015. Museums as Learning Settings, *Journal of Museum Education*, 27(1): 3-7

Museums Association 2015. *Code of ethics for museums: Ethical principles for all who work for or govern museums in the UK*. London: Museums Association

Richards, W. H. and Menninger, M. 1993. A Discovery Room for Adults, *Journal of Museum Education*, 18(1): 6-11

Smith, S. E. and Hirst, C. S. 2020. 3D Data in Human Remains Disciplines: The Ethical Challenges, in Squires, K., Errickson, D. and Márquez-Grant, N. (eds) *Ethical Approaches to Human Remains*: 315-346. Switzerland: Springer Nature

Taylor, G., Hefford, R.J.W., Birley, A. & Huntley, J.P. 2019. Identifying the "blue substance" at the Roman site of Vindolanda, Northumberland. *Journal of Archaeological Science: Reports* 24: 582-587

Tilden, F. 2007. *Interpreting our heritage*. Chapel Hill: University of North Carolina Press

van Boxtel, C., Grever, M. and Klein, S. 2016. The appeal of heritage in education, in van Boxtel, C., Grever, M. and Klein, S. (eds) *Sensitive Pasts: Questioning Heritage in Education*: 1-18. New York: Berghahn Books

Williams, R., Thompson, T., Orr, C., Birley, A., and Taylor, G. 2019. 3D Imaging as a Public Engagement Tool: Investigating an Ox Cranium Used in Target Practice at Vindolanda. *Theoretical Roman Archaeology Journal*, 2(1): 1-16

From academic research to delivery: translating knowledge to deliver accessible and captivating programmes

Barbara Birley (Vindolanda Trust)
and Bill Griffiths (Tyne & Wear Archives & Museums)

Original academic research on Hadrian's Wall can be complex, scientific and require a vast amount of prior knowledge to understand it in context. New research is imperative in moving forward our understanding of our past, but how do we take this complex information and make it accessible, without dumbing down, to the public?

To answer this question, we must remember that the public is not a homogenous group. Some people who visit historic sites have little or no prior knowledge, while others will have spent time reading books, browsing the internet or watching documentaries. The public can also include other heritage professionals, who visit sites and museums in a work capacity or as tourists. When interpreting or translating the past, we develop tiered strategies to meet differing audience needs and employ several different delivery mechanisms to help the visiting public understand Hadrian's Wall and Roman Britain.

This work of translating the past can also lead to reciprocal relationships. At museums and heritage sites we are learning from our visitors through their interactions not only with the collections and sites but also through their outside knowledge. The latter leads to important conversations, which in turn lead to museums having more knowledge to feed back to the research community. Additional mutual benefits include the increase in co-curated community-based projects, where the public have a voice in how we put on exhibitions and what matters in the retelling of the past. This work helps the public to gain greater understanding of the Wall, its place in the local community and their support in its preservation.

There are numerous different ways that we can use the research at our disposal to help Hadrian's Wall's various publics to understand the past. This chapter explores some of the techniques, from the more traditional to the utterly modern, which we use to bring the archaeology to life for our visitors.

Introduction

Interpretation is the crucial step in making a museum a place of wonder and engagement. Visitors arrive at its doors, each with their own knowledge, passions and understanding. It is the job of the interpretation specialist to take what can be complex information and produce an engaging experience for every individual. One size does not fit all visitors and the curators and heritage interpreters on Hadrian's Wall employ a full arsenal of methods to develop not only their museum exhibitions, but activities and events, both analogue and digital, to offer a variable range of experiences for people.

Some of the methods that are used are traditional, such as tiered signage and labelling around the museums, while other methods, such as reconstruction, offer academic debate and help visitors to become immersed in the world of their past. Museums must also endeavour to be relevant to those visiting, and this has led to a shift into the use of more digital technologies in interpretation, such as the use of drone footage in exhibitions or the delivery of online educational classes during a global pandemic. In this ever-evolving process, the museums on the Wall both develop their own practice and work collaboratively, reaching out to the community which surrounds the World Heritage Site (WHS) to help to bring the Wall to life.

Experimental archaeology

Often when studying history, how and why an artefact was made and used have been lost. Experimental archaeology helps us gain a better understanding of the past. In this experimental process, a specific research question is tested through the practical production, use and formation of material culture and/or archaeological features. Thus, experimental archaeology is the process

Figure 1: Graham Taylor engaging with the public near the Vindolanda replica pottery kiln. © Vindolanda Trust

of testing a hypothesis, and this usually results in more information than can be gleaned solely by external examination of the object (Exarc 2001).

This practice in turn feeds into a better understanding by the researchers and interpreters and is an incredibly useful tool to help explain complex matters simply, especially if the process is well documented with images and film footage. It helps audiences to understand the functions of and give presence to artefacts and material that we no longer use. For example, why are Roman tent pegs so thin and pointy? This might seem like an unusual question, but has been the subject of a recent experimental archaeology project at Roman Vindolanda. In its museum collection, Vindolanda has many radially split, pointy, thin, wooden Roman tent pegs. The curatorial team decided that the only way to answer this question was to ask someone with skills in working with wood, and a replica Roman tent to come to the site and try it out. Working with Ancient Britain, a local Roman re-enactor (see Brown and Robson, Chapter 12), the team experimented with different types of pegs, helping them to understand their use. The conclusion is that the pegs were quick and easy to make, the relatively thin body meant that many could be made, and the pointy top meant that they did not split when being hammered into the ground (Hackenbroich 2020).

Further work can be done through experimental archaeology to understand building techniques and industrial practices. Many Roman sites have countless fragments of Roman pottery as it is one of the most prevalent artefacts to survive. But how was the pottery made and fired? We know through archaeological evidence excavated from pottery production sites across the empire that there are variations in the size and construction of kilns (G. Taylor 2021, personal communication, 8 November). However, the understanding of how they worked in a practical sense has been lost.

Mixing modern pottery construction with research into ancient methods and then putting this knowledge into practice is the undertaking of Graham Taylor at Potted History. In 2016, a replica Roman kiln was constructed by Taylor in the museum gardens at Vindolanda to answer some of these questions (Figure 1). Working alongside him, a team of volunteers continue to fire the kiln, making changes based on academic evidence such as understanding the variations in construction seen in the archaeological record. Furthermore, the team is recording practical statistics such as how much wood it takes to fire the kiln (G. Taylor 2021, personal communication, 8 November). This information can then be fed into further academic research, thus aiding our understanding of the impact of the Romans on the landscape in Britain and across the empire. The kiln is also a feature in the gardens at the site. This means that the work Taylor and his team are doing is very much in the public focus and visitors can engage with them and find out about their process, to build on their understanding and enjoyment of their past.

Reconstructions

Interpreting the physical remains on archaeological sites for visitors, particularly along Hadrian's Wall where often no more than the foundations of unfamiliar building types survive, can prove a challenge. To enable visitors to understand archaeological sites, reconstructions are a favoured tool, be it in the form of picture or model (Figure 2). Pictures can evoke atmosphere and, on occasion, create a sense of drama. Cut-aways allow a view inside a building and can demonstrate how it might work – most famously in the reconstruction drawings of the latrine block at Housesteads (Connolly 1991: 23). Their chief limitation is that they can only operate two dimensionally. Partly

Figure 2: Reconstruction methods. Top left: Cutaway reconstruction of the commanding officer's house at Vindolanda; Top right: Full-scale reconstruction of Arbeia's (South Shields) stone gateway. © Tyne & Wear Archives & Museums; Bottom left: Model of Vindolanda's west gate. © Vindolanda Trust; Bottom right: Replica temple in the Vindolanda garden © Vindolanda Trust

for this reason, models are perennially popular as they can give a sense of the scale of a site and the way in which the structures interacted. This can be seen in the model of the fort at Arbeia, which shows the point at which the south wall of the Antonine fort was being dismantled and the fort enlarged southwards to become a supply base at the start of the 3rd century AD. This is a potentially complex story easily brought to life by an evocative model.

Illustrations and models are at their best when they are a collaboration between illustrators and modellers, and academics, working to ensure research is represented and speculation kept to a minimum. The ultimate expression of this can be found in full-scale reconstructions of buildings, in effect 1:1 scale models.

Arbeia (South Shields), Segedunum (Wallsend) and Vindolanda all feature full-scale reconstructions of Roman buildings (Figure 2). While often regarded as contentious, with the fear that they fossilise the view of a building type in the mind of the visitor, it can be cogently argued that carefully researched reconstructions are one of the ultimate translations of academic research. Archaeologists and architects need to combine forces to ensure the translation of the varied sources of evidence (building foundations, fragments of stone, sculptural evidence from other buildings, primary literary sources and figurative representations) creates a coherent functioning structure (Bidwell *et al.* 1988). Indeed, in some ways such reconstructions can also be argued to be an example of experimental archaeology. This was certainly the case with the reconstructed turf and stone sections of Hadrian's Wall at Vindolanda, where building times and practical issues were recorded (Birley 1977: 158-164).

Not only do reconstructions aid in the presentation of the past, but they also engage people much more directly with the concept of research. Put simply, show people an illustration or a small model of a building and they will likely accept it without question. However, a full-scale reconstruction is much better at challenging preconceptions, and visitors are more likely to ask how we know it is so tall, how we know what rooms were used for which purpose, and so on.

The reconstructed bath house at Wallsend proves this point. This was built to the ground plan of the bath house at Chesters Roman fort – one of the better-preserved buildings from Roman Britain. The changing room area in the reconstruction seems much, much larger than the remains at Chesters – yet they are the same size. It was only once the reconstruction had been built that it was really possible to appreciate what a significant social space the changing room area would be – akin to a good-sized village hall today. The true scale of the space is simply not something one can appreciate from the remains on site at Chesters (Griffiths 2005: 340). Again, the act of interpretation was research in its own right.

Reconstructions also allow for a much greater engagement with the evidence used by archaeologists. People often challenge the monumental scale of the gateway at Arbeia for example. However, it is based on strong evidence, such as the surviving voussoir stone on the east gate at Birdoswald, the window heads on surviving remains from the excavation of the gateway at South Shields, and so on (Bidwell *et al.* 1988). Importantly, the gateway itself incorporates a display that explains where all the evidence came from and some potential alternative reconstructions. If one is attempting a reconstruction, then it is vitally important to set out the evidence and the alternatives where possible. Time and again it is the uncertainty of our knowledge that draws people in and engages them more deeply. The reconstructed section of Hadrian's Wall at Wallsend includes a section setting out the different possible ways in which the Wall may have been decorated. One theory is that it might have been whitewashed, and excavations of a section of the Wall at Denton to the west of Newcastle suggested that it may have had a specific form of decoration known as ribbon pointing. The visitor is invited to make their own mind up, having been introduced to the uncertainty surrounding the potential evidence for decoration of the Wall (Bidwell 2018: 161).

Reconstructions are a much more widely accepted technique on the continent, with a long history. The reconstructions at the Saalburg in Germany were started in 1897. More recent work includes new interpretative reconstructions – that is to say, structures that are obviously modern but give a sense of the scale of buildings, for example, the bath house at Xanten on the Lower Rhine, where a modern structure is effectively suspended over the Roman remains (Muller 2018), and the gateway to the Roman fort at Lussonium on the Hungarian section of the Danube *Limes,* where the gateway is reconstructed as an impressionistic frame. This gives visitors an opportunity to climb the tower and experience the view a Roman sentry would have had, and demonstrates the space such a gateway would occupy. The challenges and successes of developing an archaeological park that includes reconstruction are discussed in Chapter 8 by Pausch.

Re-enactment

Historic re-enactment is a large-scale hobby in the UK. Many of the museums of Hadrian's Wall host Roman re-enactors – from bigger groups such as the Ermine Street Guard (incidentally celebrating

Figure 3: The Ermine Street Guard's display at Vindolanda, including the replica leather tents based on evidence excavated from the site. © Vindolanda Trust

their 50th anniversary in 2022) to individual practitioners, they cover many aspects of Roman life, such as cooking, make-up, metalworking, carpentry and, of course, military drill. Whether in the first person (acting as if they are a Roman) or the third person (explaining their kit and actions from a modern perspective) they undoubtedly contribute to the interpretation of a site, animating it in a way not possible with other techniques, not least via the opportunity for visitors to enter into conversation (Figure 3). Regrettably, some academics have in the past dismissed re-enactment as a valid branch of research, but many re-enactors base their replica kit on the latest research, and are often happy to engage in debate. The careful reconstruction of a leather tent, based on archaeological evidence from Carlisle and Vindolanda, has not only provided a clear visual representation for the public but has, perhaps inevitably, raised more questions about how the tent may have functioned, and in turn influenced how researchers understand future discoveries (Haines and Sumner 2000: 121-122).

Indeed, re-enactment is very much a form of research in its own right (Griffiths 2000) and offers a huge degree of overlap with experimental archaeology. The re-enactment group at Arbeia, named *Cohors Quinta Gallorum* after the early third-century garrison at the fort, have experimented with replica Roman weaponry from the gateway, gathering data about the potential effectiveness of different types of hand-launched weapons available to the Roman army. This research becomes incorporated into displays and presented to the public. Two re-enactors, who are also business owners operating on Hadrian's Wall, talk about their perspective on their work in Chapter 12 (Robson and Brown).

Digital interpretation

As the population moves to become digital natives, many visitors will not separate the use of digital technology from their museum experience, because such technologies will have infiltrated every part of life. Museums must shift to using digital technologies to aid in the interpretation of collections and heritage sites. However, it is imperative to offer a good balance and to make sure it refers back to the historical and archaeological information.

Historical games, or so-called 'edutainment', have been used for many years to help children engage with history and museums. Examples of this on Hadrian's Wall include the use of Minecraft sessions at Arbeia Roman fort in 2016 (In & Around 2016) to the newly developed Missing Dead app at the site of Vindolanda (Vindolanda Trust 2020). Games are an innovative and engaging way for children to understand the past – Chapter 10, by Stocks and Birley, talks about this topic in more depth. The global pandemic of 2020 catapulted many museums into the realms of digital engagement. Although some had been working in this area prior to the subsequent worldwide lockdowns, the pandemic created the perfect conditions for expanding this work; many museums still wanted to engage with the public, but the public, who suddenly had ample time to engage, could not physically visit (Feinstein 2020).

At the Great North Museum: Hancock, the learning team ran a series of online focus days reaching full classrooms of children. Although the days have not yet focused on a Roman theme, they have reached over 14,000 children in nine online session – with one occasion reaching 4000 children. The focus days include virtual tours of the galleries, storytelling, 'ask the expert' sessions, and workshops focusing on the collections (M. Fail 2021, personal communication, 9 November). As a collaborative project in 2022, the learning teams across the Wall are developing a joint Roman-themed focus day that will be live-streamed. This pilot will be part of the 1900th anniversary of Hadrian's Wall festival and will help to ensure that, whatever the pandemic or other future events throw at us, we are able to ensure children get to engage with the Wall at the earliest opportunity.

As a result of the pandemic, the Vindolanda Trust developed an online exhibition called *Digging up Memories* (Vindolanda Trust 2021) in order to pilot their digital community engagement work. As

Figure 4: Roman Britain in Colour on display at the Great North Museum. The display is a collaboration between the museum and the Hadrian's Wall Community Archaeology Project (WallCAP), working alongside creative studio NOVAK. © Tyne & Wear Archives & Museums

part of an Arts Council England's Designated Development Fund project 'Digitising Vindolanda's Wooden Collection', and in response to the ongoing crisis, the project digitally recorded – some with sound and some with video – the staffs', trustees' and volunteers' connections to the wooden collection. The project also worked to 3D scan several very fragile wooden objects – the educational advantages and challenges of which are discussed by Hackenbroich and Williams in Chapter 4. The project had some remarkable outcomes that went beyond collecting the digital elements. The participants felt that it broke down barriers between front of house staff, curatorial/archaeological staff and volunteers, as well as creating an enormous sense of wellbeing for those involved, at a time when communities coming together was so important.

In another example of mixing collections and digital work, the Great North Museum has brought a key selection of Roman altars to life – working with digital innovators to project colours onto them, restoring them to the way they would have looked during the Roman period (Figure 4). As well as bringing out the features on the altars the projections have been animated, in some cases providing an English translation of the lettering, and in others broader animations indicating aspects of the altars' purpose. This intimate *son et lumiere* communicates a whole new level of interpretation, and experience, to its audience (Tyne & Wear Archives & Museums 2021).

Co-curation with the community

Interpreters are tasked with the job of taking large, complex concepts and bringing them to life through storytelling. This can be done by physical or digital reconstructions or via experimental archaeology, but they must be relevant. Forward-thinking exhibitions need to create activities instead of just generating knowledge, and this can be done through innovative interactions with the public. The democratising of museums, or giving access to the collections to communities,

Figure 5: Hadrian's Cavalry. Top: 'Hadrian' leading the Turma as part of Hadrian's Cavalry. © Bill Griffiths. Bottom: temporary Hadrian's Cavalry exhibition at Vindolanda. © Vindolanda Trust

helps curators assemble many voices for their collections instead of just one. It creates 'citizen curators' who create their own connections to the museums they visit. Curators and interpreters can help visitors research, read critically and develop their own passions for not just Hadrian's Wall but their cultural heritage as well.

Several community projects have added much to our interpretation of the Wall. The Wallquest community project on Tyneside conducted research that located the position of the bath house at Wallsend, among many notable successes including publishing an alternative route to the Hadrian's Wall Trail on Tyneside, taking people on the admittedly less attractive route more directly followed by the Wall through the urban area (Hodgson 2015). A more recent example of the power of participation on the Wall is provided in Chapter 9 by Collins. Traditionally, people may think that a 1900-year-old monument does not have much to teach us about society today, but that is simply not the case. As society shifts, it opens up new areas for research to improve our understanding of the past, and museum interpretation can become a two-way bridge between formal academics and communities. Examples of this can be seen in the recent work done to engage the wider public with an understanding of the presence of Africans on the line of the Wall. This work has both inspired, and in turn been inspired by, members of the African diaspora in Northern England (Prevatt Goldstein 2021).

Hadrian's Cavalry

2017 saw the museums of Hadrian's Wall work together to create a 'dispersed' exhibition on the Roman cavalry, a subject overlooked generally in studies of the frontier, despite the fact that the majority of units stationed on the Wall were mixed units containing both infantry and cavalry, with four forts known to have been garrisoned by units that were purely cavalry (Anderson *et al.* 2017: 14-15). The ten participating museums each explored different aspects of Roman cavalry, facilitated by star loans from museums and collections across the UK and Europe. It was important to the curatorial team behind the exhibition that it was rooted in the latest research. As an element of the project, the 2016 International Roman Military Equipment Conference took the theme of cavalry in the Roman world. Academics from across Europe came together with re-enactors to consider some of the issues in our knowledge of the topic and the evidence for cavalry equipment. Much of this fed into the exhibition's associated interpretation, ensuring the exhibition set out the latest thinking on the subject.

One section of the interpretation really grabbed the public's attention, and that was 'Turma! Hadrian's Cavalry at Carlisle'. This large-scale cavalry event recreated a full *turma* (a Roman cavalry unit akin to a century of infantry) of 30 riders, possibly for the first time since the ending of Roman rule (Figure 5). Spectacular as this was, it was also an archaeological experiment, with the riders attempting to recreate the complex movements of the *hippika gymnasia* as described by Arrian in his *Ars Tactica,* the results of which were published along with other papers on aspects of cavalry in the *Journal of Roman Military Equipment Studies* (Coulston 2018). What was particularly fascinating was that the public responded as much, if not more, to the concept of this as an archaeological experiment as to the sense of spectacle of the event. This angle also involved the filming of a special 'Digging for Britain' documentary (Griffiths 2021:149).

Hadrian's Wall 1900th festival

In 2022 the Wall has its 1900th anniversary (taking the generally, but not universally, accepted year of AD 122 as its foundation). The festival that accompanies this anniversary is designed to ensure communities along the line of the WHS explore its meaning for them. The programme includes exhibitions, re-enactments, art works and much more. It offers the opportunity to explore new avenues of research in order to tell a more complete story of the frontier, for example looking at evidence of diversity along the Wall, with multicultural garrisons throughout the Roman period.

Through this project, Hadrian's Wall has a unique opportunity to bring together many different strands of the wider community. Many museums are developing temporary exhibitions and themed events programmes, but stakeholder groups are also embarking on their own collaborative projects. Despite the complexity of different governing bodies and community groups on the Wall, this project will illustrate the communal environment that is the WHS. This excellent celebration brings together not only academics and visitors, but it helps to engage the whole Wall community, including many who have not been involved in the past. Indeed, the festival is driven by a sense of community participation, with people invited to explore what 1900 years of the WHS means to them.

Keeping it all up to date

One of the great challenges for museums is presenting the latest archaeological research, theories and finds. Permanent galleries can take years to design and build, making them hard to update with new thinking. There is a further danger that the latest theories may be rejected or become outdated very quickly, particularly if not accepted by the wider scholarship base for the Wall. To this end cutting-edge theories are often avoided in museums' permanent displays. New discoveries, however, are another matter.

Excavations in 1997 and 1998 at Wallsend Roman fort saw the first complete excavation of a Roman cavalry barrack, a type of building only previously seen in excavations of sections of buildings, and, as a result, not completely accepted as a building type (Hodgson 2003: 71). However, the recovery of the full plan of two such barracks at Segedunum confirmed the theory. A reconstructed section was incorporated into designs for the museum that opened at the site in 2000, a rare opportunity for a permanent display to utilise new discoveries and present new thinking and interpretation.

In the wider museum world, it is comparatively rare to have museums located at sites where live excavations are ongoing. However, on Hadrian's Wall it is more common, with live excavations in the last decade at the majority of sites along the Wall with associated museums, including Senhouse Museum at Maryport, Tullie House Museum at Carlisle, Birdoswald, Corbridge, Vindolanda, Wallsend and South Shields. This means displays need to be changed to incorporate the latest discoveries.

Temporary exhibitions are an expedient way of presenting new theories and new information. For example, excavations at the eastern end of the Wall, beneath urban Tyneside, revealed the presence of a series of post holes between the Wall and its ditch. There was some debate about the discoveries; although the excavators were always clear that they held upright posts, some preferred to see them as *lilia*, sharpened stakes set below ground – essentially hidden traps. A temporary exhibition at Wallsend presented them as *cippi* – effectively a series of upright posts holding some form of natural entanglement in place (like barbed wire) in a 1:1 scale diorama (Bidwell 2005). Such temporary exhibitions can also invite the public to review evidence and make up their own minds. For example, in 2022, as part of the 1900th anniversary of the Wall, the museum at Arbeia will present the evidence for the theorised, but as yet unconfirmed, Hadrianic period fort at the site. The known fort there has an Antonine origin, but material recovered from the site has offered a tantalising glimpse of an earlier foundation.

All museums can present the latest finds through the medium of the temporary exhibition but in the 2011 refurbishment of Vindolanda and the Roman Army Museum, the designers worked with the curatorial team to create display cases in which it would be easy to change labels and objects round so that newer discoveries at the site could be given precedence. Due to the ongoing excavation on the Vindolanda site, new discoveries are a yearly occurrence and with each season extraordinary artefacts that tell us more about the Roman world are uncovered. The museum displays were designed so that new objects could be added in relevant spaces, as happened in 2019 when a small copper alloy votive hand was found. It was interpreted as a religious object, probably associated with Jupiter Dolichenus, and added to the museum's religion case.

Designed into the Vindolanda museum is also a case in the Archaeology room which houses new finds from the previous year's excavations. The museum has developed a social media strategy in conjunction with the archaeological and curatorial staff. Many of the best objects from the year are first shared via social media fresh from the excavations. Then the objects are conserved, and the best of the best are displayed in this case in the museum. Sometimes objects that are relatively common or even quite simple can receive the biggest following, which can be surprising for the museum staff. In 2019, the stone gaming board reached 1600 likes with 109 comments and 830 shares via Facebook, which given its simple construction and commonality on the site was a fantastic show of interest (Vindolanda Trust 2019). The gaming board not only went into the next year's 'recent finds' case but even got a blog (Penn and Courts 2019) where academics discussed more information about it. This process helps the visitors make an instant connection with the Vindolanda Trust's digital profile as well as the physical artefact when visiting the site.

Concluding remarks

We would argue that interpreting the Wall is not only about distilling research into an accessible format in order to engage with a wider public, ensuring they have access to the latest views from academia, but also to create a more symbiotic process where research questions can be grounded in public interest. More than this though, the very act of interpreting the frontier leads to new research. Questions are constantly being asked and challenged. By developing a format of varied interpretation methods, museums can work collaboratively, acting as the conduit between academic research and the public.

This is important as it creates stronger connections between society and the WHS. Put simply, the more and wider range of people who value the monument, the better able we will all be to preserve it for the future. Palpably demonstrating that it has meaning in peoples' lives today will attract much needed investment to ensure it can continue to have that effect tomorrow.

Many of the methods discussed above do not work in isolation. Re-enactors and reconstructions must be based on academic research in order to be effective. The work to produce these, through methodical use of experimental archaeology, helps to create interpretation that is as close as we can get to the understanding of our past. This process is ongoing and should be consistently challenged and explored not only by the academics through new research, but also by working with and involving the public. These reciprocal relationships help to develop a community who not only visit and work on Hadrian's Wall, but also become volunteers and advocates driving the conservation and protection of the WHS, making sure it is better understood and available for future generations to enjoy.

Bibliography

Anderson, J., Birley, B., Croom, A., Griffiths, B. Knowles, A., Laskey, J. McIntosh, F., Mills, N., Padley, T. 2017 *Hadrian's Cavalry*, Newcastle upon Tyne: Tyne & Wear Archives & Museums

Bidwell, P. 2018. *Hadrian's Wall at Wallsend.* Arbeia Society Roman Archaeological Studies 1. South Shields: Arbeia Society

Bidwell, P. 2005. The systems of obstacles on Hadrian's Wall: their extent, date and purpose, *Arbeia Journal* 8: 53-76.

Bidwell, P., Miket, R. and Ford, B. 1988. The reconstruction of a gate at the Roman fort of South Shields, in Bidwell, P., Miket, R. and Ford, B. (eds) *Portae cum turribus: Studies of Roman Fort gates*, BAR British series 206: 155-231. Oxford: BAR Publishing

Birley, R. 1977. *Vindolanda: A Roman frontier post on Hadrian's Wall.* London: Thames and Hudson

Connolly, P. 1991. *The Roman Fort.* Oxford: Oxford University Press.

Coulston, J.C.N. (ed) 2018. *Cavalry in the Roman World: proceedings of the Nineteenth International Roman Military Equipment Conference.* Pewsey: The Armatura Press

Exarc 2001. Experimental Archaeology. Exarc. Accessed on 1 November 2021 <https://exarc.net/experimental-archaeology>

Feinstein, L. 2020. Beginning of a new era: how culture went virtual in the face of crisis [online]. *The Guardian.* 8th April. Accessed 1 November 2021 <https://www.theguardian.com/culture/2020/apr/08/art-virtual-reality-coronavirus-vr>

Griffiths, W.B. 2000. Re-enactment as research: towards a set of guidelines for re-enactors and academics in Croom, A. and Griffiths, W.B. (eds) *Re-enactment as research: proceedings of the twelfth International Roman Military Equipment Conference, South Shields 1999,* Journal of Roman Military Equipment Studies 11: 135-139. Pewsey: The Association for Roman Military Equipment Studies

Griffiths, W.B. 2005. Interpretation of Roman Archaeological Sites for Visitors, in Fernandez Ochoa, C. and Garcia Diaz, P. (eds) *Unidad y diversidad en el Arco Atlantico en epoca romana,* BAR international series 1371: 337-342. Oxford: BAR Publishing

Griffiths, W.B. 2021 Hadrian's Cavalry: Strengthening Public Presentation through Partnership, in Mills, N. (ed) *Visitor Experiences and Audiences for the Roman Frontiers: Developing good practice in presenting World Heritage,* BAR International Series 3066: 145-152. Oxford: BAR publishing.

Hackenbroich, A. 2020. The Romans, camping, and me. The Vindolanda Trust. Accessed 1 November 2021 <https://www.vindolanda.com/blog/the-romans-camping-and-me>

Haines, T. and Sumner, G. 2000. Recreating the world of the Roman soldier: the work of the Ermine Street Guard, in Croom, A. and Griffiths, W.B. (eds) *Re-enactment as research: proceedings of the twelfth International Roman Military Equipment Conference, South Shields 1999,* Journal of Roman Military Equipment Studies 11: 119-127. Pewsey: The Association for Roman Military Equipment Studies

Hodgson, N. 2003. *The Roman Fort at Wallsend (Segedunum): Excavations in 1997-8.* Newcastle: Tyne & Wear Archives & Museums

Hodgson, N. 2015. *Walking Hadrian's Wall on Tyneside.* Newcastle upon Tyne: Tyne & Wear Archives & Museums/Wallquest.

In & Around Magazine 2016. Tyne & Wear Museums Announce Groundbreaking Creative Technology Workshops [online]. Accessed 1 November 2021 <https://www.inandaroundmag.co.uk/tyne-wear-museums-announce-groundbreaking-creative-technology-workshops/>

Muller, M. 2018. Colonia Ulpia Traiana: the Xanten Archaeological Park and its role in the World Heritage Site Lower German Limes, in Bruin R. de, Hertog, A. and Paardekooper, R. (eds) *The Roman Frontier along the River Rhine: the role of Museums in revitalising Cultural Landscapes*: 43-53. Netherlands: ICOM Netherlands

Penn, T. and Courts, S. 2019. Playing games at Vindolanda. The Vindolanda Trust. Accessed 1 November 2021 <https://www.vindolanda.com/blog/playing-games-at-vindolanda>

Prevatt Goldstein, B. (ed) 2021. *African Lives in Northern England: from Roman times to the 21st Century.* Newcastle: Society of Antiquaries of Newcastle upon Tyne

Tyne & Wear Archives & Museums 2021. Roman altars reimagined in vivid colour at the Great North Museum: Hancock. Accessed 17 November 2021 <https://www.twmuseums.org.uk/news/roman-altars-reimagined-in-vivid-colour-at-the-great-north-museum-hancock>

Vindolanda Trust 2019. The Vindolanda Trust Facebook Page post. 23 April. Accessed on 1 November 2021. <https://www.facebook.com/TheVindolandaTrust/photos/2163248523756278>

Vindolanda Trust 2020. The Missing Dead app. Accessed 26 October 2021 <https://www.vindolanda.com/the-missing-dead-app>

Vindolanda Trust 2021. Digging up memories online exhibition. Accessed 26 October 2021 <https://www.vindolanda.com/Listing/Category/digging-up-memories>

The role of collections management in the future of the World Heritage Site

Frances McIntosh (English Heritage)
and Elsa Price (Tullie House Museum and Art Gallery Trust)

While Hadrian's Wall sites and museums today present engaging, well researched, layered interpretations of both structures and finds to the visiting public, what can be seen on display is only the tip of the iceberg. Vast collections, with their tapped and untapped potential, their challenges and their success stories, lie in the stores of five museum bodies across the country. This chapter focuses on the collections held by English Heritage and the Tullie House Museum and Art Gallery Trust. Here, two curators explore both the daily difficulties they face – such as overflowing stores and reduced funding – and their problem-solving projects of volunteer participation at Corbridge and international research partnerships at Tullie House. They discuss what can be done, now and in the future, to realise the Hadrian's Wall collections' full potential.

Introducing the Hadrian's Wall collections

Hadrian's Wall is much more than just the monument that visitors see winding across the country; it is also the collections of objects, found along the Wall and its buffer zone, which help us populate that past landscape. To fully understand life on Hadrian's Wall, visitors must see the museums and collections as well as the sites. There are five museum bodies along Hadrian's Wall, managing 11 museums and multiple collections stores (Figure 1). As with most museums across the world, what is on display is only a very small percentage of the collections held by these institutions. Table 1 shows where the collections for each museum or site are held, and which organisation is responsible for the material.

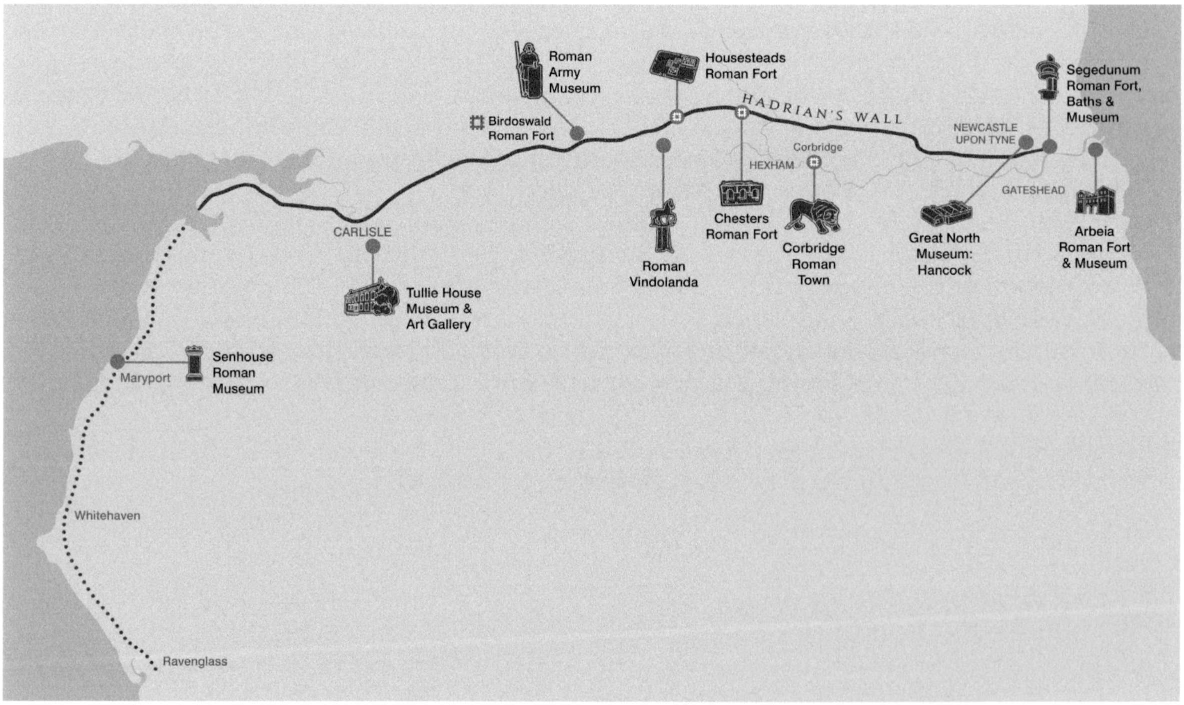

Figure 1: Map showing the location of the museums along the World Heritage Site.
© Tyne and Wear Archives & Museums

Body	Museum/Site	Stored Collection Location
Tyne & Wear Archives & Museums	Arbeia, South Shields Roman Fort	Tyne & Wear Archives & Museums stores
	Segedunum Roman Fort and Museum	
	Great North Museum, Newcastle	
National Trust, English Heritage, and Tyne & Wear Archives & Museums	Housesteads Roman Fort	Corbridge, Helmsley, and Tyne & Wear Archives & Museums stores
English Heritage	Corbridge Roman Town and Museum	Corbridge and Helmsley
	Chesters Roman Fort and Museum (the Clayton Collection)	Corbridge and Helmsley
	Birdoswald Roman Fort	Tullie House Museum and Art Gallery stores
The Vindolanda Trust	Roman Vindolanda Fort and Museum	Vindolanda
	Roman Army Museum	Vindolanda
Tullie House Museum and Art Gallery	Tullie House Museum and Art Gallery	Tullie House Museum and Art Gallery stores
Senhouse Trust	Maryport Museum	Maryport Museum

Table 1: Correlating the site (or museum), its collection and collecting body

This chapter focuses on two collections which span the central and western sectors of Hadrian's Wall: the Tullie House Museum collection and that of English Heritage. Tullie House Museum and Art Gallery (THMAG) holds more than just material from Hadrian's Wall. Besides archaeology, its collections include fine and decorative art, an Arts Council Designated Natural Science collection, local history, costume, and photography collections. Within archaeology, time periods from across Cumbria are represented, from prehistory to the Reivers, but the Roman material is predominant. Besides other key Cumbrian sites such as Brougham cemetery, Tullie House cares for much of the material from the western end of Hadrian's Wall. This includes Birdoswald Roman fort, despite the site being managed by English Heritage. Roman Carlisle, largely excavated by Carlisle Archaeology Unit (CAU) from approximately the 1970s to early 2000s, forms the bulk of the Hadrian's Wall collections. As well as formally excavated sites, THMAG also cares for material from Hadrian's Wall which has been discovered by antiquarians and amateur excavations, metal detectorists and the general public.

The English Heritage collections differ slightly from English Heritage sites due to the historic management of these sites. For example, the Housesteads archive is split between English Heritage (with part also in the Clayton Collection) and Tyne & Wear Archives & Museums, and although English Heritage manages the site, it is owned by the National Trust. Housesteads and Birdoswald are typical examples of the complex history of management and collections across Hadrian's Wall. This can often make collections access more convoluted for researchers, although communication between the Hadrian's Wall curators alleviates some of these issues. Corbridge Roman Town is the largest collection from Hadrian's Wall that English Heritage cares for, with over 59,000 records at the time of writing. It is also the collection with the largest primary archive from excavations, dating back to 1906. The final collection within the care of English Heritage is the Clayton Collection, which although displayed at Chesters, contains material from multiple sites across the central sector of Hadrian's Wall. This material was collected from excavations in the 19th century and so brings with it the issues of its time.

Excavations of Hadrian's Wall have been taking place for over 200 years, and finds have been unearthed and added to the Wall's collections throughout this period. Since documentation and record keeping were not a high priority for most antiquarians, the condition of the Hadrian's Wall collections are often not ideal or consistent. Historic collections, those which have not been recovered under modern excavation conditions, pose unique problems for curators. The Clayton Collection, for example, has no primary archive, around 20% of the material is unprovenanced and findspot information is often no more specific than a fort site. However, this material is no less important than that excavated under modern standards and deposited following up-to-date guidelines (see McIntosh 2019 for an example of using historic collections – the Clayton Collection – for research).

Despite modern standards and technologies, professionally excavated material does not always guarantee functional collections that can be readily absorbed and managed by museums. The movement over the past 50 years towards commercial archaeology can leave archaeological material, including material from Hadrian's Wall and its wider buffer zone, vulnerable. An example of this can be found in the folding of CAU, the principal excavators of Roman Carlisle in the early 2000s. The collapse of CAU left the large and significant excavations of Carlisle stranded, with excavation archives dating back to the 1980s still in the post-excavation phase. Although the material was absorbed and stored by THMAG, museums do not often have the infrastructure, expertise, or facilities to carry out post-excavation and publication work. Whilst some sites, such as The Lanes and Carlisle Millennium Project, were distributed to other commercial units for completion and publication, much of the CAU material has not been fully written up and remains part of the backlog of the museum. The folding of CAU will continue to have a long-lasting impact on THMAG as the museum works through the material left in varying stages of the post-excavation process.

Museum collections and the 'crisis in archaeology'

The CAU case is only one example of a wider national crisis in archaeology, which Hadrian's Wall's collections are not protected from despite holding UNESCO World Heritage status. This crisis has many faces, the first of which is a lack of standardisation and coordination from units, who excavate the material, and museums, who store the archive. Despite the professionalisation of both sectors, there is no national oversight of how excavated material should be prepared for museum deposition, resulting in differing standards across the country. For example, there is no enforced national guidance on which aspects of archaeological material should be retained and which should be disposed of, leading to overwhelmed museum stores when too much material is deposited. Despite the Chartered Institute for Archaeologists (CIfA) and Historic England working together to provide a toolkit for this (Chartered Institute for Archaeologists 2019), units often look to museums for guidance on a case-by-case basis, along with requests for assistance and support in other aspects of the archive.

Another face of this crisis is that museums themselves are losing specialists and are struggling to advise units on what they need. The Society for Museum Archaeology (SMA) identified in 2012 that only a third of museums have a specialist archaeology curator (Edwards 2012: 19-20). Within that third, around a quarter had other requirements within their role, such as caring for other collections outside of archaeology (*ibid.*). Given cuts to museum staffing this percentage could be even lower today, with specialist curators becoming very rare. While it is fortunate that Hadrian's Wall does retain specialist curators for archaeology across its museums, these curators have further responsibilities within their role, which restricts their ability to dedicate their time solely to the Hadrian's Wall collections. This lack of dedicated time to use expertise, has left many museums unable to draft appropriate guidelines for excavators, or negotiate box fees to cover the expense of accessioning archives into their collections (Vincent 2019). Further compounding these issues is the lack of space. With 71% of museums declaring only 20 square metres or less of space left in 2016 (Boyle *et al.* 2016), over 28,700 boxes of artefacts and ecofacts across England, Scotland and Wales were undeposited as of 2012 (Smith and Tindall 2012). Whilst in store with commercial units, this archaeological material has little to no scope for public access.

These crises and concerns affect all museums across the country, including those on Hadrian's Wall, to differing degrees. Even with the good work being done by organisations such as the SMA, CIfA and Historic England to standardise and empower institutions to care for incoming material, there is a large legacy of backlog, from undocumented antiquarian finds to incomplete and unstandardised commercially excavated archaeological material.

Figure 2: Volunteers working on the unfinished pottery type series from Corbridge, a project only possible with their time. © English Heritage Trust

The effects of the crisis

In order to share the Hadrian's Wall collections and allow people to engage with them, they need to be documented to at least a basic level. Documentation allows research enquiries, store tours, new exhibitions and digital outreach to be facilitated. If museums do not know what they have, and where it is, they cannot engage people with them. An example of this problem is pottery from Corbridge Roman Town. This is an extremely valuable resource as one of the largest pottery assemblages from the frontier, yet in its current state, it cannot be used for research as it is not sorted, or recorded, by fabric, form or context. It is therefore simply pottery in boxes: in theory, it is useless to researchers, curators and visitors. The sorting and recording of pottery from Corbridge Roman Town is a desirable yet colossal undertaking. To date, 180 boxes of Samian pottery have been catalogued by context (if the context is known) and a team of volunteers is working to achieve the same for the rest of the material (Figure 2).

Problems like this are often hidden, or unknown – there may be a site publication, and so it is assumed all materials from the site have been studied. However, it is often only highlights of the archive or part of the archive which has made it to publication stage. This may be for many reasons: perhaps funding for the publication covered only certain years (which was the case for Corbridge); the archive may be split across institutions (as in the case of Housesteads); and past politics may also have played a part in what was published. Archaeologists along Hadrian's Wall have often bemoaned the statement by Mortimer Wheeler that the only thing remaining to do in the study of Hadrian's Wall was to 'dot the i's and cross the t's'. It is a similar situation with caring for collections on the Wall; rarely has a site's collection been fully studied, or understood, despite appearances.

These gaps in documentation have left many 'star' objects and important archives in the dark. For example, scholars, archaeologists and interested members of the public can quickly point to Vindolanda's writing tablets as a jewel in the crown of the Hadrian's Wall collections. They offer us insights into the everyday comings and goings of people who lived on the frontier. However, fewer people know that THMAG holds the second largest collection of writing tablets, found during excavations on Annetwell Street and Castle Street. Although the Annetwell street tablets were published in Britannia in 1998 (Tomlin 1998), the post-excavation work and publication of the site were never completed. The tablets remain largely absent from the Roman Inscriptions of Britain catalogue despite containing significant inscriptions such as a tantalising reference to Agrippa's presence in Britain through the mention of his unit, the *ala Gallorum Sebosiana*.

Applying solutions to Hadrian's Wall – looking at the future

The issues and threats facing archaeological collections across Britain and Hadrian's Wall are very active and apparent. Museums, on the Wall and beyond, hold substantial collections of material on display, in storage or on loan to other organisations. Many report concerns about how to manage these collections over the course of the next decade. The Museums Association (MA) has drawn attention to the fact that 'overflowing storage and limited staffing and resources mean that many museum collections are in a state of stasis or even decay. Museums feel unable to undertake rigorous collections reviews, collect new material, transfer unwanted and duplicate items out of the collections, and provide adequate care for the items that they hold.' (Museum Association 2019: 5). Whilst effective collections reviews and rationalisation are required, the looming storage issues remain one of the key areas where there are few proposed solutions, with the MA themselves only offering a single sentence relating to this issue in their *Collections 2030* report, which suggests the use of shared storage as a solution (Museum Association 2019: 23).

These problems are the result of historic issues, current barriers, and systemic underfunding of the wider sector. However, there are many organisations working to find the solutions to stem the crisis

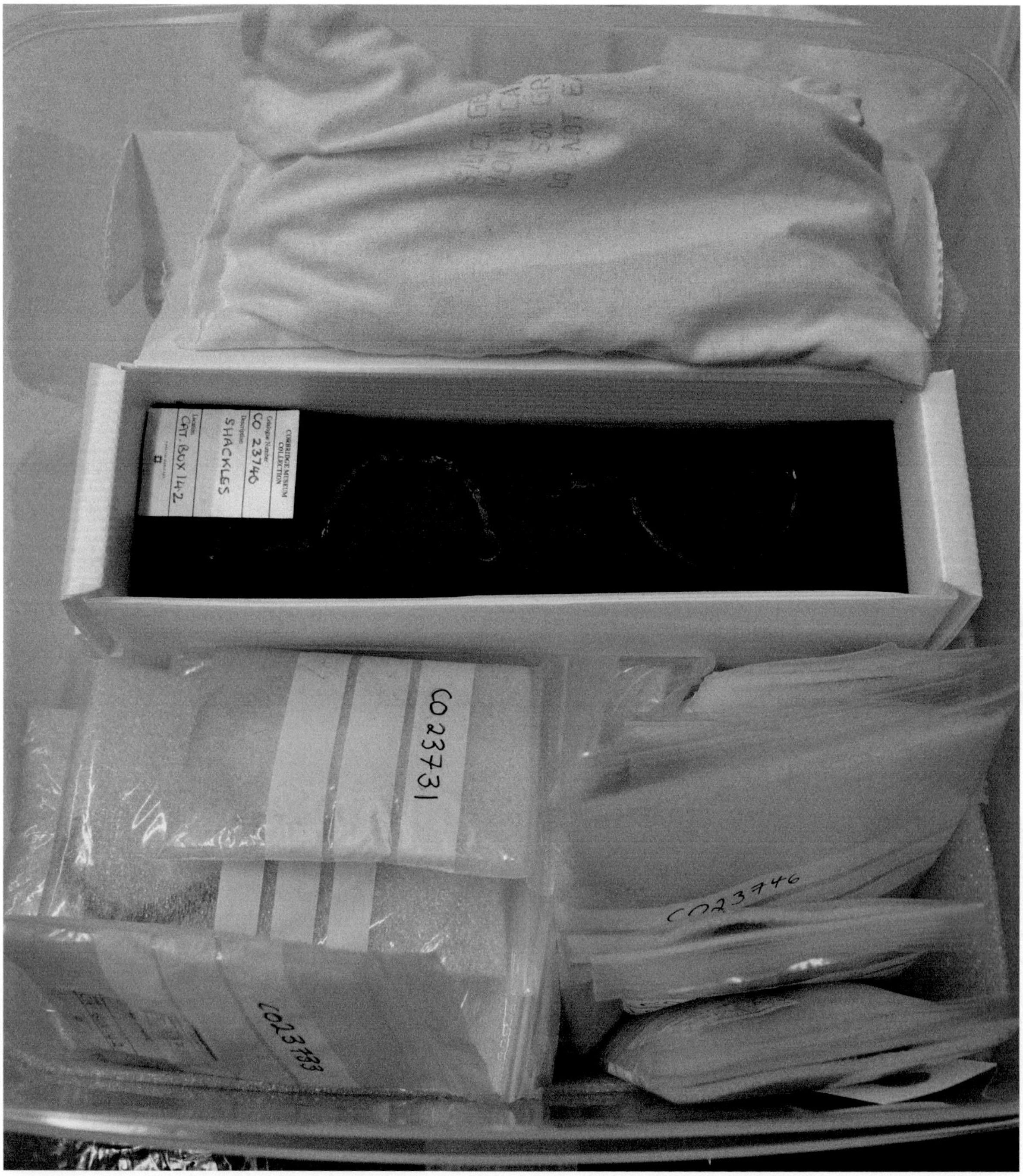

Figure 3. The repacking project of the ironwork from Corbridge, in which volunteers ensured each item was suitably stored and had a database entry. © English Heritage Trust

and convince those around them that archaeology is worthy. Sector bodies such as HE, the SMA and CIfA are working together to respond to the Mendoza review (Mendoza 2017), a government-commissioned independent review into England's museums, published in 2017. Together these organisations and others are collecting data, writing reports, and developing toolkits, training sessions and guidance on how to standardise and streamline current and future archaeological excavations, in order to ensure they can be effectively absorbed by museums going forward (see Boyle *et al.* 2016; Boyle *et al.* 2017; Boyle *et al.* 2018; Edwards 2012; Ferne *et al.* 2017; Tsang 2017).

Whilst museums continue to struggle with the constraints of finance, space and specialism, effective utilisation of box charges can ensure that documentation assistants are available to reconcile and

Figure 4: A volunteer at Tullie House, Carlisle repacking some of the organics from Birdoswald to current standards. © Tullie House Museum & Art Gallery Trust

document archives to industry SPECTRUM standards, which are set out and supported by the Collections Trust (Gosling and McKenna 2017). Documentation is the essential, and often hidden, work carried out by museums to nationally agreed standards. This documentation work allows museums to become accountable for their collections; they record what they have, where it is stored, and they can easily retrieve the information they hold about it. Without documentation, museum collections, no matter how extraordinary, are unusable and risk becoming lost, forgotten and degraded.

The work of documentation staff, curators and collections managers is often invisible, and not highly favoured by sector funders or indeed the museum sector itself, as the costs can be high and the immediate public benefit difficult to see. A key strand to help deal with documentation backlogs, unresearched collections and issues with unsuitable storage has been partnerships. These can be with other museums, who have different specialisms or resources, with universities, whose students need real material to work on and who can bring expertise, time and money, or with volunteers. The latter have increasingly become a mainstay of many museums and heritage sites worldwide, and a current PhD at Newcastle University is examining how and why volunteers work on research and excavation on Hadrian's Wall (Alberti forthcoming).

As well as volunteer work on the Corbridge pottery, a similar project with the ironwork in Corbridge's collection has equally paid dividends. By simply opening each box containing ironwork in order to individually bag each item, with padding for protection (Figure 3), over 450 new objects such as trowels, linchpins and spears were identified and catalogued. Unfortunately, it is easier to engage volunteers in the re-packing, where they get to handle objects, than the follow-up task of documentation, so whilst all the objects are now suitably stored, their documentation is not up to the same standard, although it is still better than before the project started. Some tasks are always more popular and others less so, and the management of this is a balancing act between the volunteers and the curator/volunteer manager, to ensure both sides benefit from the relationship.

Similar volunteer-led projects have been carried out at THMAG, such as the ongoing project to conserve and repack the Roman tent leather from Birdoswald, to bring its storage conditions in line with current standards (Figure 4). THMAG has also utilised and developed an award-winning international research partnership with Sapienza University in Rome (Figure 5). The Sapienza partnership sees mainly postgraduate students visiting the museum to study the collections over several weeks and months (Figures 4 and 5). Whilst the research forms part of their dissertations and project work, the Hadrian's Wall collections are being put into a global context and hidden aspects of the museum's archives are being exposed. This has included a re-examination of the

Figure 5: A researcher from Sapienza University working on the pottery assemblage of Bewcastle at Tullie House Museum. © Tullie House Museum & Art Gallery Trust

Bewcastle lamps, which are now on display in THMAG's new gallery *Occupation: Cumbria under Roman Rule*. This work, largely supported by the Curator of Human History, has only been made possible by effectively advocating to museum bodies, funders and governance structures about the importance and potential of archaeology. The significance of the Hadrian's Wall collections at THMAG has been recognised, with stores and collections facilities embedded into the upcoming Project Tullie capital development project. This will not only see physical changes to the museum, but also reimagine the future of Tullie House and its collections for the next ten to 20 years. The collections, including archaeology, are now secure within this future vision.

The Arts and Humanities Research Council (AHRC) Collaborative Doctoral Partnership (CDP) scheme has been a boon to the heritage and museum sector, allowing museums to connect with universities in formal partnerships, and offering students a funded place to gain skills, as well as a PhD (Arts and Humanities Research Council 2021). Typically, museum jobs require experience, frequently gained by volunteering, thus restricting access into the sector to only those who can afford to carry out unpaid work. The AHRC CDP scheme offers a paid six-month placement, which many students within the scheme take advantage of as an opportunity to gain valuable skills for their careers post-PhD. This is in addition to the fact that the students gain experience of a heritage organisation through their joint supervision, and the fact their research topics are based with a museum or archive, so exposing them to the world outside of academia. For example, Douglas Carr is currently working on the coins from Hadrian's Wall with supervision shared jointly between English Heritage and Newcastle University. He has also undertaken a placement at English Heritage, learning a range of collections management and curatorial skills.

The examples show that there are solutions in the making for the current crisis in archaeology and that collections on Hadrian's Wall are spearheading a march towards a better future. Our solutions are coming from many quarters including advocacy about the importance and potential of archaeology, professional development of new national standards and guidelines, and partnership working with both academic institutions and volunteers to access current collections and address museum backlogs through project work. Ultimately, however, even with the dedication of museums, their staff, partners and the public, the future of the collections of Hadrian's Wall, and the wider archaeology of Britain, will always depend on receiving national support to unlock the space, specialisms and finance required to clear backlogs and care for current and future material.

Conclusion

Despite our museums being on a World Heritage Site, we have many of the same issues faced by any other museum with archaeological collections, and so perhaps our solutions may be the same. We need to be open about what we have in our collections, and open to working with as many partners as possible to document, research and publicise our amazing material. We need to be brave in publicly sharing our concerns without bringing about reputational damage to our organisations. We need to continue to advocate for and share, where we can, the incredible collections and stories that the material culture from Hadrian's Wall has to offer, and continue to highlight the public good and benefit which can come from them.

Bibliography

Works Cited

Alberti, M. forthcoming. Volunteering for Hadrian's Wall: volunteer motivations and heritage professionals' expectations on a World Heritage Site. Unpublished PhD dissertation, Newcastle University.

Arts and Humanities Research Council 2021. Collaborative Doctoral Partnership Scheme. Accessed 15 November 2021. <https://www.ukri.org/councils/ahrc/career-and-skills-development/

supporting-universities-and-consortia-to-develop-careers/collaborative-doctoral-partnerships-cdp-scheme/>

Boyle, G., Booth, N. and Rawden, A. 2016. *Museums Collecting Archaeology (England) REPORT YEAR 1: November 2016*. Society for Museum Archaeology.

Boyle, G., Booth, N. and Rawden, A. 2017. *Museums Collecting Archaeology (England) REPORT YEAR 2: November 2017*. Society for Museum Archaeology

Boyle, G., Booth, N. and Rawden, A. 2018. *Museums Collecting Archaeology (England) REPORT YEAR 3: November 2018*. Society for Museum Archaeology

Chartered Institute for Archaeologists 2019. Toolkit for Selecting Archaeological Archives. CIfA. Accessed on 27 February 2022 <https://www.archaeologists.net/selection-toolkit>

Edwards, R. 2012. *Archaeological Archives and Museums 2012*. Society for Museum Archaeology

Gosling, K. and McKenna, G. 2017. *Spectrum 5.0: The UK Museum Collections Management Standard*. Leicester: Collections Trust.

McIntosh F. 2019. *The Clayton Collection: An archaeological appraisal of a 19th century collection of Roman artefacts from Hadrian's Wall*. Oxford: BAR publishing.

Mendoza, N. 2017. *The Mendoza Review: an independent review of museums in England*. London: Department for Digital, Culture, Media and Sport.

Museums Association 2019. *Empowering Collections 2030*. London: Museums Association

Smith, R. and Tindall, A. 2012. *A survey of archaeological archives held by archaeological practices in England, Scotland and Wales*. London: Federation of Archaeological Managers and Employers.

Tomlin, R.S.O. 1998. Roman Manuscripts from Carlisle: the Ink-Written Tablets. *Britannia* 29: 31–84.

Vincent, S. 2019. *A Survey of Fees for the Transfer of Archaeological Archives in England*. Swindon: Historic England.

Tsang, C. 2017. Gathering Information on Deep Storage Archive Facilities in England. Swindon: Historic England.

Research studies using English Heritage collections in the last five years

Banfield, L. forthcoming. Lava querns and millstones in Roman Britain. Unpublished PhD dissertation, Reading University.

Carr, D. forthcoming. Roman Coins from Hadrian's Wall and the Northern Frontier Zone. Unpublished PhD dissertation, Newcastle University and English Heritage.

Derrick, T. 2021. Glass Containers and Fluid Identities: Unguentaria And Social Practice in Roman Britain. Unpublished PhD dissertation, University of Leicester.

Gardner, C. 2019. Metalworking crucibles in Roman Britain. Unpublished PhD dissertation, University College London

Ivleva, T. 2018. GLOBALGLASS: Glass Adornments Event Horizon in the Late Iron Age and Roman Period Frontiers (100 BC – AD 250). Unpublished Marie Curie Fellowship, Newcastle University.

Johnson, E. 2019. Steering the Field. What can faunal remains recovered from sites along Hadrian's Wall tell us about human-cattle interaction within the Northern Frontier Zone of Roman Britain? Unpublished MA dissertation, Newcastle University.

Oya, N. 2018. What can the militaria from Roman Corbridge tell us about the site and Roman frontier zones? Unpublished MA dissertation, Newcastle University

Parker, A. 2022. The Materiality of Magic in Roman Britain. Unpublished PhD dissertation, Open University.

Pearce, C. forthcoming. Optimisation of Environmental Control in Museum Collections of Bone and Ivory. Unpublished PhD dissertation, University College London and English Heritage.

Rubinstein, N. 2017. An Investigation into the use of chemical variations to date worn late Imperial bronze coins using X-ray fluorescence. Unpublished undergraduate dissertation, University of Lincoln

Rubinstein, N. 2019. Catching Copies: An investigation into the identification of Constantinian copies by means of surface analysis using portable X-ray Fluorescence. Unpublished MA dissertation, Liverpool University

Rubinstein, N. forthcoming. An evaluation of the use of X-ray Fluorescence for identifying Constantinian copies in Romano British coin hoards AD 330-341. Unpublished PhD dissertation, Liverpool University

Undergraduate, Masters and PhD Theses produced within the collaboration agreement between the Department of Classics of La Sapienza University of Rome (Italy) and Tullie House Museum and Art Gallery Trust of Carlisle (UK)

Cristiano, M.T. 2019. Roman Terra Sigillata from the fort of Birdoswald on Hadrian's Wall. Unpublished Master dissertation, La Sapienza University, Rome.

Di Pastena L. 2019, Pottery from Milecastle 48 (Poltross Burn) on Hadrian's Wall: a revision (2018-2019). Unpublished PhD dissertation, La Sapienza University, Rome.

Fabiani, A. 2021. Hadrian's Wall between the Late Roman and Early Medieval period. Unpublished Master dissertation, La Sapienza University, Rome

Lombardi, M. 2018. Food supply of the Roman fort of Birdoswald on Hadrian's Wall. Unpublished Master dissertation, La Sapienza University, Rome.

Magazzino, M. 2019. Luguvalium–Carlisle: History, Excavations and Ideas of Musealisation. Unpublished Undergraduate dissertation, La Sapienza University, Rome.

Pillon, D. 2020. Roman Glasses from the Britannic limes: the fort of Old Penrith. Unpublished Master dissertation, La Sapienza University, Rome.

Pomante, S. 2021. A GIS for the archaeological collection of Tullie House Museum & Art Gallery Trust (Carlisle): the Roman fort of Bewcastle. Unpublished Master dissertation, La Sapienza University, Rome

Russo, F. 2018. Bewcastle. A Roman fort beyond Hadrian's Wall. Unpublished Master dissertation, La Sapienza University, Rome.

Scricciolo, E. 2019. Leather shoes from the Roman fort of Birdoswald on Hadrian's Wall. Unpublished Master dissertation, La Sapienza University, Rome.

Tollis, N. 2019. Coastal fortifications (milefortlets) to the west of Hadrian's Wall. Unpublished Master dissertation, La Sapienza University, Rome.

The many faces of the Wall: interpretation strategies, challenges and innovation on a multifaceted monument

A roundtable chapter by Geoff Woodward, Joe Savage, Kiki Claxton, Andrew Poad, Jane Laskey, David J. Breeze, Susan Aglionby, and Mark Richards

Hadrian's Wall is a monument with many faces, composed of many individual sites. It snakes across local authorities and counties, crossing both visible and invisible boundaries. From the east to the west, numerous organisations are involved in its interpretation. In the year of the Wall's 1900th anniversary, the organisations which manage Hadrian's Wall find a facilitator and ally in the Hadrian's Wall Management Plan, discussed in Chapter 13 of this volume.

Nonetheless, each key player on the Wall stage, and even each site, have learned their own lessons through experiences, successes and failures. The learning curve has steepened over the last decade. Technology has come to the forefront of everyday life, with personal devices such as smartphones and computers becoming widely available. They have increasingly been used in visitors' interaction with the monument, from planning a visit, to using apps to navigate the landscape, to accessing information on site via tablets and phones. New debates have come to the surface, which had previously been buried under the heavy blanket of 'archaeological scholarship'. Is archaeology all there is to the Wall? How can archaeology serve as a bridge between the past and the future? Is there only one way to interpret the archaeological evidence? What is the contribution of heritage professionals? Is it desirable that the visitor contributes to interpretation, becoming co-curator of the Wall's heritage? If so, what is the best way to do this?

Has archaeological heritage got anything to do with, or anything to reveal about, big issues such as climate change, diversity and inclusivity? Do museums need to change and evolve? And if so, how? How can they maintain existing relationships with repeat visitors, while reaching out to new and more diverse audiences? And is there any space, in this already crowded landscape, for private enterprise?

Organisations and individuals managing sites and sections of Hadrian's Wall may all have different ways of addressing priorities, but they share one concern: keeping the Wall relevant to the present, while researching and protecting its past. In this multi-vocal chapter, the many voices interpreting the Wall answer some of the questions outlined above, and set their course for the future.

Hadrian's Wall on Tyneside: the path ahead for the eastern urban sites

Geoff Woodward, Manager of North & South Tyneside Museums, Tyne & Wear Archives & Museums

The enduring perception of Hadrian's Wall is the romantic vision of the monumental frontier line snaking over a wild and desolate rural landscape. By contrast, Tyneside, at the eastern end of the frontier, with its urban intensity of industry, roads and housing, might appear to offer limited appeal to a Wall visitor, and indeed the heritage interpreter. The reality is very different. Tyneside has not just the finest collection of artefacts from along the frontier, on display at the Great North Museum: Hancock, but two well-excavated fort sites and museums at Arbeia (South Shields) and Segedunum (Wallsend). There are also a number of smaller exposed standing remains along the Wall's course through the county. The three main sites are all very accessible, as locations and as visitor experiences. The fort sites also have dynamic heritage landscape contexts. Furthermore, in recent years Tyneside has yielded some of the most important new evidence from the frontier, adding significantly to our understanding of Hadrian's Wall as a whole.

When considering how to shape future interpretation strategies on Tyneside there are some core questions. What strategies have worked well, or otherwise, over the last 20 years or so? How have our collections, sites and knowledge developed? What opportunities do new technologies offer? How have audience interests and expectations changed, and what are the likely future trends? How do we balance the interests of communities and tourists?

The fort sites present a number of challenges. Both have previously been built over and are still closely surrounded, and in part overlaid, by urban development. At Segedunum, the inspired construction of the viewing tower, coupled with a film presentation, tackles this by presenting the full fort ground plan and the wider strategic setting and landscape changes. But on the ground, there is still very limited interpretation. Self-guided audio trails were developed, but maintenance costs eventually made this unviable. At Arbeia, the recent introduction of a film with drone footage has helped enhance understanding of its plan and location. In addition, a new suite of interpretation signs was installed to tell a more cohesive and coherent story, together with a more fun and family-friendly 'Revolting Britons' trail. Pathway upgrades have improved access generally, but also highlighted under-visited parts of the site.

A major success has been the full-scale reconstructions at Arbeia and Segedunum. They present a stunning and appealing immersive experience that clearly beats any digital alternative. Yet there are caveats: inevitable compromises in construction to meet modern building regulations, maintenance challenges, and also their lack of 'Roman' people. Re-enactors and costumed interpreters bring that life and connection, but costs limit their provision.

Interpretation within the museum displays has evolved to respond directly to feedback from visitors and schools. At Segedunum this includes more information panels, a much stronger introduction to the geopolitical context of the Wall frontier as well as the post-Roman landscape, and a response to new evidence from the Wall (Figure 1), branch wall and baths revealed through excavation and research by Tyne & Wear Archives & Museums (Bidwell 2018; Hodgson 2017, 2020). At Arbeia the galleries have focused more on the engaging themes presented by the archaeology, such as the Severan invasion base, the devastating fire, and the diversity revealed in the Regina and Victor tombstones. At the Great North Museum: Hancock, a flexible display space was introduced and a recent project reimagined a number of the altars in their original vividly coloured state, challenging preconceptions and enlivening the artefacts (see Chapter 5, Birley and Griffiths, this volume).

The COVID-19 pandemic forced museums to reconsider their offer. New online audiences were reached – local, national and international – hungry for information through a digital experience. Curators and learning staff had time to focus on providing these resources in a way not previously possible. Then came the desire to return to physical visits – the real experience of Roman objects and archaeological sites. Lockdown also highlighted the importance of our culture and heritage, not just for understanding our identity and our past, but providing fundamental sustenance for our mental health and wellbeing. A welcoming, safe, engaging space for reflection, relaxation, entertainment and education helps meet this requirement.

How should all this inform our future interpretation strategies and our audience development plans? In the digital world audiences have become more sophisticated with higher expectations. Real objects and real locations have a greater value. Developing technologies provide the opportunity to significantly enhance the experience, but they need to be agile, responsive and economically sustainable. Gaming technology, discussed in Chapter 10 by Stocks and Birley, can be embraced further to recreate the forts, the surrounding settlements and the wider Roman landscape, while maintaining a clear, historical, authentic approach. Interpretative themes need to reference subjects directly relevant today, such as community, diversity, slavery, empire, plagues and pandemics, climate and the environment. This should not be tokenism or a response to fashion, but a genuine route into a wider understanding of Hadrian's Wall and the Roman world.

A personal and meaningful experience through engagement with staff and volunteers is critical. There is a need for more guided tours, more re-enactments and costumed interpretation. The latter is addressed in Chapter 12 by Brown and Robson. The hands-on experience is important too, though interactives must be robust and as maintenance-free as possible. Remains and

Figure 1: The excavated remains of Hadrian's Wall at Segedunum with the reconstructed section of Wall beyond. © Geoff Woodward

reconstructions can be reimagined with projections and audio, and Augmented Reality (AR) and Virtual Reality (VR) mobile technology, as long as free wi-fi is also available across the sites. Creative opportunities should be embraced, such as the proposed installation of renewable technology into the reconstructed bath house at Segedunum to demonstrate cutting-edge modern technology alongside cutting-edge Roman technology. The online interpretation that flourished during COVID-19 also needs to be sustained and part of the core offer, not a bolt-on. Interpretation should sit seamlessly within a strong overall visitor experience and tourism/leisure offer.

The message that only a very small percentage of the Wall has been excavated, that there is so much that we don't know and that it is a vibrant, evolving, living subject and resource, is central, as is the concept of the sites as archaeological green spaces – as community parks and meaningful store-houses of both local and world culture.

To be relevant, Hadrian's Wall has to speak to us, not just as an impressive visual concept, but as a vehicle for human connection and lasting reverberation. In many ways Hadrian's Wall on Tyneside is uniquely positioned to be able to deliver this.

The English Heritage strategy: many layers for many sites

Joe Savage, Interpretation Manager – Free Sites, English Heritage

The individuals and organisations who care for and operate Hadrian's Wall are acutely attuned to the diversity of its structures, artefacts and narratives. However, in the public's imagination and to a certain extent the media's, the Wall and its wider landscape tend to be envisaged as a unified structure with a singular story. The most significant driving force behind visits is simply a desire to see Hadrian's Wall – to be present at a site of perceived geographical and historical significance. Visitors can be unprepared for layered narratives and distinct experiences related to the Wall, and may not be aware that no individual location provides a comprehensive 'Wall experience', still less that the sprawling World Heritage Site (WHS) has distinct regional approaches. This is untapped potential: modern visitors are sophisticated and ready for complexity. If they can be assisted to appreciate the more comprehensive significance of the WHS, they may visit more widely, stay for longer and engage more deeply. This is the overall goal of English Heritage's forward interpretation strategy for the sections of the Wall and the sites in its care.

In the past, attempts have been made to synthesise a collective approach to interpretation across the WHS, linking different locations to specific stories according to archaeological evidence. Although well-intentioned, this approach was predicated on historic or archaeological explanatory messaging being the primary vector for the reception and interpretation of historic spaces. This is a limiting approach, both in principle and practice, and proved restrictive and unworkable.

A successful experience-building strategy is one which recognises that audiences bring an endless array of perspectives to their visits. As such, a much broader understanding of interpretation sees 'experience' and 'values' holding equal weight to 'understanding'. Our goal as curators and custodians of significant parts of Hadrian's Wall is to assist audiences in uncovering the meaning that feels most authentic to them.

English Heritage holds 25 free-to-enter sites in guardianship and operates a further six paid-entry sites within the WHS, four of which focus primarily on the frontier of the Roman Empire: the forts of Housesteads, Chesters and Birdoswald, and Corbridge Roman Town. Rather than focus solely on site-specific stories, a distinctive visitor experience has been created at each location to broaden audience choice and deepen potential engagement. An active, family-focused adventure is promoted at Birdoswald, where a comprehensive collection of frontier constructions can be discovered within an epic landscape, and at Corbridge – a site which holds internationally important archaeological finds – visitors enjoy a thorough exploration of an evolving Roman community through object-rich displays. At each site a balance is struck between providing sufficient general introductory information for first-time visitors to the Wall whilst allowing specific narratives and the atmosphere of the site to emerge.

Interpretation strategies are grounded by research into audience motivations and preferred types of visit. However, audience requirements change constantly, and it is important to regularly revise the approach to interpretation to ensure that the experience remains consistently engaging.

In recent times, a significant vector for change in visitor behaviour and preferences has been the impact of the COVID-19 pandemic. During its peak, outdoor spaces felt more reliable and safer than indoor spaces, a trend reinforced by mandated restrictions and social distancing requirements. Even as restrictions subside, there is a strong likelihood that visitors will maintain residual preferences and concerns. We are likely to see a continued interest in exploring landscapes and in incorporating heritage sites into family walks. Future outdoor interpretation will need to become more layered, appealing to multiple audiences rather than relying on museum hubs to provide the detail. It will take some time for visiting in large groups to feel normal again and this will have an impact on those visitors who value heritage learning as part of a social experience. We will need to consider how we can design experiences that allow visitors to feel like they are part of a wider community even if they are visiting alone, perhaps by increasing opportunities for them to share their perspectives in a way that feels meaningful.

Other developments in visitor behaviour correlate to the increased consumption of mobile and social media. Most visitors now have regular access to a wide variety of online opinions and media relating to their interests. While a strong desire remains for information at heritage sites to come from authentic and authoritative sources, visitors are also increasingly willing to engage with the idea that our understanding of the past is developing, and as such, is still open to question. Caveated interpretation is perhaps more acceptable now than in the past, and storylines and objects relating to new discoveries and radical reinterpretations are popular. For a more sophisticated audience who are keen to understand how we know about the past, future interpretation will confidently 'show its working'. At Corbridge curators will explore how the work of Edwardian excavators have informed our understanding of the site and where, in some instances, it has been misleading. The opportunity to participate in some form of engagement activity related to live archaeology will be increasingly desirable on sites.

Our audience segmentation model allows us to identify activities and storylines which may complement different motivations for a visit. For example, visitors who are primarily interested in self-improvement and learning are described as Culture Seekers. Previously, Culture Seekers were thought to be the ones that particularly liked to deep dive into their own areas of interest, but now, interestingly, it is wider than that – visitors of all types have the facility and confidence to follow their own line of enquiry and explore specific topics in more depth, though the way they want to receive that information differs. To physically cater for an array of interests in detail within the space of a single visit is untenable, so interpretation at complex sites will become, by necessity, more layered with an increased blending of online and on-site material, as data coverage allows.

Visitors' relationship with technology is complex. On one hand there is a desire to enjoy an authentic physical experience interacting with nature rather than screens, but there is also a willingness for visitors to use their own devices, at home and on site, particularly in preference to shared handsets. This opens the door to the provision of richer media and on-demand interpretation via NFC technology or QR codes, including better provision for foreign language interpretation. Integrated digital interpretation will become a core part of onsite experiences but it must be developed sensitively, intuitively and in a way that doesn't reduce the ability of visitors to interact with each other or reduce the sense of place or whatever flavour of authenticity visitors are looking for.

So what story demands are coming to the fore? As ever, visitors are looking for topics that bring history alive for them. The appeal of narratives relating to individual lives is as strong as always, but historians and curators are acutely conscious that the perspectives and voices visitors encounter need to be more inclusive and representative than is currently available. Stories of diverse communities along Hadrian's Wall are known and are being actively researched and will be more explicitly explored in forthcoming exhibitions and interpretation. Contemporary concerns and interests also include human impacts on the environment (discussed in Chapter 11 by McGlade, Pickles and Richards) – a pressing area of contemporary public dialogue but also one with historic relevance. An investigation into the way Hadrian's Wall and its associated features relate to the natural landscape and the way its builders and subsequent residents have responded to and altered the immediate environment will be a feature of ongoing projects. Topics like these, with clear contemporary relevance and challenges, benefit from our Creative Programme's adjacency to the interpretation strategy. The Creative Programme engages with artists, makers, poets, musicians and community members and enables us to bring new, sometimes contested, viewpoints and creative expression to sites. It also provides a profound output for audience and local participation, enabling English Heritage to step away from a didactic, authoritative tone towards a more questioning, value-led and experimental approach to interpreting the sites.

Since 2016, English Heritage has made significant investments in renewing the exhibitions and offers throughout its sites. However, this is just the start of the journey towards an offer that enables audiences to shape their own visits and helps to build a stronger relationship with the local and regional communities along Hadrian's Wall. A strategy that prioritises flexible, layered and re-visitable interpretation to present informative stories that also surprise, challenge and delight visitors is fundamental to these aims.

The National Trust: what is the point of Hadrian's Wall, to us, today?

Kiki Claxton, Experience and Partnerships Curator, and Andrew Poad, General Manager, National Trust

The National Trust cares for eight miles of Hadrian's Wall in Northumberland. These stretches are set in the central upland area of the Wall, within Northumberland National Park, and include Housesteads Roman Fort (operated in partnership with English Heritage) and Sycamore Gap. These eight miles follow the dramatic Whin Sill escarpment through farmland, and are important not only for the international significance of the archaeological remains, but also for the varied ecological habitats that sit alongside them and the relative ease of access to large numbers of people each year. These aspects of the area don't always sit comfortably together, and ensuring their shifting significance is relevant to society in our ever-changing world is a major part of the National Trust's role today, together with addressing climate action and making sure as many people as possible feel welcome.

We are therefore looking at new and different ways to tell the stories of our places, layering different approaches on top of the more traditional ways of engagement such as interpretation panels and the factual aspects of a site. We are trialling more inclusive approaches to, and dialogues around, contemporary identity. By doing this we can enable deeper engagement with a wider group of people, while still engaging our core audiences. Many of our National Trust sites have a multitude of different stories, histories and identities: this plurality is even more apparent at Hadrian's Wall, thanks to its 1900-year-old history, and its changing ownership and occupation throughout the millennia.

Cultural and creative programming enables us to share, celebrate and unpick some of the more complex and in some cases marginalised histories and narratives which are specific to our places, and to be more resonant with contemporary discourse. Opening up these stories enables us to better connect our work at Hadrian's Wall to people's lives today, meaning we can be more dynamic in how we deliver our new programmes. Different interventions and uses of space allow us to introduce the areas we look after along the Wall to new audiences, and to deepen the relationship communities already have with the site. It also opens up the possibility of new partnerships for us, sharing the power of delivery with other organisations who bring different voices from these places. Indeed, how could the National Trust know and understand all aspects of Hadrian's Wall's heritage and story and its contemporary appropriation? Heritage sites have many stories and working with others empowers us and others to share these and think creatively about access, participation and dialogue around the Wall's heritage.

By bringing art, culture and history together, we aim to break down boundaries as well as the idea that you need to be the keeper of all knowledge to understand a site. The Trust have been developing this intersection over the past ten years through programmes such as Trust New Art, at sites such as Cherryburn, and we have found it has a lasting impact on participants. At Hadrian's Wall these three elements – art, culture and history – came together during Hadrian's reign with the linear monument's grandiose statement of power, so exemplary of the man himself, who was as passionate about architecture as he was about military matters. The Roman 'colonisation' of Britain marked our own culture with new notions of art, architecture, religion and innovation – and of course the concept of 'empire'. Britain was partly colonised by a foreign power for nearly 400 years and the Wall would have been, amongst other things, a frontier zone between different cultures.

However, we tend now to forget to consider this through the eyes of the occupied. It is interesting to note, as Paul Frodsham points out, that our attitude to the Wall today owes much to the legacy of British Imperialism: 'It might legitimately be compared to the unlikely future scenarios of the Tibetans glorifying the Chinese, the Poles celebrating Nazi occupation, the Palestinians praising the creation of Israel' (Frodsham 2013). How those farmers felt about the occupation of their homeland is now lost, but we can explore through contemporary experiences how it might have been for them.

During 2018, we started a conversation with D6 Culture in Transit. D6 brings together artists to create art that reflects a place and its people. They seek to sustainably develop communities by connecting threads between shared experiences in our cities and regions and those internationally.[1] They wanted to look at Hadrian's Wall as a lead site for the transnational project *Contested Desires,* exploring our shared and contested colonial heritage and its influence on contemporary culture.[2] The first of three artists in residence, Monica Rikic from Barcelona, explored the Roman archives, creating a set of small robotic sculptures that represent living artificial systems from a future heritage in a post-human world. In Spring 2022, we will invite responses from visual artist Marcio Carvalho, from Portugal, and performance artist Demitris Chimonas, from Cyprus.

Contested Desires runs from 2019 to 2022 and focuses on exchange and learning; the programme offers unique opportunities for artists and communities to explore our shared heritage through research, workshops, residencies and exhibitions with local communities at each site. Working in the UK, Portugal, Cyprus, Spain and Barbados, *Contested Desires* hosts conversations and artist-led experiences to explore and reveal the links between our colonising ancestors and our cultural identities today.

Building on the work of D6, the Culture in Transit's programme *There is Beauty in this Journey*[3] seeks to redress the sensationalism and bias around migration stories. We are exploring the intersection of Hadrian's era, when the Wall was built, with society today. The Wall is often portrayed as a hermetic seal between two distinct civilisations, rather than a place where an amazing mix of cultures came together for over 300 years for communication, trade and security. Today, narratives are too often concealed around migration, diversity and cultural heritage, but through this project we can bring them to the surface and offer a space for this dialogue to be unpacked. Working with artist Henna Asikainen, D6 are able to draw out both the known and unknown historical and contemporary constructs that lead to misrepresentation and misinformation. The National Trust at Housesteads is the lead site and venue for the programme, but this is very much D6's project, shaped by the artist. Working in this way enables us to open up access to history, nature and beauty to wider audiences.

The D6 programme with Housesteads was originally made up of a series of different activities with a public engagement programme at its heart, with and for diverse and newly arrived audiences to the North East. Due to COVID-19, the programme had to shift and adapt, with much of the work happening online. A series of participatory walks have taken place, for diverse and newly arrived participants. This tried and tested method of practice is a gentle form of engagement that brings together those who might not otherwise visit heritage sites, nor have had the opportunity to visit them, and possibly make connections to their stories of migration and their connection to the past. This process informs and develops the practice of the individual artists taking part and supports participating partners to better understand the perspectives, needs and ideas of diverse and migrant communities as audiences. Hadrian's Wall, alongside a series of other creative responses from artists' month-long residencies, a digital symposium and a digital platform to serve

1 <http://www.d6culture.org/>

2 <https://www.contesteddesires.eu/>

3 <http://www.d6culture.org/there-is-beauty-in-this-journey.html>

as an alternative exhibition space to widen and extend our audiences, will be launched and freely accessible at the end of the programme.

Even though we don't know, nor should we know, what the output will be at the end of the process, we are starting to understand the impact of what our heritage sites can open up for others and the longer-lasting effect of this way of working. The way we interpret our sites is and should be changing, so different voices and stories can come to the surface. This is no quick fix and it takes time to build trust and to really engage with people and organisations in a meaningful way. What we do know is that by opening up these spaces we are taking part in a collective experience where people can access heritage in different and creative ways – something which we will endeavour to continue to develop at Housesteads (Figure 2).

Watch this space.

Senhouse Roman Museum: the jewel of the west, and how to make it shine

Jane Laskey, Museum Manager, Senhouse Museum Trust

The Senhouse Roman Museum is situated adjacent to the Roman fort and extramural settlement overlooking the coastal town of Maryport. Housed in the refurbished Naval Reserve Training Battery, the museum opened to the public in 1990 with the aim of providing a permanent, accessible home for the Netherhall Collection. The collection is owned by the Senhouse family and was first recorded by William Camden in his 1587 edition of *Britannia*. Camden and his fellow antiquarian, Sir Robert Cotton, stayed with John Senhouse at the Senhouse family home, Netherhall, in 1599 (Breeze 2018: 5). In the thirty years since the museum opened, the galleries have been refurbished and reinterpreted only once. Activities and events delivered by the staff and volunteers have

Figure 2: Illuminating Sycamore Gap in October 2017 as part of joint events with Vindolanda to mark Prejudice and Pride, National Trust

expanded both in scope and quantity to such a degree that the building has more than reached capacity. There are ambitions to refurbish the museum, reinterpret the collections and improve the visitor facilities. This is a work in progress and will be led by a robust interpretation strategy and plan.

The Netherhall Collection was essentially a gentleman's antiquarian collection. John Senhouse and subsequent generations of the family recovered Roman military altars, inscriptions and sculpture from the Roman site situated on their estate. Their house and gardens at Netherhall included stone recovered from the fort and nearby buildings, and the final rebuild included a grand portico where the collection was displayed. The collection moved into the estate coach house when the house fell derelict. In 1990 the collection moved into the Victorian Naval Reserve Training Battery, five years after the building was acquired by the Senhouse Museum Trust. Additional material, in the form of excavation archives and casual finds from the Solway Coast and West Cumbria, has since been acquired by the museum.

The current interpretation of the collections appears dated and static and the whole museum needs a complete re-evaluation. The main gallery was refurbished in 1998 and is themed around a series of Roman military altars and the garrisons stationed at Maryport (Figure 3). The Kirby Gallery was refurbished in 2012 and adds context to the collection, focusing on the Roman sites on the Solway coastal frontier and the story of the Senhouse family as collectors. However, more work needs to be done to promote the uniqueness and importance of this collection and site. The building's location adjacent to the fort and extramural settlement, overlooking the Solway Firth and the Scottish coast, provides a real sense of living on the edge of the empire. Its situation at the end of the linear Roman frontier and as a focus for the sequence of forts, milefortlets and watchtowers of the Solway Coast is an opportunity to bring this little-known aspect of the World Heritage Site (WHS) to life.

Figure 3: Senhouse Roman Museum Main Gallery with Roman military altars, Senhouse Museum Trust.

Recent planning for the future direction of the museum looked at current and potential audiences and their motivations. Internal consultation identified the local communities of Maryport and West Cumbria, prioritising intergenerational families, as a target audience. The data indicates that the majority of the museum's visitors are tourists staying in the Lake District and on the Solway Coast. Although residents of Maryport and the surrounding area are offered incentives including free entry, the local population make up only 6% of the visitors to the museum. A recent study conducted on behalf of the Maryport Cultural Consortium using data gathered by the Audience Agency suggests that people who live within a 45-minute drive from Maryport are not traditional museum visitors (Thompson 2021: 78). Any interpretation planning will need to take this into account and explore new themes that are relevant to potential audiences. The museum aims to interpret the collections in a way that is engaging and relevant to local communities and develop a deeper relationship with the museum. It is an ambition of the museum that local communities will feel a sense of ownership for the museum and discover connections and relevance to their lives in the lives of the Roman community. A number of interpretative themes identified during consultation with staff and volunteers will be explored and expanded further by a project team including audience representatives.

There is scope to explore new interpretative themes in the collections. The current interpretation is very military and academic in tone, which can exclude many visitors. Anecdotal evidence suggests that visitors engage only on a superficial level with the objects but are inspired by the more human and personal stories that can be extracted from the collection. The activity and events programme goes some way to bringing the collection to life and inspires visitors to be curious about what the collections can tell them. Lessons learnt from visitor feedback during these events will be considered when producing the interpretation plan.

We need to challenge the perception that Roman museums are all 'swords and sandals' with a very male-dominated perspective. This feedback identified a number of themes that are not explored in the current displays. Visitors are curious about the real lives of the Roman occupying presence, the native population, and how they interacted. The altars, inscriptions and tombstones include fascinating clues to the mobility of the Roman garrisons and the diversity of this itinerant population. Roman religion, the gods they worshipped and their religious practices would be a strong theme, focusing on how the altars were used and what they represented. The religious practices of the occupied population and the survival of their culture is a strong and fascinating presence in the collections. Material from a number of other sites on the Solway Coast and in West Cumbria are at present in storage. The interpretation would aim to bring this hidden world to life and encourage visitors to explore the landscape beyond the museum.

Finally, the story of the Senhouse family as collectors would be expanded on. The challenge will be the lack of objects in the collection that relate to the family. A collaboration with the Carlisle Record Office, where the Senhouse family records are held, would be an opportunity to develop a community research project, with a resulting co-curated exhibition.

The people of Maryport have a deep attachment to, and pride in, their Roman heritage. The development of the museum and the interpretation of the collections will be a partnership between the academic voice, the museum workforce and the museum's audiences. This ambition of community 'ownership' reflects the strategic direction of the principal funders, including the National Lottery Heritage Fund and Arts Council England. Both funders are essential in supporting museums to thrive.

A private enterprise: Interpreting the fragment of a ditch at Whiteclosegate, Carlisle

Susan Aglionby, David J. Breeze and Mark Richards

Susan's view

Having had a view of a short length of the ditch of Hadrian's Wall and its northern bank from my bedroom window for 32 years, I had a hankering to own this tiny fragment of the Wall. The opportunity to purchase the 23-acre field through which the ditch and its northern bank runs came up in 2020. The field adjoins my farm on two sides, so agriculturally it would be an asset to the farm. The farm is now 'Susan's Farm', a registered charity and a care farm, undertaking work with some of the most vulnerable people in our community, as well as having an extensive educational programme. It was important to me that those who visit the site were able to understand what they were looking at. I was determined that high-quality interpretation boards should be erected.

I was advised by Henry Summerson, a medieval historian, to approach David Breeze. This I did, and we found we had many connections. He suggested we also work with Mark Richards, the well-known local illustrator and author of many guidebooks, who I already knew. I have enjoyed working in this small team to enable the many visitors to the farm to understand what they are standing on! My family, I am pleased to say, would like to retain ownership of this field.

The visible archaeological features

The main visible feature at Whiteclosegate is a broad bank running approximately south-west to north-east (Figure 4). There is a substantial hedge containing large trees on its southern side,

Figure 4: The broad bank looking south-west, David Breeze

Figure 5: View of the Wall ditch and road looking south-west, David Breeze

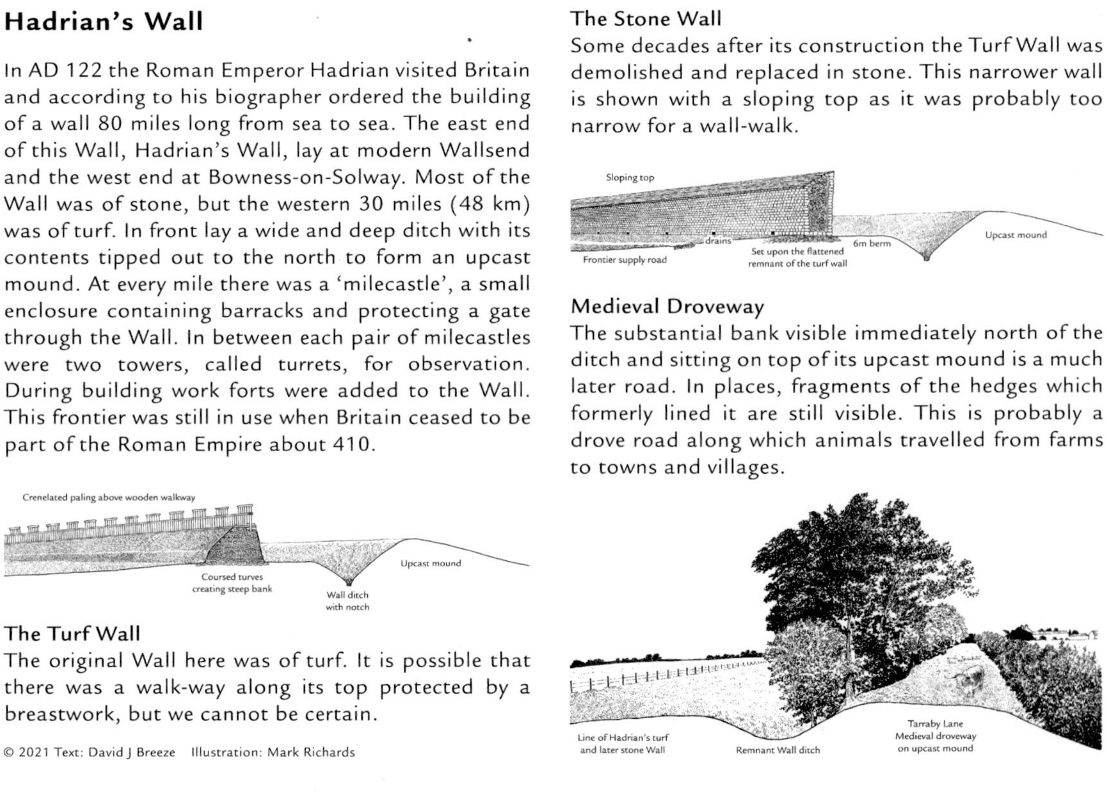

Hadrian's Wall

In AD 122 the Roman Emperor Hadrian visited Britain and according to his biographer ordered the building of a wall 80 miles long from sea to sea. The east end of this Wall, Hadrian's Wall, lay at modern Wallsend and the west end at Bowness-on-Solway. Most of the Wall was of stone, but the western 30 miles (48 km) was of turf. In front lay a wide and deep ditch with its contents tipped out to the north to form an upcast mound. At every mile there was a 'milecastle', a small enclosure containing barracks and protecting a gate through the Wall. In between each pair of milecastles were two towers, called turrets, for observation. During building work forts were added to the Wall. This frontier was still in use when Britain ceased to be part of the Roman Empire about 410.

The Turf Wall

The original Wall here was of turf. It is possible that there was a walk-way along its top protected by a breastwork, but we cannot be certain.

The Stone Wall

Some decades after its construction the Turf Wall was demolished and replaced in stone. This narrower wall is shown with a sloping top as it was probably too narrow for a wall-walk.

Medieval Droveway

The substantial bank visible immediately north of the ditch and sitting on top of its upcast mound is a much later road. In places, fragments of the hedges which formerly lined it are still visible. This is probably a drove road along which animals travelled from farms to towns and villages.

Figure 6: The panel to be erected at the same location, David Breeze and Mark Richards

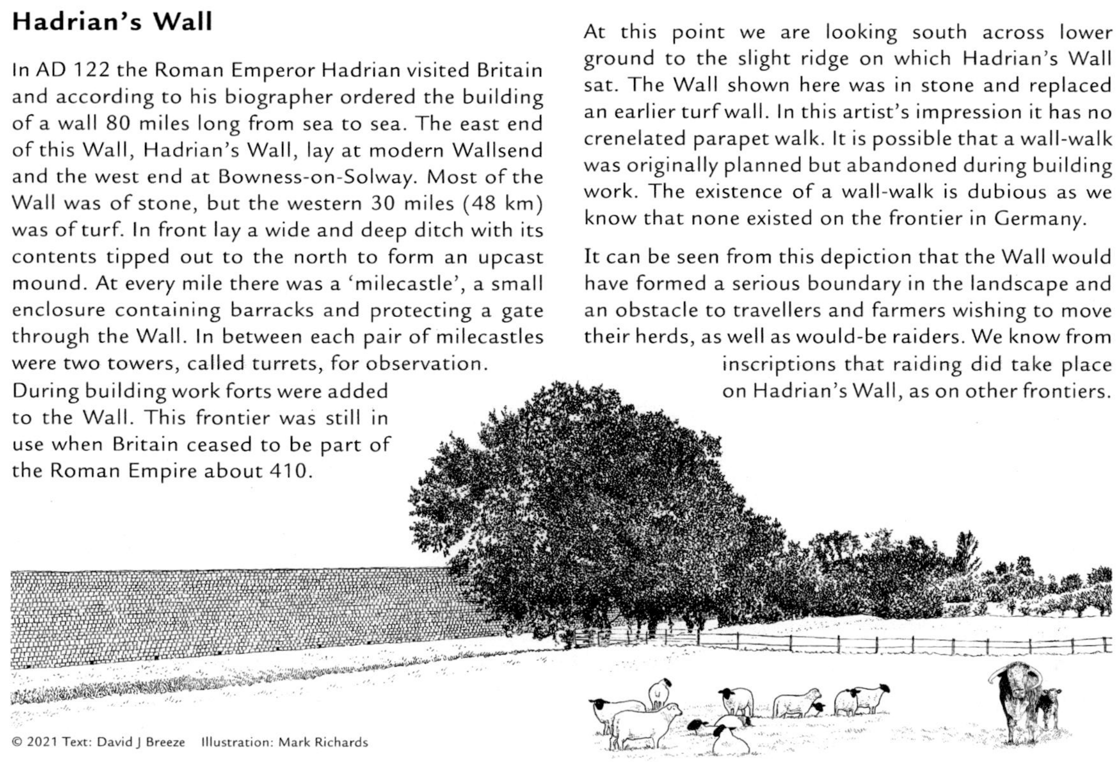

Figure 7: The panel beside the trail round the farm looking south, David Breeze and Mark Richards

with the fragmentary remains of a hedge on the north side. The southern hedge obscures a broad, shallow ditch about 8.33m wide, the normal width of the ditch of Hadrian's Wall (Figure 5). Beyond the ditch, a low mound presumably contains the debris from the Wall. No other archaeological features are visible.

Research by Bill Shannon has indicated that the broad bank is a drove road, in existence by the early 17th century It was traced south-westwards, beyond the village of Tarraby and leading towards Carlisle, during excavations in 1976 (Smith 1978). The existence of the Wall ditch in the fields immediately to the north-east of Tarraby is not recorded in early antiquarian references. However, the ditch is marked as visible on the first edition of the Ordnance Survey Map of Hadrian's Wall, published in 1964, and the second edition in 1972. English Heritage published a new map of Hadrian's Wall in 2010 and the ditch is not marked on it. Therefore, it seems that the ditch has disappeared from the written record.

The interpretation of the archaeological remains

The original intention was to place one interpretation board looking south-westwards showing the ditch and the road. During a walk on the trail around the Cumbria Wildlife Trust's land at Gosling Sike, it became clear that a second interpretative panel could usefully be placed beside the path, directing the visitor's attention to the low ridge to the south-east on which the Wall sat.

The primary panel bears three drawings by Mark Richards (Figure 6). The main drawing is a cross-section of the landscape today. This enables the visitor to engage with the visible features. This illustration was straightforward. The interpretation of Hadrian's Wall was another matter. Hadrian's Wall here is a little complicated, as there were actually two walls: the original Turf Wall and its successor Stone Wall, built later in the second century. We decided to capitalise on this situation and offer the artist's impressions of both. Since there is doubt about the way the top of Hadrian's Wall was completed, we have offered two possibilities. In the first drawing, we have shown the Turf Wall with a wall-walk, parapet and crenelations, while in the second the Stone Wall is depicted with a sloping top and no wall-walk, parapet or crenelations. The text on the board explains the reason for the different interpretations.

On the second board (Figure 7), the 'barbarian's' eye-view, the top edge of the Wall is level again with no crenelations. The date and nature of Hadrian's Wall are also discussed on both panels. We all appreciated that the depiction of Hadrian's Wall with a flat top and no patrol walk was heretical, but felt it important to show different possibilities in order to emphasise to visitors the limitations of our evidence.

For further information about Susan's Farm and Goslink Sike, see <www.susansfarm.co.uk>

Bibliography

Bidwell, P. 2018. *Hadrian's Wall at Wallsend.* South Shields: Arbeia Society and Tyne & Wear Archives & Museums.

Breeze, D.J. 2018. *Maryport: A Roman fort and its community.* Oxford: Archaeopress

Frodsham, P. 2013. *Hadrian and his Wall.* Newcastle upon Tyne: Northern Heritage

Hodgson, N. 2017. *Hadrian's Wall on Tyneside: An introduction and guide to the latest discoveries.* Newcastle upon Tyne: Tyne & Wear Archives & Museums.

Hodgson, N. 2020. *The Roman Baths at Wallsend.* South Shields: Arbeia Society and Tyne & Wear Archives & Museums.

Smith, G.H. 1978. Excavations at Tarraby Lane. *Britannia* 9: 19-57

Thompson, K. 2021. Maryport: A town of heritage, arts, and culture. Unpublished report for Allerdale Borough Council on behalf of the Maryport Cultural Consortium

Ruffenhofen, Bavaria: a new way of visualising and presenting a World Heritage Site

Matthias Pausch (Limeseum Ruffenhofen)

In 2003, construction began on an archaeological park at the Roman *Limes* fort and vicus of Ruffenhofen, in Bavaria. The terrain was not subject to any deep soil intervention or excavations, but instead was thoughtfully developed on the structures known from geophysics, to create an innovative visualisation of the Roman site as a botanical meadow. The structural layout was presented through footpaths, vegetation and selective grass management. From a viewing hill one can overlook the entire site, which includes a weatherproof 1:10 scaled model of the fort.

The accompanying LIMESEUM, which opened in October 2012, is an essential part of the strategy for the visualisation and presentation of the World Heritage Site, which stretches over 40 hectares and is now part of the Frontiers of the Roman Empire World Heritage Property. In the museum, visitors can learn everything they need to know about Roman Ruffenhofen, but also about the neighbouring forts. Further content is available via the '*Limes*-mobil' app.

This chapter discusses how unconventional and innovative ways to present archaeological heritage attractions can be applied to the Roman frontier. Non-invasive archaeological methods like those applied at Ruffenhofen protect the World Heritage Site and attract new audiences, all while contributing to the upkeep and even improvement of the natural environment, creating an ideal place for flora and fauna to thrive. What lessons can we learn from our Bavarian colleagues?

Making an invisible World Heritage Site visible – introduction

The *Limes* fort of Ruffenhofen has been known since the 18th century. In autumn 1892, excavations mandated by the *Reichslimes-Kommission* were carried out by the local *Streckenkommissar* Wilhelm Kohl. An emergency excavation in 1917 in the *vicus* remains unpublished to this day.

The knowledge and understanding of Ruffenhofen remained the same for over 100 years, with the exception of archaeological aerial photography in the 1970s and summaries of individual stray finds published in *Bayerische Vorgeschichtsblätter*. Significant new findings came from geomagnetic surveys conducted from 1999 onwards (Figure 1). These investigations were also a prelude to later measurements on the entire Raetian *Limes* in Bavaria (Fassbinder 2010; Mischka and Moneta 2012). They brought important and surprising results, especially with regard to the state of preservation of the site.

Two other factors were important for the overall development of the site, whose structural remains were increasingly destroyed by its use as arable land. General changes in agriculture resulted in a decrease in jobs in the rural sector. A territorial sub-area report was commissioned and in it, the fort site of Ruffenhofen was certified as having the potential for soft tourism. With the start of a local terrain readjustment, various measures were possible, such as area swaps and land acquisition. This led to the three small neighbouring communities of Gerolfingen, Weiltingen and Wittelshofen joining together in 2001 to form a special-purpose association for Roman Ruffenhofen. The focus was not on research, but on the development of an archaeological park.

From geophysical survey to the archaeological park

The geophysical results were first presented to the public in 2000. This was an essential step in raising local awareness of the importance of the site. At the same time, a group of expert archaeologists was formed to consider which parts of the site should be acquired and with what priority. The fort was placed in category one, and parts of the *vicus* in priority two and three.

Figure 1: Magnetic prospection of Fort Ruffenhofen. Courtesy of the Bavarian State Office for the Preservation of Monuments/University of Erlangen

Visualisation using plants

As early as 2001, the idea arose in the Limes Ruffenhofen working group not to excavate structures on a large scale or even to partially rebuild them, but to visualise them with plants and vegetation. This was initially extremely controversial among the population, as excavated and preserved walls or replicas are more often used to display Roman archaeology, and were already common practice at numerous sites in the area. Through the expertise of the archaeologists, it was possible to make it clear from the outset that excavation on a larger scale would not only be costly, but would also destroy the monument, while subsequent conservation of walls would require permanent maintenance and renovation costs, not to mention the costs for replicas. Since the sponsoring municipalities were not in a position to field these costs, large-scale excavation was very quickly discarded and the much more cost-effective option of visualisation through planting was pursued.

The land at Ruffenhofen was acquired through the Office for Rural Development in 2002 and 2003. In the summer of 2005, a small-scale archaeological evaluation took place, to deal with essential technical questions of the interpretation of the geomagnetics and to what degree the monument had been preserved (Pausch and Weinlich 2005; Weinlich 2015). A third question addressed the earlier wooden fort. While the latter could not be answered, it became clear that the information and interpretations provided by the geophysics were conclusive. This also applied to the electrical earth resistance measurements of the fort, temple and baths carried out in 2004. The results confirmed that only a pitiful remnant of the fort and building structures were left. This further helped to subdue public demand for excavations, superstructures or exposed walls.

In April 2003, the innovative visualisation process began. The fort wall was initially marked with sunflowers, and perpendicular paths were laid out within the fort, while the fields were sown as a meadow. The permanent planting of hornbeam and Siberian dogwood for the fort wall took place in spring 2004. In the area of the towers, six-metre-high poles indicate the height of the fort wall, whilst also serving as perches for birds of prey. In addition, the large edifice in the south-east of the fort, possibly an administration building measuring approximately 30m x 70m, was planted with lavender. In the completely open and unprotected terrain, weather and wild herbs caused enormous problems for the 1200 lavender plants. There were various considerations as to which plants would be suitable as an alternative, and the final decision was to plant red-leaved barberry.

The large building and the temple were visualised with boxwood, with soil added before planting to create a light embankment to help protect the walls below. In the case of the fort wall, the planting was deliberately placed slightly to the outside. The geophysical survey, carried out before planting, revealed that the fort wall had collapsed into the first ditch. It was not until the excavation in 2005 that it was found that the collapsed deposit was in fact very small and that most of the stones had been removed in the post-Roman period. There is an aerial photograph of the fort area from the 1980s showing a farmer with a hoe and wheelbarrow removing stones, probably to make better agricultural use of his field.

The inner buildings of the fort are reconstructed by a meadow that is mown once a year in spring. The surrounding open spaces are mown regularly, allowing the meadow to stand over winter and provide food and cover for small game, especially for the endangered partridges in the area. A leaching of the soil also supports plant diversity. The well-established Roman paths were laid out as footpaths. The subsoil was not deeply excavated, but their area was slightly filled in and embanked (Pausch 2008, 2010a).

The 'Mini-Castrum': A large scale-model and other interpretation features in the park

The mini-castrum has enjoyed great popularity among visitors. As early as 2005, small interpretation panels were erected, mostly inside the fort, with a virtual ideal reconstruction, as well as providing additional information on the location. This made it easier for visitors to imagine the buildings.

It was initially considered to build a tower for a better overview, but an artificially raised hill providing a view of the fort was decided upon instead. The lookout hill, planted with over 700 native shrubs in 2008, forms an important refuge for animals due to its dense vegetation.

In front of it, the fort was to be replicated on a scale of 1:10 (Figure 2).

Figure 2: Mini-castrum in the Roman Park. Courtesy of the LIMESEUM Ruffenhofen

Despite the scale, the individual buildings were deliberately built in a general, simplified manner, but taking into account archaeological evidence from the previous surveys. For example, it had been noticed that roof tiles were accumulated in the area of the fort towers, while none were to be found in the barracks. This observation was implemented in the roof design of the reconstructions, with tiles used on the towers and the common buildings (*horreum*, *praetorium*, *principia* and *valetudinarium*), whereas wooden shingles were used on the soldiers' barracks. On the hill, a sign explains the fort model and the entire site, which is easily visible from there. Signposts indicating distances in the 40-hectare area have also been set up to help visitors find their way around the site. The information system also includes a site plan for visitors, on a sign and in the form of a flyer (Figure 3).[1]

Further Roman structures were depicted in the terrain. At the main road from the fort past the large edifice in the direction of Nördlinger Ries and Augsburg, a simple trade transaction scene was created and explained with a small notice. Copies of Roman stone monuments from the province of Raetia and the *Limes* were erected at the temple, at the edge of the Roman park area near the fort, and in the burial ground. A total of 12 stone casts are distributed over the site, six of them in the area of the eastern burial ground.

There were various considerations for the visualisation of the cemetery. Ultimately, a virtual reconstruction of the cemetery in the landscape with a view towards the dominating Hesselberg mountain was developed. This image wall, measuring 20m x 2m, was given a special statically calculated flat foundation and was placed on an existing path-side ditch. As a result, it did not require any intervention to the sub-surface archaeological monument (Pausch 2010b).

[1] Since 2019, the site plan has been divided into two pages, one on archaeology with the Roman structures and one on aspects of nature.

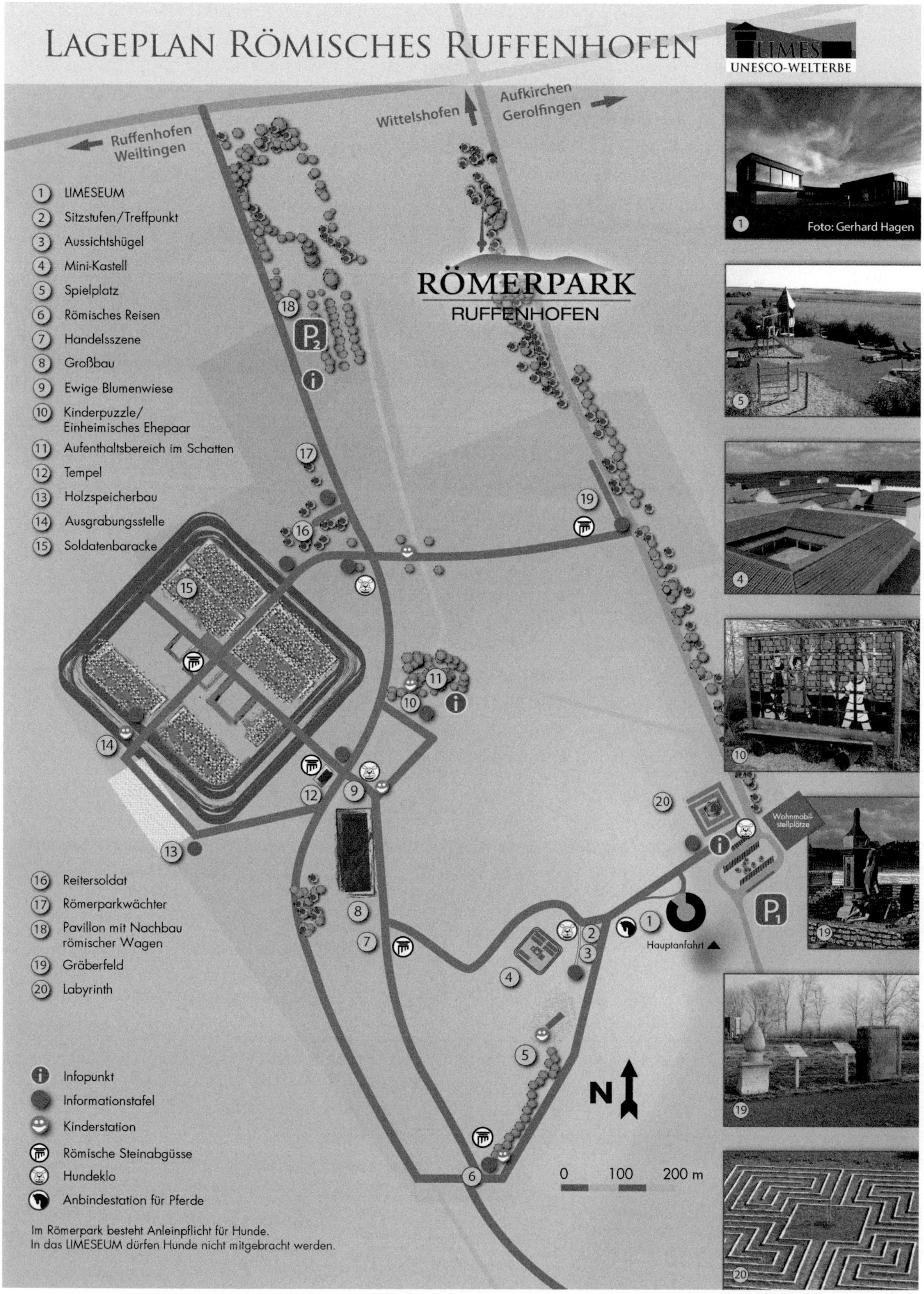

Figure 3: Site plan of the Ruffenhofen Roman Park based on geophysics. Courtesy of the LIMESEUM Ruffenhofen

Most of the other elements, such as a labyrinth made of granite stones, a playground and an educational tree trail with various other elements for sustainability (fieldstone piles and deadwood piles, an insect hotel, etc.) were deliberately placed at the edges of the site. As a result, a central line has been formed in the south-eastern part of the site – starting with the labyrinth, car park, LIMESEUM, viewing hill, mini-castrum, playground and the Roman garden with house façade that was moved there in 2020 – which is all at one level and accessible without barriers, with the exception of the viewing hill. Thus, essential elements of the Roman Park can be grasped at a glance, even when the museum is closed (for example, during the COVID-19 lockdowns).

From the archaeological park to the LIMESEUM

In autumn 2004, a small interim museum was set up in Weiltingen to show selected finds from Ruffenhofen. Based on the experience there, a new museum was planned. Because of the excellent view over the World Heritage Site, an area to the east of the viewing hill was chosen as the location. With financial support from the district of Ansbach and the province of Middle Franconia, a permanent museum operation was guaranteed. A spatial concept was also available. Thus, an architectural study could be commissioned, which, under the condition of holding an architectural competition, provided over €3 million in federal subsidies for the new building.

The ground-breaking ceremony took place at the end of July 2011, the topping-out ceremony in December, and the inauguration on 12 October 2012. With a joint effort, as well as significant financial and especially personnel support from the State Agency for Non-governmental Museums, it was possible to move the museum's construction forward quickly.

Character-led interpretation: December, a Roman soldier at Ruffenhofen

The central task of the LIMESEUM is to communicate the *Limes* World Heritage value with a focus on Ruffenhofen. The aim is to show exhibits and multimedia in a setting unaffected by bad weather. There were next to no excavation finds, and few spectacular finds overall, for the exhibition. The museum's development also considered the fact that there are two well-known Roman

Figure 4: December stamping his helmet plate. Courtesy of the LIMESEUM Ruffenhofen/Faber Courtial

museums in the nearby areas in Weißenburg and Aalen, which are branch offices of the respective Archaeological State Museums. All these museums have the same theme: Roman cavalry soldiers on the *Limes*. To complement these museums and to do justice to the significance of Ruffenhofen, a different conception for the museum was necessary. Thus, the LIMESEUM moved from the big picture to focus on a single historical person.

An introduction is provided by ten quotations with major keywords concerning the *Limes*. The first exhibition area shows a virtual ideal reconstruction of Rome and provides insights into the Roman culture that reached the area around the Hesselberg. In the second thematic area, visitors then enter the 'Raetian *Limes*' with a model, maps and photos of excavations, before continuing on to Ruffenhofen. There, a large central model on a scale of 1:200 is the main part of the exhibition. With the help of various artefacts, the exhibition also focuses on the Roman soldiers on site.

In order to convey life at that time more vividly, a soldier named December, known from a stamped inscription, was 'brought to life'. Specific details about his life and a corresponding *curriculum vitae* were created, discussed in detail and agreed by the archaeological and scientific advisory board. He can be seen life-sized at four listening stations, in several scenes in the cinematic film and at two, sometimes three places in the museum. The first insight into his everyday life is given by the young December when he is a horse-servant at Fort Ruffenhofen, hoping to continue his career as a mounted soldier. Next to the second listening station, the fully equipped December can be seen life-sized. In late 2020, a picture was added showing December stamping his name onto his helmet. This scene can also be seen in the film itself (Figure 4).

Figure 5: Overview of the Roman Park and LIMESEUM (drone picture). Courtesy of the LIMESEUM Ruffenhofen

In fact, December can be spotted in many places by attentive visitors. The film, which offers a tour from the eastern burial ground through the fort with a view towards the *Limes*, into the *vicus* and finally into the LIMESEUM, includes a journey through the life of December, who in retirement worked as a bronze-caster in the *vicus*. The permanent exhibition, the last part of which is devoted to civilian life, takes this up thematically. Here, not only is December shown with his family, but three display cases are thematically assigned to December, his wife Aurelia and their children, with corresponding exhibits. Finally, the permanent exhibition is concluded with the 'Cult of the Dead'. Here, a son of December, who has died in the meantime, has his say. At the end of the tour, a large glass area provides an overview of the entire Roman Park site.

Virtual reconstruction of the archaeological landscape

The LIMESEUM Ruffenhofen intentionally sees itself as a museum in a modern landscape (Figure 5). It was a clear direction in the architectural tender that the building should fit harmoniously into the landscape and offer many views into it. A fundamental requirement in the tender was a design with views towards the landscape-defining Hesselberg, and, through a large window, the Roman Park. The gently rising, round, glass building designed by the architects Karl and Probst achieves this. Topographical references were set up at four windows: to the *Limes* in the direction of Aalen and Weißenburg; towards the Nördlinger Ries in the context of food supply; and to Augsburg and Rome with regard to administration.

The cinematic film, which lasts about eight minutes, is a central element of the museum, providing a good experience of everyday Roman life in Ruffenhofen. The basis for the film was a topographic laser scan (LiDAR) commissioned by the Bavarian State Office for the Preservation of Monuments as part of the research into the Raetian *Limes*. Not only was the *Limes* line with Ruffenhofen included in the scan, but the geographically dominant Hesselberg as well. These features could now be virtually set in the Roman era.

The company Faber-Courtial in Darmstadt was commissioned for the complex project. The technical support was provided in close coordination with the scientific advisory board, which discussed the respective implementation steps either via film sequences made available online or in person on site. Firstly, a simple 3D model of the landscape with the dimensions of the buildings was created on the basis of the geophysics, and an outline drawing carried out (Sommer 2009). In a next step, there was a simple camera tour through the schematic cubic elements, reminiscent of a building set. For this, some specific guidelines were given for the interpretation of the buildings in question. In accordance with the dates of December's life, the years around AD 200 were chosen as the timeframe for the film, which is also reflected in the depiction of the buildings. The textures of the buildings and of the landscape were done step by step. There was considerable discussion about the extent to which the terrain had been cleared at that point in history. Even if many questions remain unanswered to this day and much detailed archaeological knowledge is lacking, the film still gives a very good insight into the landscape and life at that time.

Landscape development from pre-Roman to post-Roman times

From the beginning, guided tours also explained the development of the landscape. The first thematic complex was the culture of the Romans, who settled around the Hesselberg in *c.* AD 100. There is no archaeological evidence of any inhabitants living in the area at this time. The landscape was very sparsely populated at best, and heavily forested. The first Roman settlers felled trees and used them as timber, or cleared areas by fire. Some time around AD 100-115, the wooden fort was built, and the first buildings were erected in the *vicus*. Further insight into the time around AD 200 is provided by the cinematic film, and also by a large landscape picture, 3m x 9m, which stands directly next to the large model of Ruffenhofen (Figure 6). This picture conveys the clear

Figure 6: The landscape around Roman Ruffenhofen. Courtesy of the LIMESEUM Ruffenhofen/Faber Courtial

contrast between the image of Rome as the navel of the world at the beginning of the tour, and the appearance of Ruffenhofen at the edge of the Roman world.

There are also two post-Roman images: the depiction of the Roman-era buildings a few decades after the abandonment of the *Limes*, and of the 7th and 8th century, when the first settlers of the modern villages discovered the ruins and salvaged the building materials. Actual spolia in buildings around Ruffenhofen, including inscriptions or reliefs, could not be found. The church of Ruffenhofen, however, has to this day a floor consisting mainly of hypocaust bricks. The four landscape pictures were presented as part of a special exhibition. In order to show them permanently, they were added as commented stills to the cinematic film.

Archaeobotanical evidence, which was sporadically available through the 2005 excavation and especially through pile core sampling in cooperation with the Roman-Germanic Commission Frankfurt (Burger-Völlmecke *et al.* 2019), served as an essential guideline for the landscape changes, supplemented by approximate calculations of wood consumption in buildings by craftsmen and for heating systems. For the latter, there are various recent studies that have been taken into account (Lehar 2012; Stangl 2011). Nevertheless, we are aware that this can only provide a very schematic and general insight into the big picture.

Shifting the interpretation focus: From 'Edge of Empire' to 'Life in the Frontier Region'

In view of the planned coordination between the various *Limes* museums, the LIMESEUM was given a motto from the very beginning. The slogan 'edge of empire' was rather noncommittal. The wish of museum management had always been to focus on a concrete theme that was as lively as possible. Smaller additions to the permanent exhibition in 2016 and 2020 served this purpose. As a result, the museum motto was also supplemented and now reads: 'Multicultural society at the *Limes*'.

The first addition was essentially military, in the form of two lifelike figures showing a fully equipped soldier and one in 'light service dress'. At the same time, various other soldiers' names were depicted in addition to December, most of which are attested to by graffiti and other inscriptions at Ruffenhofen. December's *curriculum vitae* was also summarised. The point was made that the settlers at the *Limes* were Romans, but not Italians. With auxiliary troops at the *Limes*, many people came from different provinces across the entire Roman Empire. This meant that a place like Ruffenhofen could become a melting pot of cultures under the Roman umbrella. Archaeological findings are still lacking to verify this in more detail.

During the expansion in 2020, further additions were made. For example, there are now seven life-sized depictions of different Romans, who have been given names attested to in Ruffenhofen and talk about themselves in a few short sentences. The pictures were deliberately produced in such a way that they fitted in well with the various areas in the museum. In the entrance, where the museum café is located, eating and drinking Romans form the prelude, and then others follow in accordance with the different thematic areas.

Further insights and additions have also been made at various points: these include suitable quotations, for example from the Vindolanda tablets. A connection to Vindolanda is based on the fact that the Ninth Cohort of Batavians stationed there was later garrisoned in Ruffenhofen (Steidl 2016).

Other exhibits are on permanent loan to the LIMESEUM, above all those belonging to the Historical Association for Middle Franconia, which has given its *Limes* finds from the 19th century, previously presented in the Markgrafenmuseum, Ansbach. Among them are the outstanding bronze vessels from Dambach, which have been interpreted as wares from a public drinking establishment (Petrovszky 2000).[2]

Most of the changes concern the *vicus*. Here, not only can the bronze vessels be seen, but also findings on dietary habits that could be inferred on the basis of archaeobotanical and archaeozoological investigations. These include the remains of a walnut shell, a cherry pit, various cereals and a bronze fishhook. Other tools, spoons, dishes and oil lamps were also added, as well as new elements from the world of the gods, with the relief of Fortuna from Gnotzheim, the miscast of an Apollo statuette from Ruffenhofen, and other pieces.

The LIMESEUM has also developed the permanent exhibition since it opened in 2012. In future, the façade with the window niches will offer a good place to temporarily supplement the permanent exhibition. In addition, there are regularly changing special exhibitions.

In the Ruffenhofen Archaeological Roman Park, since its official handover on 1 August 2003 to the addition of the area with the Roman house façade, the garden and a baking oven, a large degree of completion has been achieved on the 42-hectare site. In the future, we expect, at most, only minor accentuations or changes. Further research on the site will now be essential, combined with monument preservation measures. The results will then continue to be presented in special exhibitions and publications.

Bibliography

Burger-Völlmecke, D., Hüssen, C.M., Pausch, M. and Radloff, K., 2019. Ein Bodendenkmal wird angebohrt - Kombinierte Prospektionsmethoden im Limeskastell Ruffenhofen, in Matešić, S. (ed.), *Interdisziplinare Forschungen zum Limes. 8. Kolloquium der Deutschen Limeskommission in Wiesbaden. Beiträge zum Welterbe Limes 10 (Mainz 2019)*: 110-120. Stuttgart: wbg Theiss.

Fassbinder, J. 2010. Von Eining bis Ruffenhofen: Auf dem Weg zu einem Magnetogramm-Atlas der raetischen Limeskastelle – Ergebnisse der geophysikalischen Prospektion in Bayern, in Henrich, P. (ed.) *Perspektiven der Limesforschung. Beiträge zum Welterbe Limes Band 5*: 89-103. Stuttgart: wbg Theiss.

Lehar, H. 2012. *Die römische Hypokaustheizung. Berechnungen und Überlegungen zu Leistung, Aufbau und Funktion*. Aachen: Shaker Verlag.

Mischka, C. and Moneta, C. 2012. Neue geomagnetische Prospektionen in den Kastellvici des Raetischen Limes, in Henrich, P. (ed.) *Der Limes vom Niederrhein bis an die Donau. 6. Kolloquium der Deutschen Limeskommission 15./16. März 2011 in Mainz. Beiträge zum Welterbe Limes 6*: 123-135. Stuttgart: wbg Theiss.

[2] In 2020, extensive X-ray examinations and material analyses were carried out in the laboratory of the Bavarian State Office for the Preservation of Monuments. The publication on this is still pending.

Pausch, M. 2008. Visualisierungen und Bepflanzungen am Limes: Erste Erfahrungen und Überlegungen aus Ruffenhofen. *Denkmalpflege-Informationen* 139: 42-44.

Pausch, M. 2010a. Möglichkeiten und Erfahrungen der Visualisierung im Kastell Ruffenhofen, in Henrich, P. (ed.) *Perspektiven der Limesforschung. Beiträge zum Welterbe Limes Band 5*: 190-201. Stuttgart: wbg Theiss.

Pausch, M (2010b) Vicus Ruffenhofen: 40 Quadratmeter Friedhof, in *Der Limes. Nachrichtenblatt der Deutschen Limeskommission 4/2*: 34-35. Deutsche Limeskommission

Pausch, M., and Weinlich, E. 2005. Die neue Abteilung „Römerpark Ruffenhofen" im Heimat- und Trachtenmuseum Weiltingen, Lkr. Ansbach. *Museum Heute* 29: 35-37.

Petrovszky, R. 2000. Eine Sonderform Römischer Bronzegefäße. Die Krüge vom Typ Dambach. *Kölner Jahrbuch* 33: 485-498.

Sommer, C.S. 2009. Kastellvicus (Marketender- oder Zivilsiedlung) in Pausch, M. (ed.) *Römisches Ruffenhofen. Entdeckungen am Welterbe Limes*, Augsburg.

Stangl, G. 2011. Der Holzverbrauch in der Antike als Teil des ökologischen Fussabdrucks, in Scherrer, P. (ed.) *Lignum. Holz in der Antike, Keryx 1*: 73-86. Graz: Uni-Press Graz Verlag GmbH.

Steidl, B. 2016. Ein Militärdiplom aus dem vicus des Kastells Ruffenhofen am raetischen Limes. Zur Dislokation der cohors VIII Batavorum milliaria exploratorum. *2. Jahrhundert n. Chr, BVbl* 81: 147-170.

Weinlich, E. 2015. Die Forschungsgrabung 2005 im Limeskastell Ruffenhofen. *Bericht der Bayerischen Bodendenkmalpflege* 56: 115-187.

From MOOC to WallCAP: engaging non-academic audiences with Hadrian's Wall

Rob Collins (Newcastle University)

The most traditional (and time-honoured) way to experience Hadrian's Wall, its archaeological remains, its collections and its landscapes, has long been an in-person visit to the World Heritage Site. However, such a traditional approach poses some challenges, which the last decade of managing the Wall have brought into stark relief. How do we inspire Hadrian's Wall's many publics to learn more about the frontier when a global pandemic strikes, and all travel is restricted? How do we attract and engage interested audiences from across the world, with a mixture of ages, abilities and backgrounds? And is there a space for sustainable community archaeology on the Wall? This chapter explores the lessons learned by the author through his involvement in two Newcastle University projects: the Massive Online Open Course (MOOC) titled 'Hadrian's Wall: Life on the Roman Frontier', and the Hadrian's Wall Community Archaeology Project (WallCAP). The traditional way of approaching Hadrian's Wall is alive and well, but what alternatives, or enhanced opportunities to engage with the history and archaeology of the Wall, are out there?

Introduction

Hadrian's Wall is justly celebrated as World Heritage, and its long-term history of investigation spanning centuries has ensured that it is a very well-researched monument. However, the depth of our understanding of the Wall is not always appreciated or understood by non-scholarly audiences, who often approach the monument with varied, even factually incorrect knowledge. This distinction between *recognition* and *understanding* is important, not least as this influences the ways in which audiences engage with the Wall, as well as the benefits such engagements bring. While there is an august tradition of communicating with wide audiences in Wall studies, not least epitomised by the decennial tradition of the Hadrian's Wall Pilgrimage (Bidwell 1999: 1-6), a number of changes with the turn of millennium have generated new opportunities to engage with a wider audience than ever before. The growth of community archaeology and broader awareness of the role of heritage management are important, but the advent of the internet has exponentially increased the potential for Hadrian's Wall to reach new audiences. Since 2013, Newcastle University has led on two initiatives that aimed to engage the public and enhance understanding of Hadrian's Wall. First, a Massive Online Open Course (MOOC) was designed, constructed and run from 2014 to 2020; 'Hadrian's Wall: Life on the Roman Frontier' reached 64,563 registered learners in 170 countries over its six years of life. Second, the Hadrian's Wall Community Archaeology Project (WallCAP) ran from 2017 to 2022 with more than 375 registered volunteers and significant research and conservation interventions undertaken at 20 sites. The MOOC and WallCAP both made use of pedagogic methods and planning, and provide an opportunity to assess the effectiveness of new forms of public engagement, highlighting challenges and successes that serve as lessons for future work.

Hadrian's Wall via global online education

The Hadrian's Wall MOOC was a collaboration between Newcastle University and FutureLearn, a company owned and funded by the Open University. The partnership combined the research and educational expertise of staff from Newcastle University with FutureLearn's digital platform, technical support and pedagogic experience of online delivery of teaching. Within Newcastle University, three groups cooperated to produce the Hadrian's Wall course. A dedicated MOOC team of 2.5 staff from the (then) Learning and Teaching Development Service (LTDS) was supported by three professionals from the university's Digital Media service, who provided filming and editing. Ian Haynes and Rob Collins were responsible for overall educational course design, content and delivery. While the lead educator (Haynes) and secondary educator (Collins) were prominent within the course, the development and production of the course was largely cooperative across the subject expertise, media professionals and the MOOC team from LTDS, which ensured the educational aims and delivery were consistent and professional in execution. The entire course was designed, written, filmed and produced between March and August 2014. The core aim of the course was to provide a reliable foundation for understanding the archaeology of Hadrian's Wall through a familiarity with the evidence and methods used to gather data. The data provided below is derived from the final report of the MOOC (Garland 2020), and further discussion of some of the pedagogy and details of content and structure can be found elsewhere (Collins *et al.* 2018).

Designed as a six-week course, the MOOC first ran from 22 September through 2 November 2014, with a further 12 deliveries between June 2015 and June 2020. During each run of the course, a small number of 'mentors' were paid to review the online platform regularly to answer questions and provide interactivity for registered learners. The mentors worked in shifts of two to six hours across seven days per week for the six-week duration of the course.

Each of the course's six weeks was designed following best-practice guidance established by FutureLearn from their previously completed MOOCs. Each week combined mixed media – text, videos, exercises and quizzes – with the intent of requiring approximately four hours of time to complete by a registered participant (known as a Learner). Furthermore, the course had to be self-contained such that it could be completed exclusively from course content; other web-based resources could be incorporated but had to be treated as optional extras. A final condition was that no previous knowledge of archaeology or Hadrian's Wall was to be assumed for the Learners; thus,

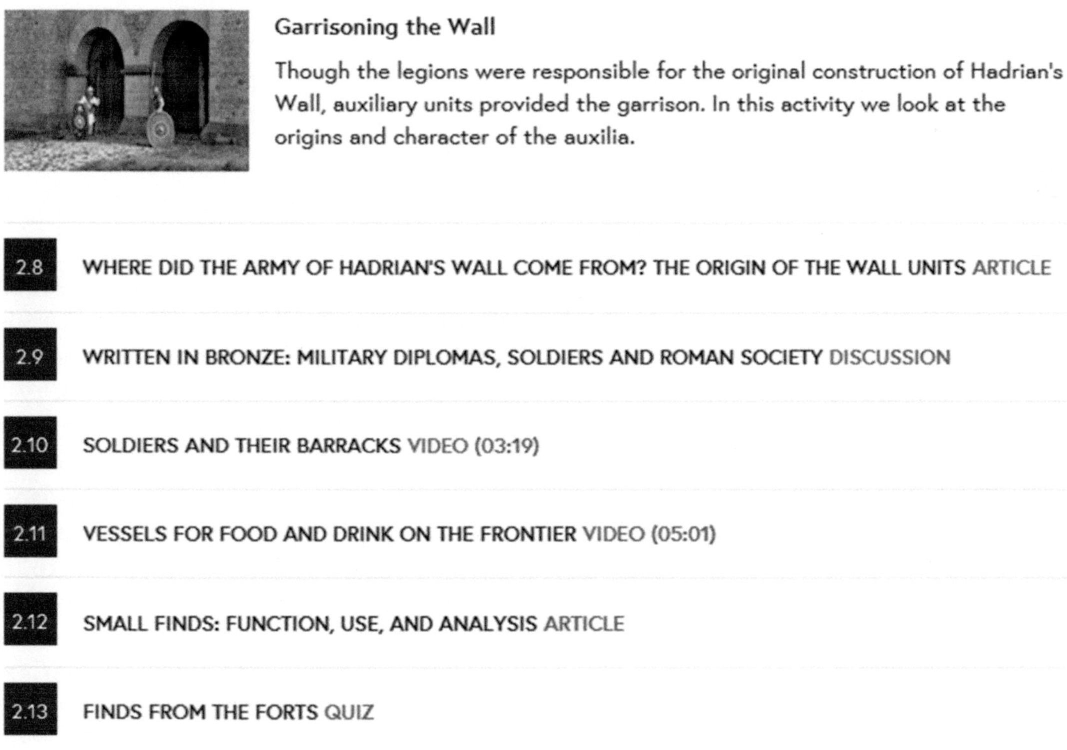

Figure 1: An example of an Activity or subject-block from the Hadrian's Wall MOOC, as it appeared on the FutureLearn platform. The image and text at the top introduces the topic, and the individual Steps that build up the learning of participants are seen below, with the medium of the Step noted in the grey text. Image: Rob Collins.

Week 1
Welcome to the Wall
Wall Essentials
Life Before the Wall
The Stanegate
Clues to the Wall
Week Summary

Week 2
The Invasion Force
Garrisoning the Wall
The Late Roman Army
Cold case: The Head in the Ditch

Week 3
Frontier Landscapes
Populations
Identity on Roman Frontiers

Week 4
Naming and Seeing the Gods
Syncretism
Digging Ritual
Honouring the Gods
Christianity Along the Wall

Week 5
Severan Period
A 3rd Century Crisis?
The 4th Century
A 4th Century Banquet
The Value of Visualisation

Week 6
The End of the Wall
The Antiquaries
The Modern Landscape
Conclusions

Figure 2: The course content in terms of Activities by Week for the Hadrian's Wall MOOC. Image: Rob Collins.

the course was presented at the difficulty level of secondary education, though the content itself was representative of university-level education.

The six-week structure provided the framework (designated Week 1 to Week 6). Within each Week, there was a number of Activities or subject-blocks, and each Activity consisted of a number of Steps. Individual Steps provided focused information, with short sequences of Steps contributing to a broader topical Activity (Figure 1). The Activities then reinforced each other in addressing a thematic focus for the Week (Figure 2). Steps and Activities cross-referenced and reinforced each other across Weeks, with information readily accessible for further review. Though the numbers varied slightly week by week, the four hours of coursework per Week were generally achieved with approximately 20 Steps, yielding six Weeks of 122 total Steps separated into 35 Activities. Minor changes were made to the original course structure to improve the Learners' experience, and while the majority of Steps delivered content developed by the educators, additional experts were featured to highlight the community of scholarship.

Individual engagements with Learners in each Step used a variety of media, but were also constrained by the need to achieve the correct level of educational intensity. Videos were the primary medium, supported by discussions, quizzes and articles. Videos were almost always less than five minutes in length, while articles were approximately 600 words. This limited length for videos and articles challenged the scholars and experts that contributed to the course to distil complex topics into a concise but coherent offering. Multiple choice quizzes and tests provided a means of assessing the extent of participants' comprehension, and other activities included interactive discussions or exercises. For example, Learners were asked to identify key archaeological features through the interrogation of the Maryport geophysical survey plot superimposed on a Google Earth image. Each Step also had the capacity to record Learners' comments and questions in line with social media platforms, enabling digital interactivity with the broader learning community as well as mentors and educators. Comment threads also provided the capacity for hyperlinking to digital materials outside the course, allowing educators and Learners to support each other. Across all runs of the MOOC, it was significant that the educators and mentors interacted with the Learners on the platform; such engagements consistently reinforced continued participation by Learners.

Participants, or Learners, in the course were distinguished from registrations. The first run of the MOOC, for example, boasted 18,076 registrations, but only 64.9% of these participated in the course as Learners. Of these Learners, further distinctions could be made between Active Learners (who ticked the 'complete' button per Step), Returning Learners (those who completed Steps in more than one week), and Fully Participating Learners (those who completed the majority of Steps in the course). Social Learners, who made comments and asked questions, were also distinguished. The percentage of these varied with each run, but Learners (of all sub-types) totalled at 64,563 people from 170 different countries. Of this impressive selection, the majority of Learners were from English-speaking nations, namely the UK, USA and Canada, though a number of participants were explicit in stating that they used the course as a means of improving English-language skills. Social Learners provided a qualitative means of assessing understanding of course content, but did not represent the majority of Learners in any run of the course.

The web-based delivery of the course allowed a number of metrics to be captured and analysed. Quizzes and tests provided simple assessments of understanding, as in a traditional classroom, while numbers of comments and media views were quantified per Step, providing a means of identifying the Steps that were most frequently (re)viewed and/or generated the most positive or negative social interest. Across numerous metrics, the Hadrian's Wall MOOC was highly successful, consisting as it did of high numbers of registrations, consistent participations/completions of the course, and high levels of social engagement. These metrics have also yielded important insights in understanding how a global audience perceives and learns about Hadrian's Wall.

Over 98% of active learners reported that they learned something new, and 85-95% had shared this knowledge with others. A survey of participants (n=3823) revealed that around 70% pursued further interest in Hadrian's Wall after completing the course: some were inspired to take degree programmes, whereas a majority visited museums or pursued further reading (80%). Of these, 35% reported purchasing those reading materials, 30% of whom spent more than £30. A majority of participants reported that the course inspired them to visit Hadrian's Wall itself (60%). Numerous testimonies provide indirect evidence of the regional financial benefit stimulated by the MOOC, with one example from a European participant here: 'So, after the FutureLearn course I have spent money buying books, employed local travel agents, some B&B's and restaurants and found Britain as a travel destination again ... Also our local adult education center thought about organizing a hiking trip there.'

WallCAP

The Hadrian's Wall Community Archaeology Project (WallCAP) was funded by the National Lottery Heritage Fund across two discrete phases from 2017 to 2022. The project was structured on the premise of community archaeology (citizen science) to address a series of heritage management concerns and research questions. The project benefitted from a core team of seven individuals that led on specialist roles. For example, the Volunteer Coordinator and Community Liaison Officer was responsible for initiating and maintaining communications with project volunteers, while the Community Archaeologist coordinated and directed any archaeological fieldwork. At the heart of the project was the identification of three key audiences and each of these audience's agendas/interests. Heritage professional audiences were concerned with the degrading physical condition of some locations along the Wall, as well as sharing an interest in better understanding

Theme	Skills Learned	Testimonial (participant quote)
Archaeological fieldwork / training Volunteers: 1,095 Attendees: 5,931	Geophysical survey; topographic survey; archaeological excavation; standing buildings survey; archaeological illustration; historical information/knowledge; IT skills; photography	"I enjoyed finding out about LIDAR. I learned how to excavate a site methodically and appreciate how much work goes into organising such an event." "[I learned] how to decide whether a particular site should be investigated and how to determine exactly where to focus and the best method to carry out further work - even knowing that nothing is there is useful!" "Discovery of local previously unknown (by me) interesting sites to visit and share with family...who are all of course as interested as I am."
Geological fieldwork / training Volunteers: 603 Attendees: 5,163	Rock identification; geological formation; quarrying techniques; masonry techniques	"Signed up to a geology training course that I wouldn't have known about if it wasn't for WallCAP." "Learning about the different types of stone, how quarried etc. Adding to my overall picture of Roman and other life on the Wall."
Interpretation and management Volunteers: 122 Attendees: 1,357	Source assessment; critical reasoning; outcome-based communication; audience interests and bias; professional practice	"I was surprised to learn all the different processes involved in planned a new gallery at the Roman Carlisle event. We analysed the current gallery, discussed at length what we liked and also what we thought didn't work. Naturally none of us agreed, so a fascinating discussion followed. It was quite an insight to hear other people's views on the gallery."
Well-being and inclusion Volunteers: 446 Attendees: 2	Mindfulness; appreciation of place; position of heritage in communities	"It's had a massive impact, I would have gone into real deep depression without it." "I work full time so struggle to get along to digs and other archaeological events and activities. As such the GIS project offered flexibility, in particular given home working due to Covid19, to undertake elements of research for the project." "I appreciated the opportunity to take part in an indoor activity as I sometimes worry my fitness may let me down during outdoor sessions."

Table 1: A thematic breakdown of WallCAP activities, indicating the numbers of Volunteers and Attendees, the skills learned, and supporting testimonials. The testimonials are kept anonymous, but used with the permission of the speaker/provider.

contemporary threats to the monument (Frodsham 2016); research audiences had questions pertaining to understanding of the Wall in Roman and more recent centuries (Symonds and Mason 2009); and local communities had an interest in not only better understanding the Wall, but also a desire to have opportunities to actively engage with archaeological and heritage practices (Norman and May 2014). Though identified as discrete audiences, the needs of each group were not mutually exclusive, and the underlying benefit of the project was to invite local communities and volunteers to be part of the solution to management, conservation and research 'problems'. WallCAP has brought together nine stakeholder organisations (including Historic England, English Heritage, the National Trust and the local planning authorities) with five community groups and 375 registered volunteers. The numbers present here are accurate at the time of writing in December 2021; final project statistics are bound to increase by the end of 2022.

As with the MOOC, WallCAP was designed to provide opportunities for people to participate and engage with the Wall, regardless of any previous experience or knowledge. Throughout the course of the project, various events and activities were designed and implemented that provided training, intended to function both as a one-off activity for those participants that wanted a 'light touch' experience but which also fitted into a larger suite of activities for those desiring more consistent involvement. Events and activities were also planned and designed with specific participating audiences in mind. WallCAP participants are separated into three discrete categories: volunteers, intended as individuals that registered with the project; the general public, consisting of individuals with no defined relationship with the project; and professionals/experts/researchers, who were both participants that contributed to some events and audiences or beneficiaries of some activities.

WallCAP coordinated 232 digital and in-person events across its lifespan (as of December 2021), totalling 14,719 individual participations, consisting of registered project volunteers, members of the public and professionals/researchers. These events can be analysed in various schema (e.g. by participant demographic, by beneficiary, etc.) but are presented here thematically (Table 1), such that an indication of various skills learned and knowledge gained can be summarised. It is important to distinguish between the participants as registered project volunteers relative to other attendees, also separated in Table 1.

Figure 3: The WallCAP excavation at Walltown Crags, viewed from the east with the 20th-century quarry in the background. The Wall curtain sits at the forward edge of the crags, and work along the north face was slippery under wet and windy conditions. Image (by Kathryn Murphy): WallCAP.

Events that were structured for volunteer participation were typically more interactive, with volunteers engaged in active learning or the generation of work and/or results. In contrast, events with attendees can be viewed as more 'passive' activities, such as talks, papers or exhibitions: these, however, still resulted in some learning by attendees. Project volunteers typically attended events that were open to the general public. The key distinction, however, is that project volunteers engaged with, shaped and benefitted from a larger programme of activities and events that generated a growth in knowledge and skills pertaining to the Wall, indicated in Table 1. For example, volunteers were able to build a well-rounded appreciation of the full process of archaeological fieldwork. Training sessions included 'Why and when do we [archaeologists] excavate' alongside practical experience in undertaking geophysical survey and excavation, supported by training and participation in other essential activities, such as archival research and data entry. Communicating 'why' various activities were necessary was as important as the 'doing', and in fact resulted in greater attention to detail and appreciation for tasks that could be considered as boring or routine.

In-person events were often defined in their scale and outcomes by the activity being undertaken. For example, excavations could only host a set amount of people on any given day, depending on the size of the trenches, or even the safety of the work. Limited excavation at Walltown Crags was followed by a period of further consolidation of the curtain, but the location of the trenches at the top of the crags coupled with very windy conditions made it unsafe to include volunteers in the activity; therefore, only WallCAP staff and necessary contractors engaged in the work (Figure 3). By contrast, excavations at Corbridge in 2019 and 2021 were extremely popular, with 169 volunteer engagements.

In addition, in-person events required the ability of any participant to be able to travel to a given location in the World Heritage Site (WHS); obviously, this limited participation (generally speaking) to people living locally to the Wall or within North-East and North-West England. Digital events, however, were not so constrained and opened WallCAP up to a global digital audience, effectively enhancing the project through non-local and international participation. The project has reached audiences in Australia, Japan, China, Poland, Romania and California (USA), to name only a few examples. Social media, too, has promoted the project to a global audience, and enhanced awareness with UK-based audiences: for example @Wall_CAP (Twitter) had 2528 followers and its posts resulted in 1,971,600 impressions. That said, small-scale digital interactions were also well-attended and, particularly during periods of lockdown during the COVID-19 pandemic, not only furthered the aims of the project but provided entertainment and support. WallCAP's Volunteer Coordinator instigated a monthly 'volunteer tea break' online event, which continued until the end of the project, where no work or structured activities were undertaken – it was simply a chance to chat. Similarly, the running of a monthly book club and periodic meetings of a film club by WallCAP allowed volunteers to approach the Wall, the Roman period and this region of England as portrayed in print and film media; these meetings were often filled with laughter and good cheer.

WallCAP facilitated and delivered a number of benefits to stakeholders and local communities, but perhaps the most easily communicated benefits were to those sites designated as Heritage At Risk. Fieldwork was undertaken at 12 sites: Port Carlisle; Drumburgh; Cam Beck; Thirlwall; Walltown Crags; Mucklebank turret; Steel Rigg; Cats Stairs; Green Carts; Portgate; Corbridge; and Heddon-on-the-Wall. The fieldwork typically not only generated new archaeological knowledge and therefore understanding of Hadrian's Wall, but often also left the monument in a better condition. At Port Carlisle, for example, archaeological assessment revealed the extent to which a surviving above-ground length of stone curtain had been historically demolished, while also repairing the upstanding *in situ* Roman fabric. Significantly, this fieldwork has revealed more clearly the extent to which the Wall curtain has been interfered with in recent centuries in contrast to what was previously believed to be a largely surviving stretch of the monument.

Survey and excavation at Cam Beck revealed for the first time how the Wall crossed a 'minor' watercourse, and this new knowledge will better inform future management of the location. Such engagements were usually beneficial to landowners and conservation authorities such as Historic England, but equally importantly provided opportunities for communities and volunteers to directly and positively impact their local heritage – coming to understand a given 'issue' and why it was important to address it. Though difficult to quantify, it is also worth noting that volunteers often reported increased feelings of wellbeing from participating in such activities.

Discussion

A number of insights can be drawn from the Wall MOOC, with its digital global audience, and WallCAP, with its focus on community archaeology. Both endeavours have been highly successful, and a review of feedback and evaluation data highlights key takeaways for future engagement, not least those involving educational aims. The scale of these endeavours should also be appreciated. To reach the 64,563 registered learners on the MOOC would have required teaching the equivalent traditional university campus-based course (consisting of 35 students on average) a total of 1,845 times; even if taught continuously in autumn and spring semesters, that means 922 consecutive academic years! This underscores the importance of assessing key conclusions for future work.

First is the combined importance of expertise and accessibility. Consistent feedback from both the MOOC and WallCAP is that participants enjoyed having *interactive* access to individuals with scholarly credentials and expertise in the subject of Hadrian's Wall and archaeology. To be clear, an *expert* is attractive to audiences, which further underscores that people do value the knowledge and experience of experts. While the expertise should not be dismissed, it should not be seen as secondary to accessibility. In this case, accessibility bears more than one meaning.

The experts needed to be willing and available to engage with the respective audiences, but more importantly, the experts needed to be able to communicate and deliver material at the appropriate pitch to those audiences, whether the interaction was in-person or digital. Scholars used to lecturing for periods of 45 minutes or more and reading and writing short papers of 5000+ words found the limited lengths of MOOC videos and articles shocking. However, short videos and articles could be watched or read in a relatively short amount of time, which is beneficial for non-traditional learning environments. Furthermore, short offerings are less daunting for learners, especially those not engaged with academic education and research. Three-minute MOOC videos allowed for a distillation of the key concepts, facts and significance to be communicated. If the information could not be conveyed within three minutes or 600 words, this indicated either an excessive amount of information or that more than one Step would be required. In seeming contrast, WallCAP's digital learning engagements were more episodic (e.g. monthly lectures of approximately one hour) or a brief-but-concentrated offering (e.g. two to three-hour digital sessions), and occasionally longer commitments (e.g. two-day workshops/conferences). However, while WallCAP's digital offering initially contrasts with those of the MOOC, it is worth highlighting that WallCAP benefitted from a much longer duration that allowed for both sustained and developed social relationships alongside those individuals that only wanted to attend a single event or drop in and out of selected events. Regardless of the commitment levels of participants, however, was a consistent offer and perception of accessibility in both the MOOC and WallCAP.

A second takeaway is of the benefits accrued from a diverse 'offer' provided by the MOOC and WallCAP, both in terms of knowledge and types of activities. For the MOOC, topical Activities and thematic Weeks were able to introduce Learners to new subjects, challenging their expectations and expanding their knowledge – all of which contributed to the reported very high levels of learning. Furthermore, the inclusion of experts and scholarly voices beyond Haynes and Collins highlighted the community of scholarship, allowing non-experts to see different perspectives, approaches and interpretations – in other words to identify a broader discourse underlying leading interpretations. Polyvocal representation of the Wall added dynamism and suggested to audiences that there was/is space for them! Similarly, in WallCAP the diversity in types of activity provided opportunities for people to try something new and/or continue to hone skills through repeated practice. In both cases, the 'diverse offer' reduces the potential for boredom on the part of participants while concurrently meeting the needs or interests of people with different aptitudes. Exposure to a greater range of experts and diverse skills and activities also resulted in a greater appreciation by participants that there is not just one 'type' of archaeologist, or one way of interpreting data. In short, providing a diverse offer in terms of content and activities is broadly inclusive and results in greater levels of satisfaction.

These benefits should not be dismissed, but it is also fair to highlight that achieving them requires concerted effort, explicit identification of aims and outcomes, and resource commitment. The MOOC benefitted from significant financial investment in Newcastle University staff and resources, not only of the educators, but also from the digital media and LTDS teams. The happy marriage of knowledge/expertise, sound pedagogy and professional presentation underscored confidence on the part of Learners. WallCAP was very thoughtfully structured after considerable consultation with numerous stakeholders, and a key 'asset' of the project was dedicated staffing for volunteer and community engagement.

A further challenge, pedagogically, is that of the threshold concept. A threshold concept is a fundamental concept that, once understood, transforms the understanding of the student, and once learned and understood cannot be 'unlearned' (Meyer and Land 2003, 2005). Specific threshold concepts, or rather the lack of understanding of them, can inhibit the progress of any learning. Hadrian's Wall, as an archaeological monument, has a number of threshold concepts that quite simply need to be learned to achieve a more complex understanding of the monument. These relate both to archaeological methods and principles as well historical and cultural knowledge of the Romans. Three brief examples of a threshold concept were shared by both projects: stratigraphy; time-depth; and 'Roman'. Stratigraphy is a fundamental principle to the practice of field archaeology and interpretation, and without understanding this concept a person will struggle to understand how experts are able, for example, to determine the building sequence of the Wall complex. Similarly, archaeologists and heritage professionals are used to thinking in terms of time-depth and contextualising the date of an event; for non-experts, however, the remote past is often compressed due to its very abstract distance from the present. A fairly typical comment from many Learners on the MOOC is that they had not really considered that the Roman army and its soldiers would change over the 270 years or more that Hadrian's Wall was occupied. The final example, that of 'the Romans', is also challenging, as it requires someone to confront their own expectation or definition of what a Roman person is, and providing evidence that allows them to understand that being Roman was more of an umbrella category for identity, in some ways akin with modern uses such as European or American.

It was essential for these threshold concepts to be identified and to provide training and opportunities for people to engage with them. For WallCAP volunteers, the principles of stratigraphic formation and relationships were essential to their understanding of excavation methods and interpretation, and this was communicated and taught in a combination of online digital sessions, as well as practical experience in the field. To accomplish successful teaching and embedding of such fundamental concepts outside of a structured educational environment requires a combination of appropriate staffing and time (note also observations about accessibility above), but undeniably yields longer-lasting benefits to those participating.

Conclusion

The MOOC and WallCAP have been able to achieve an enhanced public understanding of the Hadrian's Wall World Heritage Site. Digital platforms have generated a truly global audience, while those participating in fieldwork and other in-person activities have been able to build up new skills and knowledge along the Wall itself. Future projects that seek to make Hadrian's Wall more accessible to non-experts should always be embraced. However, it is encouraged that such efforts be explicit in the audiences to be reached and the outcomes desired. Deliberated design and structure is not only good pedagogy, but also essential to success. Furthermore, while the potential of digital technology and platforms has yet to be fully realised, audience expectations and needs must also be assessed. Resourcing appropriate to production value and engagement – whatever form it takes – is also essential and instils confidence in the audience. No doubt future projects will surpass the successes of the MOOC and WallCAP, but it is hoped that these have contributed to the high standard on offer that is typical of Hadrian's Wall.

Bibliography

Bidwell, P. 1999. *Hadrian's Wall 1989-1999*, Kendal: Cumberland and Westmorland Antiquarian and Archaeological Society and the Society of Antiquaries of Newcastle upon Tyne.

Collins, R., Davis, N., and Hardy, S. 2018. The 'Virtual' Wall: Building global interest in Roman frontiers through digital outreach, in Sommer, C.S. and Matešić, S. (eds.), *Limes XXIII. Proceedings of the 23rd International Congress of Roman Frontier Studies, Ingolstadt 2015*: 387-391. Mainze: Beiträge zum Welterbed Limes Sonderband 4.

Frodsham, P. 2016. Hadrian's Wall Heritage At Risk Survey, unpublished report for Hadrian's Wall Community Champions project, Tyne & Wear Archives & Museums.

Garland, N. 2020. Hadrian's Wall: Life on the Frontier MOOC – Evaluation Report, unpublished report, Newcastle University.

Meyer, J.H.F. and Land, R. 2003. Threshold Concepts and Troublesome Knowledge (1). Linkages to ways of thinking and practising within the disciplines, in Rust, C. (ed) *Improving Student Learning Theory and Practice - 10 Years on: Proceedings of the 2002 10th International Symposium Improving Student Learning*: 412-424. Oxford: Oxford Centre for Staff & Learning Development.

Meyer, J.H.F. and Land, R. 2005. Threshold Concepts and Troublesome Knowledge (2). Epistemological considerations and a conceptual framework for teaching and learning, *Higher Education* 49: 373-388.

Norman, K. and May, S. 2014. *Hadrian's Wall WHS Consultation Report.* London: University College London.

Symonds, M. and Mason, D. 2009. *Frontiers of Knowledge: Hadrian's Wall Research Framework*, Durham: Durham County Council.

Gaming and Hadrian's Wall: a future of digital possibilities

Claire Stocks (Newcastle University) and Barbara Birley (Vindolanda Trust)

For many, the content of console and computer-based videogames, as well as games played on smartphones and tablets, can offer a first encounter with past cultures and peoples. This extends to experiences of the ancient world, including Hadrian's Wall and its sites, with the result that a digital encounter with the past will often precede an actual visit to a site. This trend has become more pronounced in recent years due to changing perceptions linked to global issues, such as environmental concerns. As a response, heritage sites have been working extensively on developing their digital profiles, including exploring the role that games can play in their educational offering. This short paper considers the benefits of serious gaming for sites along Hadrian's Wall, focusing on the case study of a mystery game, created for the site of Roman Vindolanda and targeted towards Key Stage 2 students.

Introduction

The videogaming industry has long made use of material from the ancient world as a back-drop to some of the most popular games on the market. *Rome: Total War*, for example, together with its sequel *Rome II: Total War*, produced by Creative Assembly (now part of the SEGA Group), have sold millions of copies since they were released in 2004 and 2013 respectively[1], and the enduring popularity of the games was illustrated by the release of a remastered version of the original in April 2021. The franchise *Assassin's Creed*, produced by Ubisoft, similarly makes use of this material following the release of the game *Assassin's Creed Origins* in 2017, set principally in the world of Ptolemaic Egypt. Ubisoft also released a 'Discovery Tour', which allowed players to 'explore Ancient Egypt without being interrupted by combat or quests', suggesting that the subject matter of the game was of as much interest to users as the gameplay itself.[2] Hadrian's Wall has also featured in AAA games, notably in *Assassin's Creed Valhalla* (2020), set in eighth-century AD Britain, where game-makers appear to have side-stepped the problem of representing in painstaking detail the archaeological remains of Housesteads by covering the landscape in snow. A Discovery Tour mode was also released for this game in October 2021, but this time functioning as a role-playing game (without combat) that allows users to explore the world of the Vikings in the guise of various characters completing quests, reinforcing the importance of entertainment alongside education.[3]

For many people, games such as these may serve as their first introduction to Hadrian's Wall and the ancient world before they have an opportunity to visit a site in person. This new way of approaching archaeological sites brings with it some important benefits, amongst them increased engagement with the ancient world from the general public and younger generations, the latter often being the hardest audience to reach. There are also many potential disadvantages; for example, audiences view the ancient world, and Hadrian's Wall within it, from the perspective of the game makers. Game makers in turn have made a choice as to how to represent the ancient world, and their choices may be guided by interests other than scientific knowledge. Nonetheless the possibilities for using digital resources and games in particular to reach new and established visitors to Hadrian's Wall are extensive and can serve as a valuable tool for educational purposes – what is known as 'edutainment' (e.g. Maugard 2019).

[1] In the case of Rome II: Total War alone, SEGA reported the sale of 1.13 million units of the game between its release in September 2013 and the publication of its financial results in March 2014 (Karmali 2015).
[2] See Ubisoft's webpage on this discovery tour; they describe this game mode thus: 'purely educational, the mode is a virtual museum with guided tours and historical sites to discover' (Ubisoft 2021a).
[3] 'Explaining a time period is very interesting if you are seeing it from all perspectives and we think that showing it from a Nordic saga and an Anglo-Saxon chronicle, it helps to better understand the richness and complexity of a time period' (Ubisoft 2021b, 1min10 – 1min22)

Hadrian's Wall (Archaeopress 2022): 92–99

In this chapter we consider the possibilities for employing games and game mechanics at historic sites along the Wall, discussing some of the work that has already been done – notably the creation of a mystery game at the site of Roman Vindolanda, geared towards Key Stage 2 students. We also assess the possible scope of employing digital games in the future as a means of engaging new audiences and in terms of thinking about Hadrian's Wall as a monument that can be experienced and interpreted in a number of ways.

Gaming at the Wall: Vindolanda and the child's skeleton

'Edutainment' is the term used to describe games used for educational purposes, and it complements the umbrella term 'Serious Gaming', used for games that serve a purpose beyond entertainment (e.g. Mahony *et al.* 2012; Malaka 2014). Games have been used in a wide variety of areas for serious purposes, such as in the medical field to aid patients with physical recovery and rehabilitation (e.g. Ushaw *et al.* 2015a, 2015b), as well as in military and police training.[4] Increasingly, we see the heritage sector and museums making use of digital resources and games for educational purposes on site (Ioannides *et al.* 2017; Veermeren *et al.* 2018) but also as a means of engaging new audiences remotely, especially when working towards sustainable tourism.[5]

Museums, not unlike other parts of modern society, have been forced to develop new interactive ways to engage their audiences, and this has been made all the more relevant in the last few years, when physical access has been limited or even impossible due to the COVID-19 pandemic. Whether the interaction is based on the use of Artificial Intelligence (AI) – as seen in the recent online and games platform at Birmingham Museums Trust, *Occupy White Walls* (Kendall Adams 2020), and at the National Portrait Galleries' *Who do you think you were?*, an online quiz to 'discover your inner Elizabethan' (Bell 2018) – games allow users to interact actively with the collection instead of the sometimes passive experience a visitor might have in museums and galleries. Examples of this on Roman frontier sites in the UK include the use of Minecraft sessions at Arbeia Roman Fort in 2016 (In & Around 2016) and the Antonine Wall app, which allows users to access GPS navigation with alerts for nearby points of interest, discover and 'handle' 3D objects and models, and view 360° virtual reconstructions (Antonine Wall 2021). In the autumn of 2020, the Vindolanda Trust released a game (playable on Android and iOS) and a series of four activity packs (free to download from the Vindolanda Trust website) aimed at Key Stage 2 students (7-11 year olds). The game was funded by the Arts Council England and produced in collaboration with Newcastle University. The packs are a collaboration between the Vindolanda Trust, Newcastle University and Creative Assembly. While the project started well before the beginning of the global pandemic, it evolved in light of it, and so can offer some insights into the benefits of digital games and resources for learning both on site and at home or in the classroom.

The Missing Dead: designing a game for Roman Vindolanda

Roman Vindolanda is a military site established in *c.* AD 85 that continued to be occupied well into the 5th and 6th centuries. Its ongoing excavations offer a wealth of material culture and archaeological remains to fuel the imagination of visitors. In 2017, the Vindolanda Trust was looking for new and innovative ways to engage and interact with its audiences. They collaborated with colleagues at Newcastle University to develop a game for mobile devices, originally designed to be played on the site (Figure 1).

For the Trust, any digital interpretation had to have a strong foundation in the collection and history of the site, and it was vital that the research and archaeology was reflected in the work.

[4] See, for example, Bournemouth University's 'Plus Project' on the use of serious games for police training (Bournemouth University 2015).

[5] The ways in which the Heritage sector is using serious gaming and virtual resources to respond to the challenges of the global pandemic are constantly evolving. For discussion on some of these responses, see, for example, Resta et al. (2021).

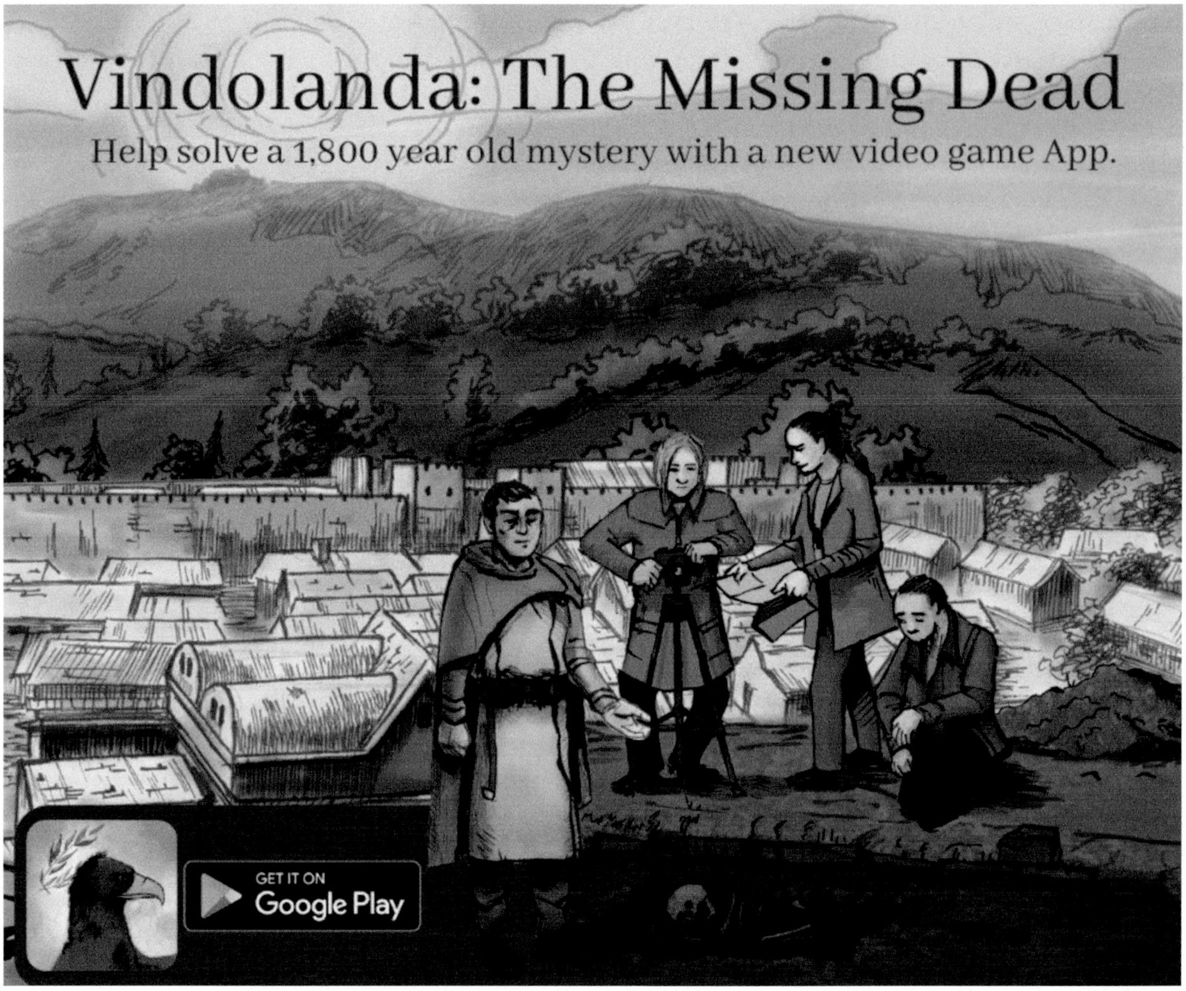

Figure 1: Promotional image used for the game's launch October 2020, Newcastle University and Vindolanda Trust

During the excavations in 2010, an unexpected discovery was made: a child's skeleton was buried in a shallow grave in one of the third-century barracks inside the walls of the fort. Working with forensic anthropologists, the archaeologists were able to determine some basic facts behind the child's identity. Through scientific analysis, including DNA testing and lead isotope analysis, it was determined that the child was female, 8-10 years old and had recently moved to Vindolanda from the Mediterranean area. How and why the child was buried in this very atypical way has led to several possible answers, and the open-ended questions served as a foundation for the development of the game's narrative. From these beginnings, the project developed into a mystery game which takes our fictional detective, Marcus the Tribune, on a journey around the Vindolanda site in *c.* AD 230.

Called 'The Missing Dead', the game and accompanying activity packs take the moment of discovery of the child's skeleton as the starting point for the game's story. Using hand-drawn, 2D animation, we begin in 2010, on site, as the archaeologists make their discovery, before taking the user back to AD 230, where they assist Marcus as he attempts to solve the mystery of Vitalis' missing slave (Figure 2).

The target audiences of the game are Key Stage 2 students (7-11 years) and their families. From the outset, therefore, we had to consider carefully how we presented this subject matter in a sensitive manner which nonetheless acknowledged the realities of life in the ancient world. The approach was to cast the player in the role of co-detective and hence co-'archaeologist'. By beginning with

Figure 2: Vitalis in the bath house – image from The Missing Dead game, Newcastle University and Vindolanda Trust

Figure 3: Vindolanda's *praetorium* in a rainstorm as seen in The Missing Dead game. This image is used when Marcus reports to the commanding officer regarding the outcomes of his investigation, Newcastle University and Vindolanda Trust

the discovery of the skeleton, the user learns from the outset that we are dealing with a death, but they are simultaneously distanced from that death by situating it within the context of an archaeological dig in the contemporary world. The player is thus aware of the end result before they are transported to the past – the mystery lies in how we get to this point. As they play the game, therefore, students learn about the past in a way that is designed to make them ask their own questions as they piece together the clues to help them solve the case; this approach is meant to replicate the process of discovery and investigation employed by archaeologists. The overarching narrative of the game is fictional, but it is populated with real people, buildings and objects from Vindolanda, based upon the source material discovered on site. This content ensures that the game world remains authentic and serves as a lead-in to the more detailed stories about Vindolanda's population that can be explored on site in the museum (Figure 3).

The use of 2D animation in the game was cost-effective and in part influenced by the outdoor environment of the archaeological site, which would have made the use of Virtual Reality (VR) difficult due to trip hazards and variable weather conditions. There were also connectivity issues for devices due to the rural nature of the location. An additional reason was the desire to create a resilient product that could be used by Vindolanda for a number of years. It is hoped that the 2D animation, drawn in a style reminiscent of comic-books and graphic novels to create a vintage feel, will date favourably. Accompanying the game are online activity packs, developed during the pandemic, which can be used to support Key Stage 2 learning in the classroom or at home (Figure 4). These packs were produced in collaboration with Creative Assembly and offer more detail on the game's background (e.g. life in the Roman Army, life at Vindolanda) as well as offering students further resources for learning about how game designers recreate the past in games such

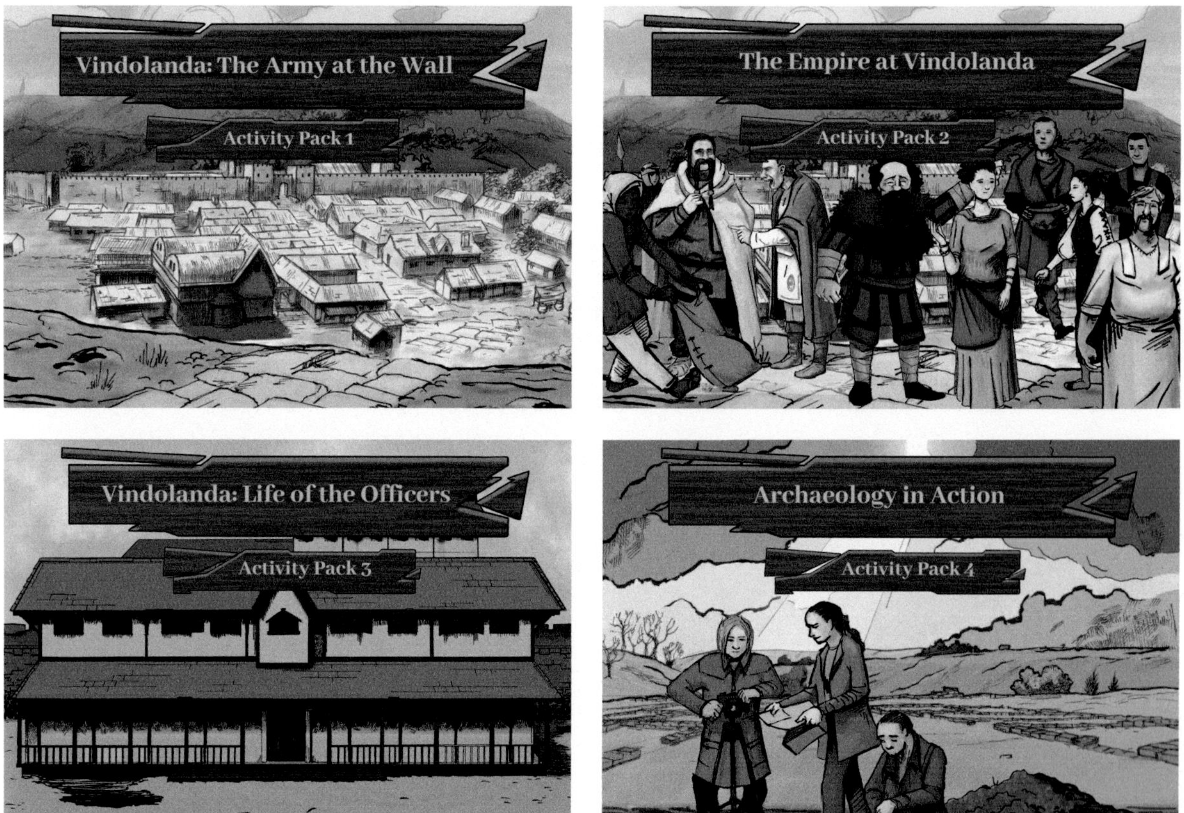

Figure 4: The Missing Dead's activity pack, which can be downloaded at <https://www.vindolanda.com/the-missing-dead-app>, Newcastle University and Vindolanda Trust

as *Rome: Total War*. The final activity pack also includes a section on careers in the heritage sector and gaming industry so that students can see for themselves the wide variety of options available to them through the study of history, computer science, etc.

Where we go next: evaluation, reflection and future development

Feedback on the game has been very positive, and the analytical data from Google Play, Apple Stores and the Vindolanda Trust indicates that some users are playing the game multiple times and off-site, indicating the potential of future games to reach new audiences, who will then be encouraged to visit the site of Vindolanda. Opportunities have also been created for reflecting upon the ways in which such games could be improved in the future. While the use of 2D graphics in this game has been successful, it limits the angles from which people can perceive an object. Had 3D reconstructions been viable then users could have had the opportunity to view an object from any perspective they wished, offering a level of accessibility that is often impossible when the artefact is on display in a museum case. A VR experience, whilst difficult to implement, could go one step further, transporting users into a game environment in which they can 'touch' these objects and see them as they would have been in ancient times.

An additional benefit of placing the objects, albeit in a digital form, back into their original environment, through the creation and playing of the game, is that it offers another way of connecting audiences to the past by overriding the artificial separation created by displaying an object in a museum. This is not to underestimate the value for the visitor of seeing the 'real' artefact with their own eyes. Rather the hope is that such digital experiences can provide a new layer of meaning for audiences, as well as extending the reach of the Vindolanda Trust's collection to visitors for whom coming to the site regularly, if at all, may prove difficult. In 'The Missing Dead', the intention was to include in the game only objects that the user – having played the game on-site – could see in the museum. This means that the user could see both the real object and the digitally reconstructed object in its original environment, enriching both experiences (see also Birley and Griffiths, Chapter 5 in this volume).

The game uses a mechanic that focuses on narrative play, allowing the user to choose their own story-path. This approach proved popular with a test audience from Newbrough School as well as with users following the game's release. The concept of involving students in the progression of the game's narrative was developed further in the accompanying activity packs, which encourage them to develop their own stories based upon the game's narrative. 33 children tested the initial content of the packs, and, using them as story-starters, wrote a wide variety of short stories. In these stories the children took basic elements from the original game's plot (e.g. the names and the story of a missing slave) and developed their own narratives that reflected their interest in (among other things) the Roman army, life in the town, hunting, and even time-travel!

Giving students the opportunity to develop their own stories proved beneficial to their learning experience; their stories reflected the information that they had learnt through reading the packs and studying the Romans in school, so reinforcing this information. Additionally, the children's stories offered fresh perspectives on how archaeologists can interpret the material remains of the past. While these stories are fictional, they encourage us to re-evaluate the information that we have at our disposal. Here 'citizen science' (or 'citizen humanities')[6] can play a role; involving students and the general public at large in both the design of future games and the narrative possibilities within them encourages people to invest in the collections of heritage sites and to be involved both in their preservation and in reaching new audiences.

[6] 'Citizen humanities' is the term that has been used for citizen science in the humanities, and the emergence of digital humanities has presented new opportunities for including the general public in academic research, from working with archives to offering new perspectives and insights on human culture (Heinisch et al. 2021).

Conclusion

Digital games are increasingly an important resource for heritage sites. They offer a way of remotely engaging new audiences with museum collections, and new ways of experiencing what an archaeological site has to offer. In the case of Hadrian's Wall and the sites along it, such games can revolutionise the way in which we experience these monuments: an encounter with the Roman past is no longer limited to the physical experience of seeing a site 'for real' but can be experienced at home and at a distance. Feedback from the game 'The Missing Dead' demonstrates that we need not fear that a digital encounter will replace the real. Rather, the two experiences can complement and enhance one another, with the digital encounter often encouraging users to visit and experience a site for themselves.

All digital resources can be valuable in preserving an ancient site and extending its reach to new audiences. Games in particular can offer an additional benefit – not simply the concept of education through entertainment, which has proven to be such a popular format in the videogaming world, but the idea of involving new audiences in telling stories about the past. As archaeologists we make choices about which 'stories' about an object we will prioritise over others. Involving a wider audience, and particularly students, in this process not only gives them the skills of evaluation needed to become future archaeologists, but can have a positive influence upon how we interpret this material. Through the world of digital gaming, the reach of Hadrian's Wall and its sites are no longer limited to a stretch of land between Wallsend on the River Tyne to the shores of the Solway Firth – they encircle the globe.

Bibliography

Antonine Wall 2021. Download the app. The Antonine Wall: Frontiers of the Roman Empire. Accessed 7 January 2022 <https://www.antoninewall.org/visiting-the-wall/download-the-app>

Bell, F. 2018. Games in Museums and Cultural Spaces, blog, Thrive, 16 July. Accessed 7 January 2022 <https://wewillthrive.co.uk/resources/blogs/museums-and-games>

Bournemouth University 2015. PLUS project: Serious games for police training. Bournemouth University. Accessed on 6 January 2022 <https://www.bournemouth.ac.uk/research/projects/plus-project-serious-games-police-training>

Heinisch, B., Oswald, K., Weißpflug, M., Shuttleworth, S., and Belknap G. 2021. Citizen Humanities, in Vohland K., Land-Zandstra, A., Ceccaroni, L., Lemmens, R., Perelló, J., Ponti, M., Samson, R. and Wagenknecht, K. (eds) *The Science of Citizen Science*: 97-118. Switzerland: Springer Nature

In & Around Magazine 2016. Tyne & Wear Museums Announce Groundbreaking Creative Technology Workshops [online]. Accessed 1 November 2021 <https://www.inandaroundmag.co.uk/tyne-wear-museums-announce-groundbreaking-creative-technology-workshops/>

Ioannides, M., Magnenat-Thalmann, N., and Papagiannakis, G. 2017. *Mixed Reality and Gamification for Cultural Heritage*. Switzerland: Springer Nature

Karmali, L. 2015. SEGA Financials Reveal Total War: Rome 2 as Best-Seller. IGN, 6 October. Accessed on 6 January 2022 <https://www.ign.com/articles/2014/05/09/sega-financials-reveal-total-war-rome-2-as-best-seller>

Kendall Adams, G. 2020. Online game enables users to curate Birmingham Museums collections. *Museums Journal*, Museums Association. Accessed 7 January 2022 <https://www.museumsassociation.org/museums-journal/news/2020/11/online-game-enables-users-to-curate-birmingham-museums-collections/#>

Mahony, S., Tiedau, U. and Sirmons, I. 2012. Open Access and online teaching materials for digital humanities, in Warwick, C., Terras, M., and Nyhan, J. (eds) *Digital Humanities in Practice*: 167-192. London: Facet Publishing.

Malaka, R. 2014. How Computer Games Can Improve Your Health and Fitness, in Göbel, S. and Wiemeyer, J. (eds) *Games for Training, Education, and Sports. 4th International Conference on Serious Games, Game Day 2014, Darmstadt, Germany, April 1-5 2014. Proceedings*: 1-7. Switzerland: Springer Nature

Maugard, N. 2019. Fundamentals of Serious Games, in Akhgar, B. (ed) *Serious Games for Enhancing Law Enforcement Agencies: From Virtual Reality to Augmented Reality*: 15-41. Switzerland: Springer Nature

Resta. G., Dicuonzo, F., Karacan, E., and Pastore, D. 2021. The impact of virtual tours on museum exhibitions after the onset of Covid-19 restrictions: Visitor engagement and long term perspectives, *Scientific Research and Information Technology; Ricerca Scientifica e Tecnologie dell'Informazione* 11, Issue 1: 155-166

Ubisoft 2021a. Discovery Tour Mode of Assassin's Creed: Origins. Ubisoft. Accessed on 6 January 2022 <https://www.ubisoft.com/en-gb/help/assassins-creed-origins/gameplay/article/discovery-tour-mode-of-assassins-creed-origins/000062699>

Ubisoft 2021b. Discovery Tour. Ubisoft. Accessed on 6 January 2022 <https://www.ubisoft.com/en-gb/game/assassins-creed/discovery-tour#6IeDi0phETkbe6sGHkd0TS>

Ushaw G, Davison R, Eyre J, Morgan G. 2015a. Adopting Best Practices from the Games Industry in Development of Serious Games for Health, in *DH '15: 5th International Conference on Digital Health*: 1. New York: Association for Computing Machinery

Ushaw G, Davison R, Eyre J, Morgan G. 2015b. Benchmarking Motion Sensing Devices for Rehabilitative Gaming, in *The 30th ACM/SIGAPP Symposium On Applied Computing. 2015, Salamanca, Spain.* New York: Association for Computing Machinery

Vermeeren, A., Calvi, L., Sabiescu, A. (eds) 2018. *Museum Experience Design: Crowds, Ecosystems and Novel Technologies.* Switzerland: Springer Nature

Exploring Hadrian's Wall: the management and limitations of a National Trail, and the challenges for sustainable tourism within a World Heritage Site

David McGlade (Hadrian's Wall Path National Trail Officer, 1995-2017), Gary Pickles (current Trail Manager, Northumberland National Park) and Mark Richards (guidebook author and curious walker)

Hadrian's Wall attracts thousands of visitors each year, not just for the outstanding history and archaeology one can see, but for the recreational enjoyment of walking in some of the most impressive, and in parts physically challenging, landscapes of Britain. The creation of the National Trail along the length of the Wall in 2003 set new standards in heritage access management. The essential balancing of archaeological and countryside management expertise created a Trail that aimed to protect and promote the archaeology at the same time as giving visitors a full appreciation of the natural environment.

In this chapter, two leading figures in Trail management past and present discuss the extensive research behind the creation of the Trail and the issues that can arise from increased visitors. The challenges of sustainable tourism are discussed through the ongoing conservation management of the National Trail, and how it endeavours to engage and educate visitors on the part they play in helping to maintain the World Heritage Site for future generations.

We also hear the experiences of the walkers: is the National Trail too limited? Is there yet more that should be explored in the wider area? To be sustainable, Hadrian's Wall tourism might also consider ways to guide visitors away from the linear stone Wall, through more environment-conscious transport links, to promote the nearby and often overlooked areas. These surrounding areas have their unique histories and offers, from the monastic sites and villages built with stone from the Wall, to the beauty spots offering unparalleled views of the Wall running across the landscape. The Wall in Roman times was mutually supported by a wide network of communities. Might 'Hadrian's Wall' tourism today benefit from the same, to give visitors a deeper understanding of the natural landscape and human history of Northern Britain?

The Hadrian's Wall Path National Trail and the challenges of sustainable visitor management – David McGlade

Introduction

The Hadrian's Wall Path National Trail was always going to be different. The Submission Document for the Trail to the Secretary of State for the Environment (Countryside Commission 1993) made sure of that with the pledge:

'The most appropriate surface is a green sward path. This will be aimed for wherever practical, using vegetation management techniques as part of a regular maintenance regime. Where this is not possible engineering solutions will be used but these will be kept to a minimum'.

Engineered paths were the accepted response to path erosion on the already established National Trails in England and Wales, but the Hadrian's Wall Path was to follow a different course, with the Submission Document acknowledging the World Heritage Site (WHS) status of the majority of the proposed route. The 'green sward path' would define the Trail's implementation project, and beyond, and it raised expectations for new standards in sustainable environmental management. The reasoning was simple: an unbroken natural grass surface would protect both any buried near-surface archaeology as well as the actual setting of the WHS. The Submission Document's aim was clear enough, but it was weak on delivery. Just how the thousands of new visitors to this free-to-access heritage trail in the north of England, with its seasonally saturated soils, would square up with the idea of an unbroken green sward path remained unclear. The lessons learned about footpath erosion on the Pennine Way (opened 1965) and Offa's Dyke Path (opened 1971) National

Trails indicated that a new approach to visitor management, with policies supported by the wider tourism industry, was required.

The Trail project can point to both moments of success (generally when it was well funded) as well as more challenging times (generally when it was underfunded), when the green sward appeared to be beyond reach. So far in its short life it has experienced five distinct phases:

1. Pre-Secretary of State approval in 1994
2. From approval to Trail opening: 1995 to 2003
3. Between 2003 and 2005
4. The second period of innovation: 2006 to 2014
5. Events since 2014

Pre-Secretary of State approval in 1994

The Trail was originally referred to as the 'Roman Wall Track', one of six 'Long Distance Routes' to be established in the post-war period as part of the nation's reconstruction effort. The aim was a laudable one: to give a weary population the opportunity to fill its lungs with clean air with the enabling legislation, the National Parks and Access to the Countryside Act 1949, paving the way for a stable of reforms. The Act led to the creation in England and Wales of today's network of Public Rights of Way, National Parks, National Nature Reserves, Areas of Outstanding Natural Beauty (AONBs) and National Trails.

By 1994 the network of National Parks and AONBs that we know today was almost complete and the ranks of the National Trails had swelled to ten. However, the countryside management profession, albeit on a rapid learning curve, was still coming to terms with the challenges of coping with high visitor numbers in environmentally sensitive areas, with the word 'honeypot' often used to describe visitor destinations that were over-heating. For example, the Yorkshire Three Peaks Project (1992) was set up with 'the sole remit of developing a range of practical solutions to prevent further erosion and restoring those areas that were already damaged' (Enact 1993: 19). The eroded peat moorland soils of the popular twenty-four mile walk around the summits of Pen-y-ghent, Ingleborough and Whernside required urgent attention. Its report evaluated experimental techniques, ranging from mechanical hydro-seeding to the use of various ground-reinforcing materials, with the ultimate aim of sustainable management solutions.

Hadrian's Wall was no exception, and by the 1970s the same erosion issues, in particular on the central section of the Wall within Northumberland National Park, were obvious. Here, however, the problems were more serious because footpath erosion was causing the archaeological record to tumble, unrecorded, down the slopes of the Whin Sill. The Countryside Commission (succeeded in 1999 by the Countryside Agency and in 2006 by Natural England) engaged the Dartington Amenity Research Trust (DART) to report on the issues, with the ensuing report (Dartington Amenity Research Trust 1976) documenting a catalogue of chronic visitor-oriented erosion problems coupled with inadequate visitor infrastructure and facilities. It also highlighted a vacuum in planning, long term, for sustainable public access to the Wall's sensitive archaeology and its setting.

A succession of project officers then set about researching a route and in 1993 submitted its recommendation for a 'green sward path' to the Secretary of State. It presented an opportunity for the Hadrian's Wall Path to set new standards, to become a beacon, a case study across the world in heritage access management. When in 1994 the Secretary of State approved public funding to establish the Trail, the project could point to government policy for the green sward. Thereafter, hard landscaping, or engineered path surfaces, were to be limited to the areas already damaged beyond repair, mostly the slopes within the central section of the Wall between Wall Miles 37 (Housesteads) and 40 (Steel Rigg). Maintaining a green sward was considered to be the best way of protecting both near-surface archaeology and the setting of the WHS, as well as farmers' grazing land.

From approval to Trail opening: 1995 to 2003

This period was a time of innovation. A successful application by the Countryside Commission to the Heritage Lottery Fund meant that project was well funded, with the countryside units of Cumbria and Northumberland County Councils able to employ countryside officers and field staff and, when required, call upon legal teams, land agents, and so on. Additionally, many of the Trail's long-term management systems were thought through and developed.

When the implementation project began in June 1995, the archaeological community were united in their opposition to the Trail because at the time no comparative model existed anywhere in the world. They cited the decision made in the 1960s to locate parts of the Hadrian's Wall segment of the Pennine Way on the crest of the masonry Wall (sections between Rapishaw Gap to Steel Rigg – Wall Miles 37-39) and the Wall mound at King Arthur's Well in Wall Mile 44, where Wainwright, in his *Pennine Way Companion* (1968: 39), described the Pennine Way as being 'on the foundations of the Roman Wall'. The ladder stiles were still perched on the Wall mound in 1995, so it was understandable when they queried if more of the same was to be expected of the Hadrian's Wall Path. Likewise, would the footpath erosion on Offa's Dyke, caused by the decision in the 1960s to site the Offa's Dyke Path National Trail on the crest of the Dyke itself, be repeated on Hadrian's Wall? Today, some fifty years since the latter's opening in 1971, some 20% of the damage on Offa's Dyke can still be attributed to recreational use: wear lines, erosion scars and pinch points around footpath infrastructure within the Scheduled Monument area (CADW 2018, section 6.2.2.7).

How would the soils of those sections of Wall hitherto visited for recreation only informally, or in some cases not at all, cope with the introduction of several thousand pairs of walkers' boots for 12 months of the year? The answers were still some way off, but initially at least there was strategic level cooperation between organisations. The elevation of Hadrian's Wall onto UNESCO's list of World Heritage Sites in 1987 certainly provided a welcome level of scrutiny beyond that of the National Trail's own steering group, and a very helpful triumvirate comprising the National Trail Officer (NTO), English Heritage's WHS Coordinator and the Hadrian's Wall Tourism Partnership Officer was established, with all three also attending the WHS Management Plan Committee. Discussions at their regular meetings left no stone unturned and the willingness of all sides to take a long-term view was refreshing.

The Trail's basic implementation strategy, which evolved over a period of around 12 months, was based on sound countryside management principles supported by research based on lessons drawn from other UK archaeological sites subject to intense visitor pressure. An early visit to Stonehenge demonstrated the principles of proactive grassland and visitor management in the maintenance of a continuous green sward, including, where required, the use of artificial ground-reinforcing products and attempts to influence visitor behaviour. At the request of English Heritage (today's Historic England) the Countryside Commission agreed to fund an independent archaeological consultant for the Trail, with the contract awarded to Oxford Archaeology North. It not only brought another level of scrutiny and discipline to the project but also forged an alliance of archaeological and countryside management expertise. The consultant evaluated every post hole for every item of path furniture for their likely impact on the monument and made a significant contribution to the Trail's Generic Scheduled Monument Consent. The Generic Consent proved itself to be a linchpin for the Trail project, one of the contributory factors behind the second great period of innovation and creativity, post-2006; it enabled staff to respond to situations in real-time in the field with the confidence that what they were doing was legal. Under constant review as new ideas for techniques and materials for grass sward management were introduced, by 2017 it was operating under Version 7. The appointment of the consultant therefore demonstrated to

Figure 1: Conservation tip from Every Footstep Counts © Natural England

the archaeological world that the National Trail project was not going to tread rough shod, as was feared, over the WHS.

Countless discussions with the archaeological consultant about the green sward led to the realisation that the project needed to engage the visitor with the conservation process, and that without a means of periodically resting the path, especially during the wet winter months, the archaeology would soon become compromised. The region's seasonally high rainfall was a given, so a solution based on science was required. The Met Office obliged with monthly soil moisture deficit data (the MORECS service) for the WHS, which, when compared with the 30-year mean, revealed that the soils were at field capacity or saturated between November and April each year. Of course, some years would be atypical, with wet summers or drier winters, but the 30-year mean pointed to general trends and the data provided a rationale for explaining to the general public that saturated soils posed a significantly greater risk of damage and erosion in the six-month winter period. Met Office soil moisture deficit data was used already in farming and by National Parks to predict the risk of moorland fires, but its use to influence the management of a WHS was possibly a first.

The Trail project took the lead with the public consultation and publication of *Every Footstep Counts*, the WHS's own code of respect for visitors (Figure 1). It communicated basic conservation messages about not walking on the top of Hadrian's Wall and about following circular day walks instead of linear there-and-back walks, but also asked visitors, in particular long-distance Trail walkers, to consider in winter months, avoiding footpaths that ran alongside sensitive archaeology. The code is entirely voluntary and the National Trail is legally open 365 days of the year, but it pointed out to visitors that they had a role to play in helping to conserve the WHS for future generations. Soil moisture data also influenced the decision to introduce a seasonal Trail Passport scheme for its opening in May 2003 (Figure 2).

By 2017, annual sales of Passports were approaching the 5000 mark, with walkers able to access the seven stamping stations between the months of May and October only – that is, during the

Figure 2: Hadrian's Wall Path Passport cover, English Heritage and Mark Richards, © Northumberland National Park

Figure 3: Erosion tip from the National Trail team © David McGlade

drier months of the year. The Passport was a source of amusement and provided a talking point for walkers, but it also demonstrated that it was possible to enter into a discussion with the general public about the fragility of the WHS's archaeology and to engage them in its conservation. For some visitors at least the Passport did influence the seasonality of their visit, and all proceeds of Passport sales were ploughed back into the project.

A simple message for walkers to walk side-by-side instead of in single file emerged from a conversation with the archaeological consultant during one of the early annual condition or 'snagging' surveys (Figures 3 and 4).

The side-by-side message effectively doubles the carrying capacity of the sward at nil cost, and if sufficient numbers of people follow the advice then it does make a difference. The annual surveys were an opportunity to review every idea, management plan, proposal and decision, to learn from successes and mistakes and to think outside of the box.

Effective monitoring is essential to a project's success. The Trail's fixed-point photographic monitoring regime commenced in 1996 when just a handful of sites were established. Additional points were added over time as new sections of Trail were established, until eventually every Wall Mile between Rudchester (Wall Mile 13) in the east and Bowness-on-Solway (Wall Mile 79) in the west had at least one monitoring point. The exercise was repeated every spring, summer and late autumn, thus capturing the condition of the Trail surface and its archaeology at different times of the year and in response to different weather conditions and visitor numbers. While it is important to try to understand the reasons behind short term fluctuations in ground condition, it is the medium to long-term trends that should be used to influence major decisions.

Between 2003 and 2005

Following the opening of the Trail in May 2003, the Heritage Lottery Fund award drew to a close and the Countryside Agency's own funding proved insufficient to pay for the proactive grassland management that the NTO's research had demonstrated was going to be necessary if the Trail was to enjoy a sustainable future. While there was an initial shortage of accommodation for walkers, new private sector entrants into the B&B market soon met demand, and visitor numbers increased. However, within only a few months the failure to invest in practical field-based management resulted in the appearance of pinch points and wear lines, precisely the situation that everyone connected with the project had wanted to avoid. In 2004, the Countryside Agency agreed to engage on a self-employed basis a practical field-based 'lengthsman', tasked with enacting proactive management, but it soon became clear that the role was beyond the scope of one person.

Then, without warning, the Trail received some unwelcome press attention. An example follows:

Figure 4: Visitors walking side by side along a mown section of path in Wall Mile 30
© David McGlade

> ***'Walkers put Hadrian's Wall on road to ruin. The World Heritage Site survived invasions and battles but is being wrecked by a surge in tourism.***
>
> *Hadrian's Wall is in such a dire state of deterioration that parts of it should be closed to the public, a report has concluded. Peter Fowler, an archaeologist and a World Heritage consultant for Unesco, said in his report that the Roman wall's condition is much worse than he has feared and that sections of the 73-mile frontier need immediate attention. "By immediate, I mean this week, today - now," he said. "Very little is being done to stop the destruction of such an important World Heritage Site. The situation is desperate".'*
> Alberge, The Times, 2005

This criticism cut deep. The NTO, consultant archaeologist and County Council countryside staff were conscious of the wear lines in the new sections of path where before there had been none.

The second period of innovation: 2006 to 2014

In 2006, the Countryside Agency responded to the criticism by employing a second lengthsman. It proved to be a wise decision, because within only a few months it was evident that the general condition of the Trail was gradually improving. Professor Fowler followed up with a second unpublished report (2006) criticising what appeared to be the slow rate of improvement, but the investment had begun to pay back. Within a couple of years, the complete package of proactive grassland and visitor management techniques and materials permitted by the Generic Scheduled Monument Consent, together with the Trail Passport, the walk side-by-side rule and other conservation tips, resulted in almost all of the new wear lines and pinch points being brought under control. Some of the wear lines that pre-dated the Trail project would continue to present a challenge, but the lengthsmen demonstrated that investment in skilled personnel and in materials, and a willingness to experiment and try something new, always under the watchful eye of the archaeological consultant, offered hope for a more sustainable future. This was the Trail's second great period of creative innovation, when everyone concerned eagerly looked forward to their field work, especially the annual snagging surveys when the year's work was looked at in the round and plans made for the next. It was a time of experimentation with micro-management techniques, of research site visits to other heritage sites, of mapping (and unblocking of) centuries-old drains, and of continuing to borrow and learn from other specialisms and areas of expertise.

It was during this period that the team demonstrated the correlation between the Trail's fixed-point photo-monitoring condition scores, seasonal visitor use and climate.

In Figure 5, the path's condition is seen to deteriorate after the Trail opened in 2003, with some improvement after the appointment of the first lengthsman. Following the appointment of the second, the trend was towards a steady and consistent improvement. There were small-scale

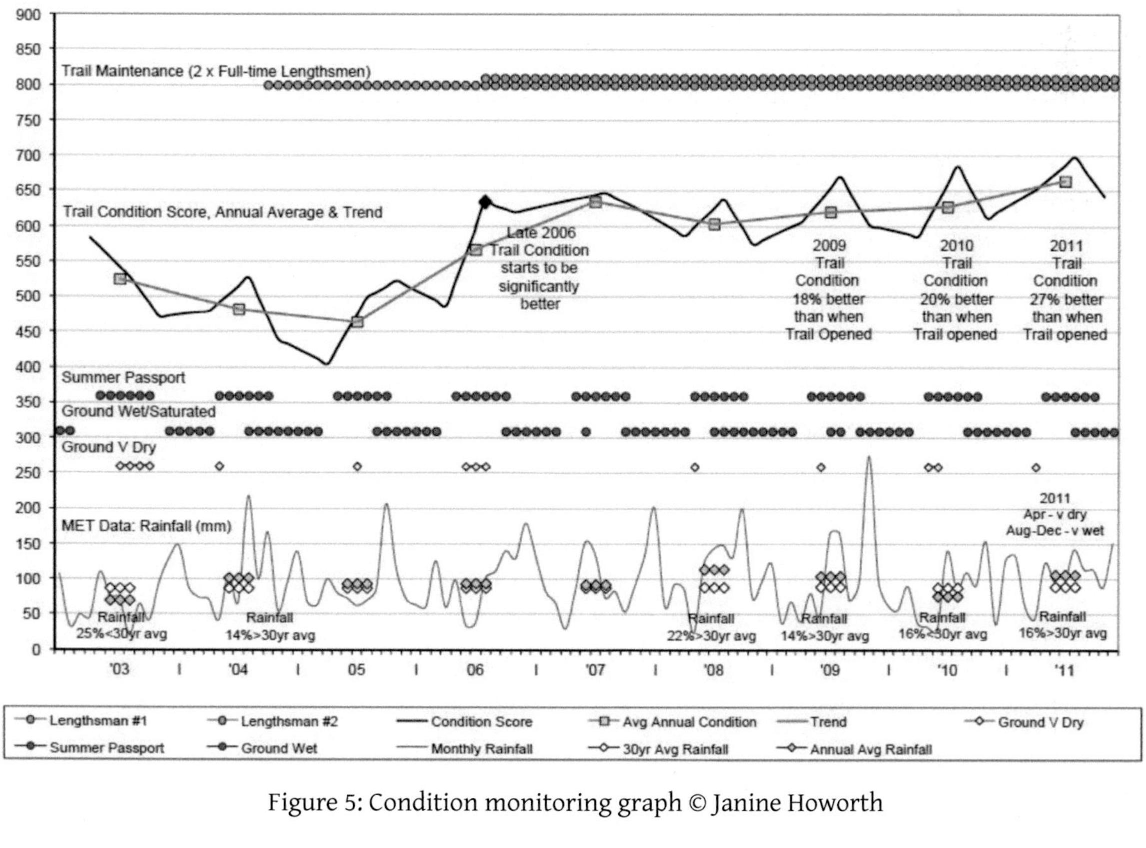

Figure 5: Condition monitoring graph © Janine Howorth

fluctuations in the November photo-monitoring scores, reflecting the increased seasonal rainfall and the pounding of the year's walking boots, but the August scores in years 2008-2011 show that the sward responded both to the new growing season and to the cumulative grassland management effort. The Trail team felt that they had arrived!

Events since 2014

The project team that had brought so much creative thinking, innovation and confidence building was broken up. The contracts with the two field lengthsmen and archaeological consultancy were drawn to a close and Natural England introduced new a funding formula for National Trails together with a new governance model for local Trail Partnerships. At the same time the NTO's attendance at the WHS Partnership Board ended. The new arrangements consisted of one new Trail field officer, with archaeological advice provided by the Northumberland National Park archaeologist.

In 2017, when the NTO post was made redundant from the National Park, the role became a part-time one. Since then, Trail Field Officer Gary Pickles, accompanied by his seasonal assistants and with input from Cumbria and Northumberland County Councils, has exercised considerable skill in delivering the practical maintenance of the Trail and WHS.

Managing the Hadrian's Wall Path National Trail today – Gary Pickles

At the time of writing, there are 15 National Trails throughout Britain which have been designated by the government and are managed to a set of quality standards that separate them from other routes. Each trail uses a network of footpaths, bridleways and roads to create a linear route across varied landscapes. You'll recognise them by the acorn symbol marking the route. Think of them as footpaths where the trail managers go the extra mile for the visitors' use and convenience.

National Trails in England and Wales are administered by Natural England, a statutory agency of the UK government, and Natural Resources Wales (the successor body to the Countryside Council for Wales), a Welsh Government-sponsored body. In Scotland, the equivalent trails are called Scotland's Great Trails and are administered by NatureScot.

The Hadrian's Wall Path National Trail today is an 84-mile-long (135km) National Trail stretching from coast to coast across Northern England – from Wallsend, Newcastle upon Tyne, in the east to Bowness-on-Solway on the west coast, following the line of Hadrian's Wall. The unique archaeology and landscape require us to go that extra mile to fulfil certain additional standards to maintain and sustain the Trail. Today we need to ensure that the Hadrian's Wall Path is:

- Useable: it's got to be fit for purpose
- Sustainable: it's got to be able to withstand the actual usage over a reasonable period of time
- Sympathetic: it's got to sit within the protected landscape.

To achieve these aims one of the *modus operandi* of the Hadrian's Wall Path National Trail continues to be the 'green sward'. This is the effective management of the grassed surface to create a durable and sustainable path – a 'wearing membrane' that will separate the walker from the archaeology below.

By understanding the environment that the Trail passes through we can be effective in our management (Figure 6). No one surface is appropriate for all shoes; if we were to imagine a green path through urban Newcastle, it would not fulfil any of the above criteria. At the same time, a concrete path within the National Park would not be appropriate.

There are also certain areas of the Trail that require minimal management, for example the Wylam Wagonway or the aggregate path through Carlisle – both these surfaces are 'solid or hard wearing',

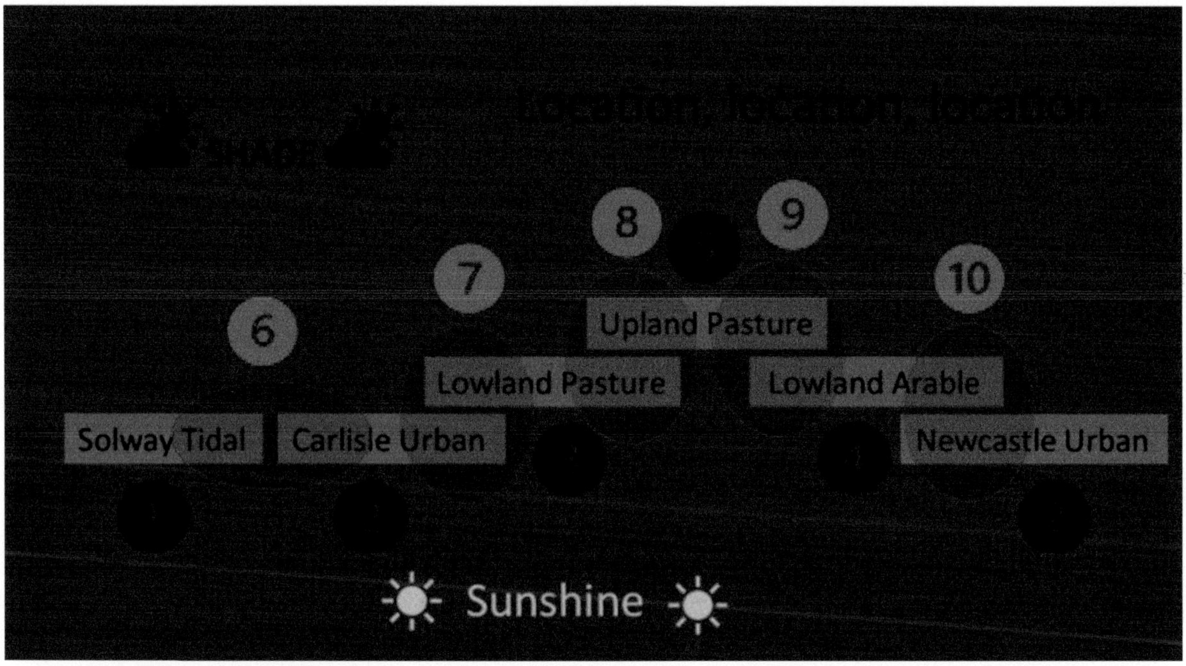

Figure 6: The differing environments along the Wall. © Northumberland National Park

Figure 7: An example of the Trail at Iron Sign, which demonstrates how access and archaeology can co-exist with the initial correct design and subsequent correct maintenance. © Northumberland National Park

so walkers are unlikely to have any impact upon its condition. What we need to do is manage the areas that are most susceptible to erosion and to understand what factors contribute to this 'susceptibility'. The ideal ingredients for the path would be a relatively flat, wide field margin with a southern aspect, on arable land to ensure no ground poaching from hoofed animals (Figure 7).

If we change some of these ingredients, then we start to see an effect upon the surface. If the path has a northern aspect, it's much harder to maintain a good grassed surface as we can't recreate sunshine. Similarly, we can't level a slope or widen a narrow margin. We must also take into consideration the 'honeypot' areas – those that have great views or accessible Roman sites, or even just good parking. These areas draw visitors to a higher degree and so have a higher level of usage. The example above works in its location as it's remote and so only has local users and Trail walkers; if we were to transport this to an area with higher visitor numbers, then it may no longer be sustainable.

Managing the National Trail

Having touched on what the Hadrian's Wall Path National Trail is, and what constitutes the ideal surface, we now need to look at how we currently manage the path on a yearly basis. We can look at that through three recurring tasks:

- Grassland management
- Vegetation management
- Repair and replacement of the infrastructure

Figure 8: The Trail with sufficient width to walk side-by-side.
© Northumberland National Park

Figure 9: Green Carts gorse management on monument, 2006. © Northumberland National Park

Figure 10: Green Carts gorse growth if left unchecked, 2014. © Northumberland National Park

Having established a healthy green sward on the Trail, a large part of our work is in cutting and maintaining the grass. Shorter grass tends to be of a tighter knit and so is more durable. It also clearly delineates the route and helps keep users on the 'managed surface' as opposed to free roaming over the various locations. When using a footpath, people almost invariably use the central point of what's available. Given enough space, users will tend to walk side by side. This is highly desirable as it in effect halves the level of usage and helps sustain the grassed surface. Figure 8 shows how the available width is dictated by the hedge and the fence-line. As the hedge is still growing then without yearly management it will encroach on the available space, and the available walking width will get narrower with each passing year.

Side vegetation can also become a problem if it is allowed to spread unchecked. At Green Carts, the gorse regeneration over a ten-year period seriously encroached on the Trail (Figures 9 and 10). Finally, we need to look to the skies. If left unchecked, they can become full of tree canopy. This creates shade which means reduced grass growth. By lifting the canopy, we can allow more sunlight to reach the surface. This has a two-fold effect of promoting grass growth and drying out the surface quicker. If you've ever been caught out in a shower, you head beneath a tree to shelter, and this is true for animals as well. By creating less shelter, we reduce the risk of damage to the grass and underlying soil by livestock standing or walking on it for prolonged periods in wet conditions.

Alongside the yearly grass surface and vegetation management, we undertake a program of infrastructure renewal of the many gates, stiles and signs along the route. As the Trail is nearing

Figure 11: Erosion developing on underlying archaeology. © Northumberland National Park

Figure 12: Soil is collected from molehills and mixed with grass-seed to repair the erosion.
© Northumberland National Park

its 20th year, a lot of the infrastructure is beginning to fail. This isn't an issue in itself, but it's not desirable to have to undertake all the infrastructure work in one go. Perhaps 10% replacement each year is a realistic and a sustainable level of maintenance. We look to create a more 'age-diverse' range within these structures. Every piece of 'furniture' on the Trail is assessed every year for condition and is either classed as 'good', 'monitor' or 'replace'. All the information is accessible through our mobile phones and as such is constantly being updated as we monitor the Trail.

Owing to the underlying archaeology along the Trail, we have to maintain structures on a like-for-like basis. Any time a structure is installed in the Scheduled Monument Area, even a small gate post or signage panel, a trained archaeologist will supervise. If we strayed from this remit, we would be digging into potentially archaeologically sensitive ground. This can create challenges if we look at trying to improve the access along the Trail, say with larger gates or fewer stiles. We have had to add archaeological supervision as an additional but necessary resource when maintaining and improving the Trail.

Our final task in the year-round maintenance is repairing the surface when moles have been active. We collect the material (soil) from the molehills, which we can use to repair erosion on other areas and re-build the surface. Figures 11 to 14 show some of these maintenance works.

All the types of works described above are covered through a document called the Generic Consent, which allows us to undertake work on a Scheduled Ancient Monument by establishing 'ways of working' that comply with the legal status of the Monument. There are four types of intervention allowed under the Generic Consent:

Figure 13: A flexible membrane covers the repair to allow the new grass/root system to become established. © Northumberland National Park

Figure 14: The membrane is removed once the grass/repair has become durable enough to withstand usage. © Northumberland National Park

- Type 1: General maintenance and grassland management
- Type 2: Aggregate paths and repairs to the grassed surface
- Type 3: Replacing structures on a like-for-like basis
- Type 4: Stand-alone projects that vary significantly from the existing issues

We've looked at the first three types, but works that comply with type 4 are longer-term projects that can require significant resources of time and money. As such, these tasks fall beyond the role of 'maintenance' but in some ways also present great opportunities to improve and enhance the National Trail going forward.

We must keep in mind that the work we do to maintain the Trail is subject to government funding. It is therefore crucial that our work is part of the long-term planned management. We should not be repairing an issue on a year-by-year basis if we have the ability to repair the issue for the longer term. We must work closely with all our partners (Northumberland County Council, Newcastle City Council, Northumberland National Park Authority, Historic England, English Heritage and Cumbria County Council) for future management. The phrase 'a stitch in time' carries significant weight when looking at the whole Trail over a long period of time. Cutting grass is much easier if the grass is already well managed – less cutting reduces the thickness of the green sward and also means that when you do cut, you have to go slower as the machines need to work harder. Perhaps it's a case of swings and roundabouts, but from experience consistent management is superior to sporadic management. What we do should allow the work that follows to be done to the same standard but more easily, and this will, in part, mitigate the variables of funding.

The final piece that can bring all these strands and techniques together is having the consistency of personnel to deliver these goals. Having the ability to reflect on the work undertaken the previous year and assess whether it's been successful (and if not, why not) is of great benefit when working within such a potentially fragile environment. The opportunity to undertake work over a period of years can make achieving difficult goals realistic – smaller achievable goals can, if part of a greater scheme, deliver the 'difficult' goals. This also holds true with gaining agreement to implement change with the various landowners along the National Trail, who are perhaps initially wary or reluctant to accept change. Stakeholders can witness what we do and see the consistency and high standards of maintenance, which helps them become more receptive to change – even if this is just reducing the number of kissing gates to install more accessible wicket gates, or the removal of a gate altogether.

The term 'stakeholder' is most commonly applied to organisations and groups of individuals who 'hold a stake' in the management of Hadrian's Wall Path. It is worth reminding ourselves that, while not carrying out general maintenance, farming the landscape or managing archaeological heritage sites, walkers and visitors are also stakeholders in the Path. Without their (amongst others) cooperation and input, successful management remains theoretical and detached from daily experience of visiting the Wall. What follows is the perspective of a 'walking stakeholder'.

Hadrian's Wall and the curious walker – Mark Richards

For the last 30 years I have repeatedly been drawn to explore and describe Hadrian's Wall and its greater cultural setting. My writing, photography and graphic art has primarily been directed to the creation of practical walking guides, including my most recent guide to the mountain landscapes of Cumbria. But Hadrian's Wall has long had a special fascination. My interest in frontiers can be traced back to when I prepared the first ever practical walking guide to the Offa's Dyke Path in the early 1970s. So, when in 1991 my publisher Cicerone invited me to realise the same for Hadrian's Wall I was more than excited. This was an opportunity to explore a frontier from the Classical Age, enigmatically cast coast to coast across the northern neck of England (Figure 15). This was a dozen years before the Hadrian's Wall Path National Trail was opened in 2003 and I considered

Figure 15: Mark Richards walking Hadrian's Wall. © Mark Richards

myself lucky to have witnessed quiet passages of curious walkers, whereas now there is an almost ceaseless intensity of Trail walkers – perhaps only matched when it was a living Roman frontier!

My 1991 aim was to prepare a guide tracking the course of the linear Wall frontier. I began with next to no knowledge of the area but soon got the antiquarian's bug in my search for a largely 'lost' Wall. The frontier stretched out across a landscape redolent with at least 1900 years of human life coping with a damp, chilly climate. The Wall and surrounding environment is an interface of history, part pastoral, part industrial and shielding hints of troubled times as a fierce borderland. When visiting the Wall, one soon grasps that for all the Romans left a major monument, no less fascinating is the succeeding unfolding landscape. That said, the presence of a good three hundred years of research of the Roman Wall and Northern Frontier lends to the area a uniquely important place in the history and the culture of Britain.

My Wall Walk in 1991 was an original heritage hike as there was no defined route. Tyneside was completely unknown to me and after choosing to walk the Wall from east to west, I made my way first to Wallsend and then double-walked every stride to Bowness-on-Solway. I soon learnt the value of walking eastwards in terms of the weather too. Teasing a coherent route on or near the dashed line of the Wall on the OS map, especially through the great conurbation of Newcastle, was genuinely fascinating (Figures 16 and 17).

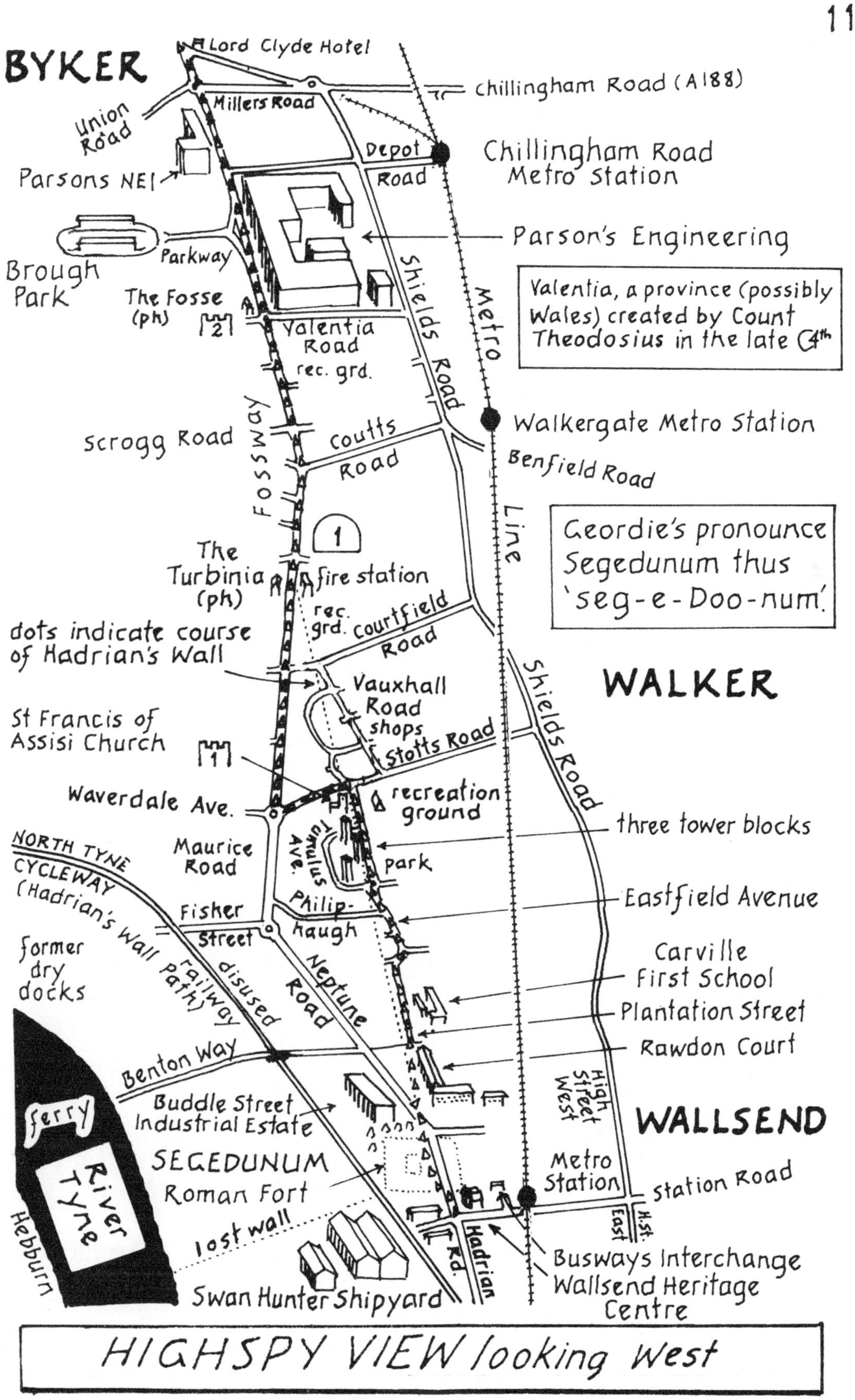

Figure 16: Richards 1993 Guidebook map of the Wall from Wallsend to Byker. © Mark Richards

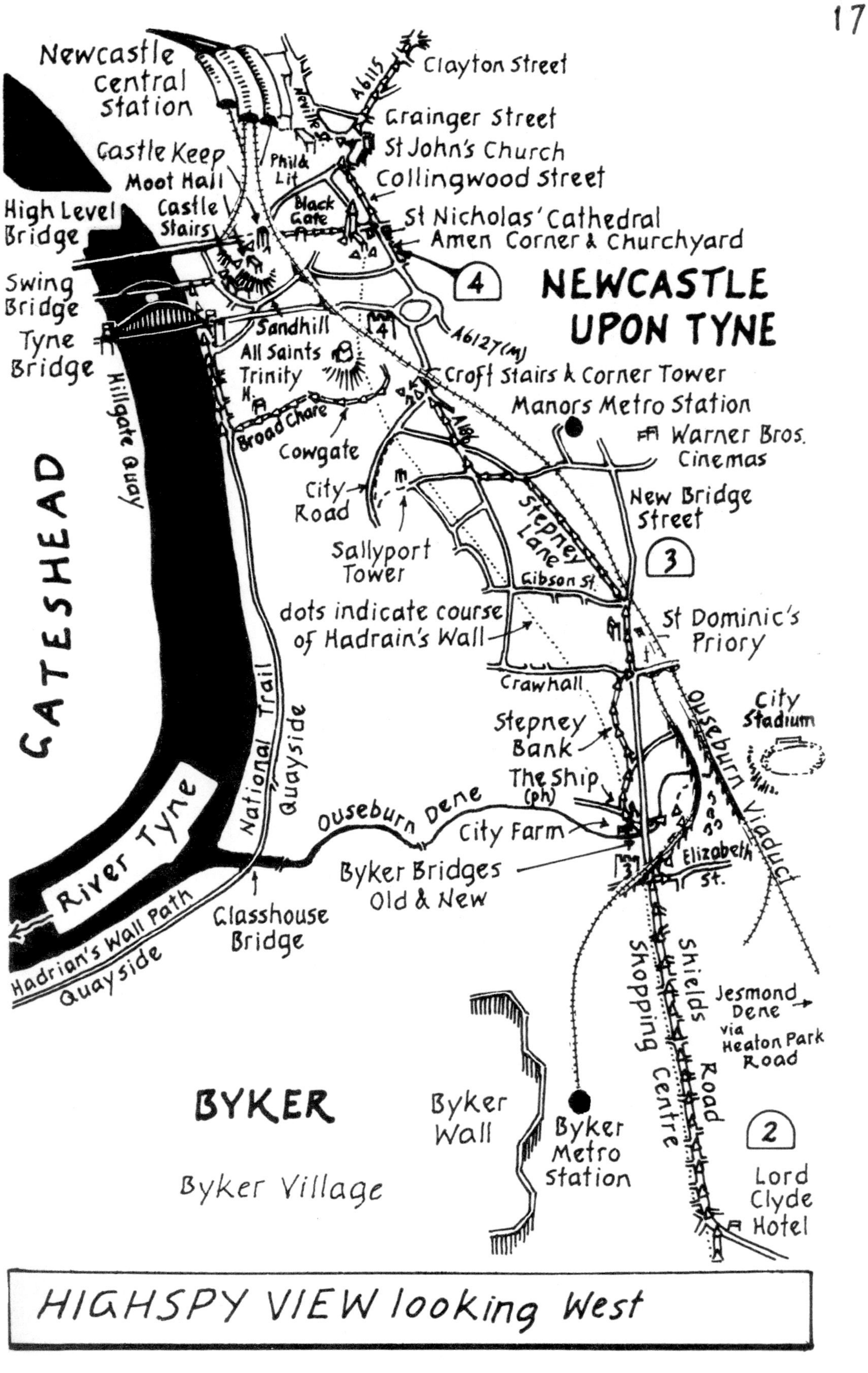

Figure 17: Richards 1993 Guidebook map of the Wall through the east end of Newcastle.

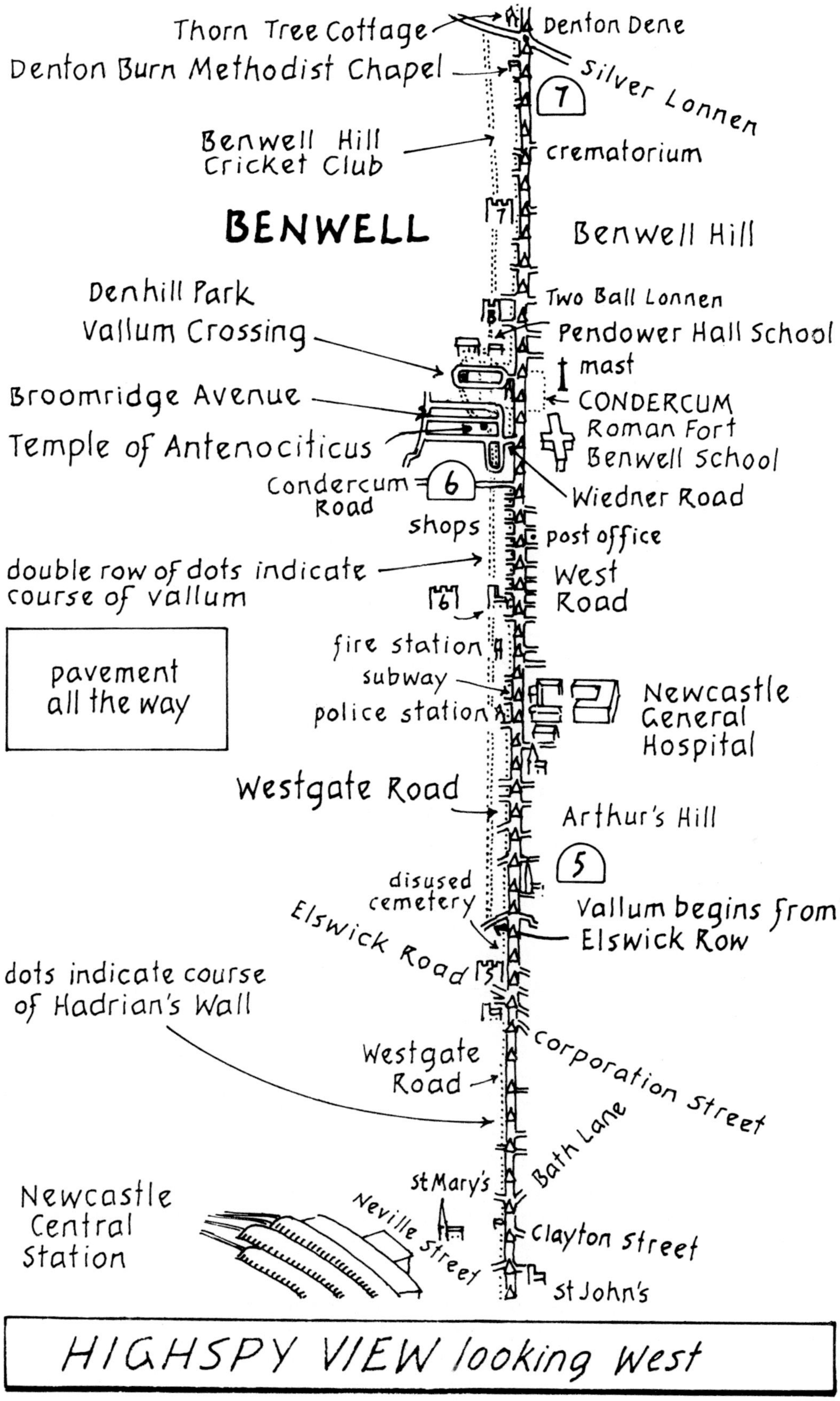

Figure 18: Richards 1993 Guidebook map of the Wall through the west end of Newcastle.
© Mark Richards

That the subsequent National Trail chose to ignore it at this eastern end gives a stark reminder of the thinking and objectives in creating a recreational route, which by definition is more casual, where fresh air and exercise have equal importance to the qualities of the journey (Figure 18).

Strictly, the justification for the creation of a National Trail is to nurture a tourist economy where previously there was little or none. This is why the Pennine Way came into being. Hadrian's Wall has been a pilgrimage destination for as long as heritage tourism has existed and has never needed boosting; of far greater concern is the welfare of the monument itself. Yet in 2003, the Hadrian's Wall Path National Trail was inaugurated and has continued to attract a strong flow of long and short-distance walkers precisely because it is waymarked intimate to the Roman Wall and is constantly given high-profile publicity.

Yet I have long been of the opinion that the creation of a waymarked coast-to-coast route was difficult to square with the long-term care of the monument. My own Wall Walk guide was published a decade before and although Hadrian's Wall regularly attracted walkers and tourists, once the National Trail came into being, the walking visitor numbers exploded. Inevitably it has attracted people who swarm upon a promoted trail. But that is not the same as nurturing a desire to know and try to understand what can be seen. Energy needs to be directed to steer visitors to appreciate the unique qualities of the region, to engage physically with it and to draw lasting value from their time gently rambling in the wider landscape that contains multiple layers of human influence.

My reaction was to create new Roman-themed routes guides away from the immediate vicinity of the mural frontier, including circular walks in the countryside to the north and south in a bid to introduce curious visitors to the wider heritage setting. But without official status and marketing they had little or no impact. How can this be improved? On a personal level, I constantly seek to find new ways of communicating through social media but by far the best devices are audio and visual means. My fortnightly podcast Countrystride, though centred on Cumbria, serves to outreach an appreciation of people and landscapes, and for 2022 I am presenting a sequence of videos tracing the course of the National Trail east from Bowness with Catherine Jarvis of Handy History, projecting a shared love of this remarkable landscape and its communities.

There is undoubtedly a need to cultivate practical ideas to develop the use of public transport and reduce reliance on the private car. I would relish the development of linear green walks – walks that are easily accessible by scheduled bus or rail services – springing from the Tyne Valley Line and AD122 bus services that operate across the country along the route of the Wall. We should encourage the spirit of 'roam from home', even if the visitor's 'home' is their holiday accommodation.

Future attention also needs to turn to elevate the concept of Hadrian's Wall as part of a monumental landscape, reflecting how the frontier functioned with a wide supportive network of roads, forts, administrative and civil settlements, thereby widening the vision of the region in context with the most important landscape statement of classical history in Britain. Initiating a broad conservation corridor approach and creating lateral east to west connections to the north and south of the strict line of the Wall will facilitate these aims and open a greater appreciation of the area. Other walking journeys should be cultivated on a great range of themes and defined circular trails to link communities, other sites and heritage features to convey the deeper chronological history of the wide region.

Conclusion

Although the Hadrian's Wall Path National Trail has yet to reach its twenties, the ambition is for this resource to exist for much longer. The benefit of having a long term objective to care for the Trail is that we can use the time at our disposal to make our goals usable, sustainable and sympathetic to all the varied environments the Trail passes through, across the breadth of the country.

However, the key lesson to be learned from the rollercoaster of the Trail's setup and upkeep is that sustainable management carries a financial cost, and that the opportunity loss in terms of erosion to the archaeology and damage to the WHS reputation is potentially greater. The tourism wheel is turning, and it cannot be stopped. To succeed long term, the archaeology of the WHS and the needs of the National Trail must be afforded equal weighting with a corresponding guaranteed continual investment in staff, research, innovation, practical field-based management and, crucially, inter-organisational cooperation. Everyone, from the WHS Partnership Board to government agencies, local authorities, universities and the Wall's tourism industry, needs to buy into this. They should also keep a watchful eye on climate change and its effect on the WHS and its soils. Finally, the walker on Hadrian's Wall needs to be recognised as a stakeholder, and be engaged with. The increasingly popular 'slow travel' movement pays attention to the environment it crosses, and many walkers do profoundly care about the preservation of the places they visit – so much so that they initiate their own routes and find new ways to experience the challenge of walking the Wall. These laudable efforts should be encouraged, supported, and integrated with the Path's management efforts.

Bibliography

Alberge, D. 2005. Walkers Put Hadrian's Wall on road to ruin [online], *The Times,* 9 August. Accessed 2 February 2022 <https://www.thetimes.co.uk/article/walkers-put-hadrians-wall-on-road-to-ruin-nfkg5btn0xd>.

CADW 2018. *Offa's Dyke Conservation Management Plan.* Cardiff: CADW.

Countryside Commission 1993. *The Hadrian's Wall Path Submission to the Secretary of State for the Environment* (CCP 409). Cheltenham: Countryside Commission.

Dartington Amenity Research Trust 1976. *Hadrian's Wall: A Strategy for Conservation and Visitor Services* (CCP 98). Cheltenham: Countryside Commission.

Enact. 1993. Failing Footpaths on Three Peaks. *Enact,* 4: 19

Fowler, P. 2006. Hadrian's Wall and the National Trail. Notes on a Visit 5th April 2006 (unpublished report).

Wainwright, A. 1968. *Pennine Way Companion; A Pictorial Guide.* Kendal: Westmorland Gazette.

Hadrian's Wall: a lifeline for living history practitioners, event organisers and business owners

Robin Brown (Legio VIII Augusta MGV) and Kevin Robson (Ancient Britain)

Hadrian's Wall is not just a monument, a visitor attraction, or even a cultural and archaeological resource. For the people who live and work along it, Hadrian's Wall is a lifeline, a place where they can practice their passion and share their skills and knowledge in creative ways.

Local business owners, and not just the large heritage institutions, are stakeholders in the World Heritage Site: their work and support are vital in promoting the history, archaeology and landscape of the Wall to new audiences, which traditional archaeological scholarship may fail to reach. Business owners and heritage organisations on the Wall should work together for mutual benefit, not only to share the Wall's archaeological heritage with the widest possible audiences, but also to protect the astounding natural environment that the World Heritage Site is set in.

In this chapter, two businessmen and living history practitioners discuss their experiences of working on the Wall. Through their eyes, we see how grass roots and first-hand experience of the Wall are an essential resource for education, sustainable tourism and personal engagement, but can often be neglected by the very stakeholders who would benefit from a partnership.

The view from a Roman re-enactor – Robin Brown

I have been the Events Coordinator for the Legio VIII Augusta MGV Roman Living History Society ('The Eighth Legion') for over 20 years. We are a small society based in North Wales who perform regularly on Hadrian's Wall and elsewhere in the UK. I have lived in Carlisle for the past 30 years and am passionate about promoting and presenting Hadrian's Wall and the Romans to anyone who will listen!

The fact that you're reading this means that you probably have more than a passing interest in the unique and diverse landscape of Hadrian's Wall country – an area that runs right across Northern England, linked by the remains of the Roman military zone. When I moved to the area I sought out and joined a Roman re-enactment group, where I could share my passion with like-minded people (Figure 1). In the years since, I have helped to deliver many events along the Wall, including opening the National Trail, Illuminating Hadrian's Wall, The Living Frontier, Hadrian's Cavalry, and countless others.

Roman re-enactors, people who "dress up as Romans", are an integral part of the Hadrian's Wall experience. Look in any leaflet and you'll find us there. Visit one of the museum sites in the summer and you'll often find us performing, entertaining, and educating visitors. We act as ambassadors for the World Heritage Site (WHS) and as local guides, helping to bring the remains to life and creating lasting memories for those who come to enjoy the experience we offer. Many visitors assume that we are regular employees but in practice, we are more like swallows, in that our clients just expect us to reappear every summer! Some are professionals who make a living from this work. The vast majority are volunteer enthusiasts, who are members of societies operated either as charities or unincorporated associations; the latter provide everything needed for the performance usually for little more than expenses. Professionals tend to operate as individuals or just a few people, and generally cater towards school visits, small-scale museum demonstrations, or work as tour guides. The larger volunteer organisations are the ones who provide weekend events involving an arena display plus tent-based presentations of various aspects of Roman life (Figure 2). The term 'volunteer' should not imply that we are any less 'professional' than our full-time colleagues, as we have often spent years researching and making armour, clothing and replica items and presenting them to our audiences.

Hadrian's Wall (Archaeopress 2022): 122–134

Figure 1: Robin Brown, or 'Squamatus' due to the scale armour, once a relatively rare sight. Photo by Dave Foster

Animating the Wall

Re-enactors can be an effective means for Wall sites to generate extra visitor numbers, yet despite being a key component in the Hadrian's Wall 'brand', the quality and historical accuracy of performers is completely unregulated, and surprisingly rarely features in booking negotiations. Every Roman re-enactment group has been formed by a group of enthusiasts who have set their own criteria in terms of period, activities and historical accuracy. The most common principle, inherited from the Ermine Street Guard – the first Roman re-enactment group – is that everything should be evidence-based as far as is possible. A lack of historical evidence means that in many areas we must make an educated guess, but as new evidence is found, or existing finds are reinterpreted, reconstructions become obsolete and need to be re-made. This is an ongoing process, and the time and costs associated with this philosophy means that it is often impossible to achieve in practice. This is equally true for museum displays, where the cost of refurbishing or upgrading a display is a significant investment. My approach to dealing with this reality is to try to always be

Figure 2: Legio VIII on the march at Vindolanda. Photo by Dave Foster

up front about the evidence that supports our presentations – what is interpretation, and what is speculation.

There is no requirement to follow these practices, and what is presented is often driven more by levels of personal influence within the re-enactment world and with clients than actual evidence. We also have to contend with public expectations, as the image of the sandal-wearing, *lorica segmentata*-clad legionary in a red tunic has dominated public perception since the Hollywood epics of the 1950s. The reality is that the Roman soldiers who built Hadrian's Wall only resembled this image for perhaps a century after its initial construction, and those that manned the forts were likely very different from the outset. For most of the Wall's history, the garrison was made up of auxiliary troops, and therein lies much uncertainty, as their ethnic origins suggest a whole range of different arms and equipment, costume details, religious beliefs and tactical deployment, which for the most part we can only speculate about (Figure 3). Whether there should be more of an effort to show this reality strikes to the heart of the question of how the WHS should be presented and promoted.

Figure 3: A Batavian Auxiliary Soldier. Photo by Dave Foster

Authenticity, collaboration and costs

To aim for authenticity, re-enactors must work closely with the archaeological evidence, and archaeologists themselves. However, the relationship between re-enactors and professional archaeologists is variable. Whilst there have been instances of collaboration, these are still inhibited by the mutual lack of understanding and the restricted opportunities to interact on a formal basis (Bishop 2013). The field of experimental archaeology represents a potential crossover point, even if to the layman it can sometimes appear to be people making a career out of learning from scratch something that a traditional craftsperson already knows how to do! On the other hand, some re-enactors mistake what they do as experimental archaeology. The reconstruction, use and repair of clothing, tools and equipment can provide insights into the accuracy and correct use of an item if the breakage and wear matches that of the original, but without experimental design and control, this evidence remains anecdotal. The amateur nature of re-enactment combined with the absence of any means to establish recognised credentials or credibility will likely always remain a barrier to collaboration. This is a great pity as ultimately archaeology relies to an extent on ongoing

Figure 4: Scorpion, with bolt in flight, Birdoswald. Photo by Chris Lee

public interest to generate funds to carry out research, and so showcasing the results in a publicly accessible way through reconstruction and interpretation would be mutually beneficial.

Ultimately, the level of quality and accuracy is driven by the enthusiasm and resources of individuals and societies. This too is an evolving situation, as many of the people who 'invented' modern Roman re-enactment some 40 to 50 years ago are being replaced by a new generation. The hobby has always struggled to recruit, and there is no guarantee of continuity during this process. An important difference is that nowadays it is possible to buy costume and equipment of variable quality over the internet. In the past, if you wanted it you had to either make it yourself or find one of the few craftsmen around and join their waiting list. The administrative overheads created by modern legislation in terms of health and safety, compulsory insurance and weapons control are a constant headache for society managers that are likely to put many off taking up the hobby (Figure 4).

This older generation of re-enactors, and many of the present one, have developed lost specialist craft skills from first principles, or applied existing skills to the accurate reconstruction of artefacts. (Figures 5 and 6). Without a mechanism for passing on these skills, they risk being lost once more, as it's easier to buy in than to make from scratch. This is where the expansion of craft demonstration workshops and the expansion of experimental archaeology mentoring could prove vital. Often the limiting factor is the lack of a suitable venue. There is huge scope for 'out of season' courses for local people and students to be encouraged and equipped with the skills to fill the gaps between re-enactment societies, archaeologists, and traditional heritage management roles.

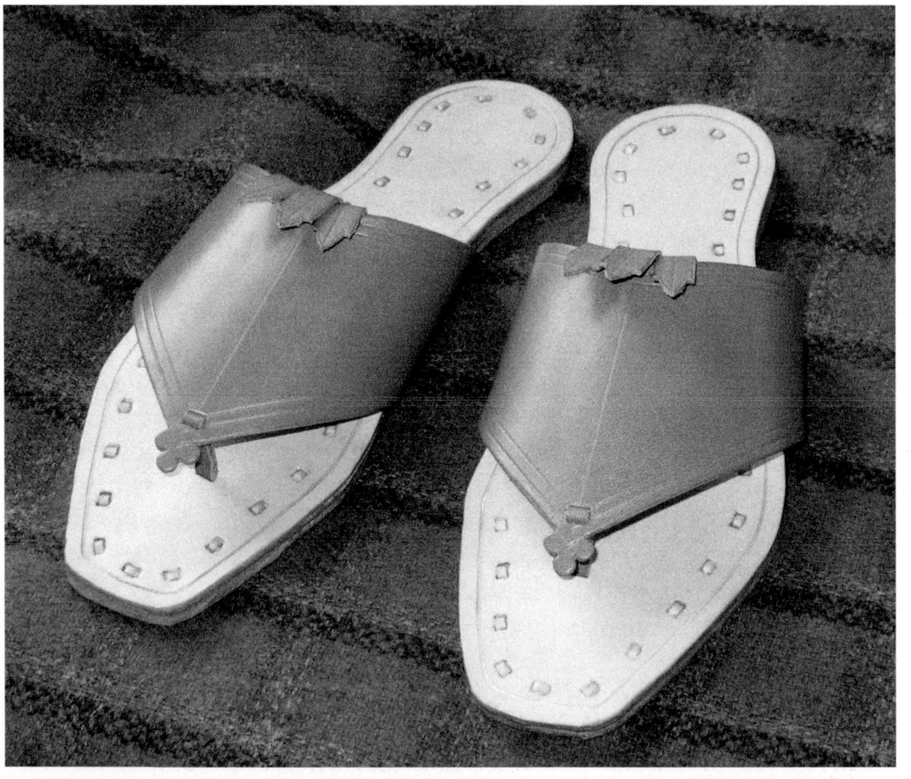

Figure 5: Interpretation of Sulpicia Lepidina's slippers from Vindolanda. Shoes and photo by Robin Brown.

Figure 6: Interpretation of 'Balmoral' type boots from Vindolanda. Boots and photo by Robin Brown

Issues and opportunities for historical interpretation

From the perspective of managing and promoting Hadrian's Wall, this leaves the future of re-enactment, and the visual representation of life on Hadrian's Wall during the Roman period, down to blind chance. Whilst the general public may not have the level of knowledge to discriminate good re-enactment from bad, a WHS should ideally be aiming for the very highest quality interpretation, and from this viewpoint, there is still a great deal of room for improvement. Large-scale events are often commissioned as 'one-offs' by organisations who may have little understanding of what performers can offer, and who then define the parameters without any consultation, leaving the performers to deliver on the detail. This situation is down to the very informal relationship between re-enactment societies and Wall managers. Re-enactors are seen as a pool of useful volunteers, who will always be available to be hired at minimal cost to provide whatever spectacle is required, without the need for any nurture or investment in return. There seems to be an increasing divide between the research and conservation and the venue management professions on the Wall, with the former only interacting with the public at excavations and the latter not making use of the potential quality control these experts could provide when producing publicity material or hiring performers. Re-enactors and site staff, who share a public-facing role, almost without exception get on tremendously well, but these usually aren't the people who decide whether to hire us again.

As re-enactment societies are made up of volunteers, rather than employees, it is a constant struggle to ensure that enough members will be able to deliver an event. The fees charged by societies generally cover overheads and wear and tear on group equipment. Many potential clients seem to believe that we sit in costume waiting for any opportunity to travel anywhere at a moment's notice to look scenic at whatever brief event or photo-call they have in mind. Many inexperienced potential clients tell us what they want us to do, rather than ask us what we can do, or have expectations not remotely matched by their budget. Many societies have been operating

Figure 7: Packed up and ready to go home after a long weekend. Photo by Dave Foster

for several decades, and so we do know what we are doing. The reality is that most of us travel hundreds of miles before and after an event and have full-time jobs that help pay for personal expenses and the cost of personal costume and equipment. This means that society organisers like me need to look for interesting events at interesting venues to motivate our members to put in the effort to attend. The actual event is only a tiny part of the effort involved. Most venues have next to no facilities, certainly less than you would expect to find at a public campsite. Setting up and taking down an encampment is hard work, as is wearing heavy armour and talking to visitors, providing demonstrations and maintaining an upbeat attitude all day for two or three days in a row, especially with a 200-mile journey either side (Figure 7). I find the best event managers are those who have experience as re-enactors; they are so much easier to work with as they have the necessary understanding of the logistics and practical considerations.

I have seen re-enactment evolve over the last 30 years or so as client budgets, the popularity of the hobby and the availability of costumes have changed. The 1990s saw a drive towards larger and larger events, which presented logistical challenges, yet highlighted that such events saw a

Figure 8: 'Have your name written in Roman script!' A popular keepsake for many visitors. Photo by Dave Foster

lot of performer redundancy outside of the main arena displays. You simply don't need a hundred soldiers to present more intimate 'living history' show and tell. The more recent trend is towards smaller, more family-friendly events. One of the key roles of the interpreter in engaging with a visitor is to make their presentation relevant to the individual. Thus, the approach will vary according to the audience, but should be open to a change of direction based on the response. The goal is to leave the visitor with a nugget of information that feels relevant and interesting to them. We have also found that a small souvenir of their experience maintains the memory of an event and encourages repeat visits (Figure 8). However, for re-enactors the provision of 'family friendly' events can risk the criticism that history is being excessively dumbed down or sanitised.

One of the key themes of recent years has been to present the diversity of the Romans on Hadrian's Wall, and yet re-enactment struggles to recruit from the ethnic minorities whose geographical ancestors contributed to the Roman garrison of Britain – most re-enactors are white, middle-aged men. There is also an emphasis on the military, with every society basing itself on a chosen military unit. This is not to say that the civilian side is not represented, but there are a lack of women and

Figure 9: Fun and friendship – what it's all about! Selfie by Robin Brown

child participants. This is a real pity, as their presence greatly enhances an event and enables greater audience engagement, allowing more parallels and relevance to be demonstrated. There is no simple solution to this reality, but the first steps may lie in encouraging and facilitating local friends' groups and students to participate in workshops and courses which break down these barriers. It should be emphasised that such local volunteers would not be expected to undertake the journeys or use the makeshift accommodation that itinerant re-enactors make do with.

We also need to foster closer relationships with the local communities. Whilst people travel from all over the world to see the Wall and to walk the National Trail, many local people regard it as 'something for the tourists' and haven't visited since their school days. I can understand this attitude: it applies to many other tourist destinations, as people seldom appreciate what is on their doorstep. Large-scale Wall events have always been planned using a top-down approach, which leaves many local people feeling like the event has been done 'at' them, rather than 'with' them. These projects often set out to involve local people, but the delivery on the ground has not provided the legacy outcomes hoped for in their planning stage. Further efforts need to be made to engage with local people who are not directly involved in the tourism industry, and in fact may feel inconvenienced by it, to clearly demonstrate the boost to the economy provided by visitors. We can do this by making use of local produce, goods and services, and by facilitating arts and heritage festivals and activities within local communities to promote social cohesion and the feeling of community ownership and involvement.

Hadrian's Wall attracts tourists for many reasons, but the bottom line is that these visitors spend their money in the local area. There is a maintenance cost for the archaeology and facilities, overheads in promoting and interpreting them, plus the ongoing product research and development, which includes events, exhibitions and even archaeology. Re-enactors contribute to all these areas, and yet we are seen simply as a resource, as hired-in subcontractors. We are not involved or consulted in any of the strategic management decisions for Hadrian's Wall, as we have no recognised stake in the physical real estate of the WHS. Our experiences and expertise are ignored or taken for granted, and even our continued existence is left entirely to chance. Most of these issues could be mitigated if only the various parties could begin to actively collaborate. Hadrian's Wall country has colleges full of trainee archaeologists, tourism managers, artists, fashion designers and actors. Imagine what could be achieved if these talents were put to work on collaborative projects which would not only provide vocational training for those involved, but would facilitate the refreshing of displays, improve the level of interpretation, and provide a Wall-wide resource to boost the tourism offer and attract inward investment to the region (Figure 9).

The benefits of re-enactment – Kevin Robson

At Ancient Britain, the company I founded with my wife Sara, we have been providing tours of Hadrian's Wall and the surrounding museums for almost ten years. We also provide education sessions for schools, museums and events. We deliver our tours and sessions in costume with a focus on the peoples of the Stone Age, Iron Age and Roman eras (Figure 10).

Re-enactment is a fantastic way of engaging visitors, and this can be a great service for museums and venues along Hadrian's Wall. Re-enactment events have become increasingly popular in recent years, including both large-scale displays at the museums and forts along Hadrian's Wall and more personal, focused presentations to visitors, such as guided walks with a 'real-life' Roman soldier. At Ancient Britain, we interpret the past by wearing modern versions of Romano-British clothing and footwear, as well as demonstrating reconstructions of tools, weapons and armour. Whilst it is impossible to recreate the past, and difficult to reproduce items from the past, we aim to provide a good visual representation. We understand that metallurgy, weaving technology and manufacturing in general have changed considerably over the past two millennia, so creating exact copies of historic items is very rare. Even so, this can become a great talking point and we

Figure 10: Kevin of Ancient Britain in traditional Romano-British dress

can provide insight into how these technologies have changed. Our interpretation of re-enactment is to show how some aspects of life have changed, though in some ways people remain the same, with the same daily needs, the same hopes, fears, dreams and aspirations, as we have today.

My learning path towards these skills has been relatively unconventional. Having spent considerable amounts of my childhood with my headmaster, outdoors, hunting to supplement our weekly food, I gained a good understanding of skills that would now be termed bushcraft or survival skills. This included preparing game, making hunting nets, using hand tools and gaining an understanding of nature and weather. Some of these skills have not changed for thousands of years. Growing up in a working-class family, university was not considered, so I turned my attention to travelling. Visiting Australia and New Zealand and looking at the lifestyles of Aboriginals and the Maori encouraged my interest in bushcraft. Being very young when I travelled, money was in short supply, and so we spent months living outdoors, cooking on open fires and trying a variety of foraged food.

Upon returning home, the Roman period and the Iron Age and prehistory became a hobby. During the week, I ran my own building company and visited archaeological sites in my spare time. These two aspects of my life were not completely separated. The building company enhanced my understanding of traditional construction techniques, as many of our projects were the refurbishment or repair of old buildings, farmhouses, water mills and, occasionally, stately homes. If you look at the construction of a Northumbrian farmhouse with sandstone roof slates and lime-mortared walls, the basic methods have remained unchanged for hundreds, if not thousands, of years. The construction business has helped greatly in my interpretation of archaeological sites and this approach to learning allowed me to focus on the areas and topics I really enjoyed. After a time, we decided to set up a business focusing on our hobbies and interests, with the intention of creating a lifestyle which we did not want to escape from on a weekend, and one where I could share my knowledge and passion for the archaeology and environment of Hadrian's Wall.

Through the activities and events we offer with Ancient Britain, we aim to encourage new ways of learning and promote a more inclusive and interactive way of connecting with the past and people of Hadrian's Wall. I consider myself more as an educator than a re-enactor, and I am sure many other re-enactors feel the same. However, many of the skills we demonstrate have been hard won. To provide a good understanding of the past for our guests, we too require a good understanding of the past. Before demonstrating a new skill, we first research it, then try it out for ourselves, until we become competent enough to demonstrate it. The research can be hard to find and even harder to become competent with – we have many scars as proof. I spend a lot of time reading the classical writers, the latest publications on the Wall, and books about farming, mining or geology. This helps link the rich tapestry of events both above and below ground where Hadrian's Wall stands. We attend lectures, visit museums, speak with the archaeologists, share ideas with other educators and we also spend time overseas visiting archaeological sites. Our tours and sessions are continuously evolving as we include new information. It also means we can take the session in a variety of directions depending upon the questions we are asked or the interests of a group.

We never re-enact battles or display fighting. We simply use the costumes, armour and reproduction equipment as a visual aid so people can better understand life in the past. The original artefacts are unique and valuable in many ways, so by their nature they cannot be used in daily handling. Re-enactment fits very well with the fantastic museums and the outdoor sites of Hadrian's Wall, and it can enhance the experience of visitors by making the past seem more tangible and vivid. By wearing traditional clothing and armour, we break down boundaries – we breathe life into inanimate items and form a bridge to the past, and visitors feel comfortable approaching to ask questions or to discuss ideas. We also learn about the functionality and practicality of the equipment. We do realise that reproduction items are a modern interpretation on archaeological finds, and we wear them for relatively short periods, so whilst we gain a better understanding we couldn't claim to fully understand them. We are constantly adding to our sessions with new information or new skills. This keeps it fresh for us and in turn for our guests.

If you have studied archaeology or ancient history, you may have a better understanding of the earth works, quarry sites and archaeological remains of Hadrian's Wall. But many visitors to the area have limited formal knowledge of this. Many visitors see Hadrian's Wall as a walking trail with some archaeology. We always endeavour to reverse this view. We provide in-depth sessions weaving a narrative of the daily life of civilians and the local population from the past, through the stories from the classical writers and the archaeological evidence, by displaying scenes of daily life or providing hands-on activities for guests to try for themselves, for example, fire lighting or preparing and cooking game. These skills were everyday tasks for Roman soldiers and native Britons alike. In our sessions we can demonstrate these skills and show how aware of the natural environment the soldiers and civilians were. Our activities also help to promote the diversity of life on the Wall. It is easy to view Hadrian's Wall as British history due to its geographical nature. The reality is that Hadrian's Wall shares heritage with North Africa, central Europe and the Middle East. Many of the soldiers stationed on Hadrian's Wall and some of the civilians travelled vast distances to the frontier, bringing their own culture and world views with them. They mixed with the local population and remained here after their military service. In fact, Hadrian's Wall has a very multicultural aspect. By sharing this information, we have noticed a positive visible change in attitude from both national and international guests when they realise that Hadrian's Wall is not an abstract or detached monument and is part of many heritages outside of Britain. We, as re-enactors, help to provide the public with a better understanding of life on the Wall, and we often see visitors' views of Hadrian's Wall change – from a simple walking trail to an important archaeological site.

Our time spent wearing clothing, armour or displaying reproduction pottery or tools is limited to our session times, though visitors respond very well to our costumes and storytelling. This in turn can renew interest for visitors. Many of our guests have reported visiting other sites and museums or looking for Iron Age hillforts after attending one of our sessions. Our lifestyle and business rely on repeat visits and a growing audience. Increasing visitor numbers can be of immense benefit to the local economy, but can also bring pressure on sensitive areas. By working on the UNESCO WHS of Hadrian's Wall, we all have a responsibility protect the environment. This can be achieved by informing guests of the importance of the archaeology and by providing information on the Countryside Code: closing gates, keeping dogs on leads, showing guests how to spread out to avoid erosion on the National Trail, and encouraging a 'leave no trace' attitude. Information panels can be of great benefit to visitors who are new to the countryside or new to the area by showing suggested walking routes and designated car parking sites.

Having a personal guide, weaving a narrative of the sites and providing the cultural, spiritual, environmental and political context, can significantly increase the public's understanding and appreciation of Hadrian's Wall. In turn, each generation becomes the custodian of our heritage. Everyone involved with Hadrian's Wall, in large or small part, has a responsibility not only to leave things in the same condition that they found it but to leave it in a better condition. Through education of the general public and the creation of a better understanding of the landscape, archaeology and heritage, people will care for, protect and enhance Hadrian's Wall. This will share the responsibility for preserving the rich heritage we have around us.

Bibliography

Bishop, M.C. 2013. Re-enactment and Living History – Issues about Authenticity, in Mills, N. (ed) *Presenting the Romans: Interpreting the Frontiers of the Roman Empire World Heritage Site*: 23-30. Woodbridge: Boydell & Brewer Ltd.

The next 1900 years: a future for Hadrian's Wall World Heritage Site management

Nick Henderson (Hadrian's Wall Partnership Development Officer)

In 2022 we celebrate the 1900th anniversary of Hadrian's Wall. As with any anniversary we remember and celebrate the past, but also consider the future to ensure the World Heritage Site endures for at least another 1900 years. Hadrian's Wall is in a strong position looking towards the future – this chapter discusses the Hadrian's Wall Partnership, and Hadrian's Wall Management Plan, from the point of view of a Development Officer. Through discussing the origin and evolution of the Plan, this chapter touches upon the challenges and successes intrinsic to working across the mosaic of partners and organisations that form the World Heritage Site. We also take this chance to explore how the Hadrian's Wall Management Plan relates to, and can help with, long-standing initiatives, as well as possible future funding and governance of the Wall.

The Hadrian's Wall Management Plan consultation process

The Management Plan (MP) secures our World Heritage Site (WHS) status and provides the framework and foundation for WHS developments. Beginning with archaeological matters in 1996, the first plan was unique to a UK WHS, with every subsequent plan involving greater levels of consultation and participation with wider groups of stakeholders, to represent the broad range of interests of the Wall's communities (Young 2013). As part of the Frontiers of the Roman Empire (FRE) WHS, created in 2005 (Brough and Scott 2013) the MP is further of international significance. Continued expansion of stakeholders is essential to the Wall's future. Plans have incorporated broader initiatives, and since 2014 include a section on 'Aims for the Management of the World Heritage Site during the next thirty years, 2015-2045'.

The Management Plan goes digital

The 2014-2019 plan (Hadrian's Wall Partnership 2014) was the first in the UK to be entirely available online and open for public scrutiny. The consultation (Norman and May 2014) prioritised a practical plan, with 15 varied objectives falling under the umbrellas of Conservation, Understanding, and the Visitor Economy. Participants engaged in public workshops and online consultation, with public and stakeholder panels along the WHS. Due to COVID-19 social restrictions, this type of hybrid consultation wasn't possible for the 2021-2025 plan, so the primary form of public consultation was through online surveys designed to encourage participation and dialogue and collect quantitative data and feedback around the MP's objectives.

Reflecting the impact and roles the WHS covers, subjects consulted upon were varied. They ranged from public perceptions of UNESCO WHS status, to community involvement, such as volunteering, awareness, conservation and accessibility. Other topics regarded future developments, visitor experiences and understanding, economic development and challenges such as illegal metal detecting and climate change.

What do we learn through consultation?

The consultation is an opportunity to gauge what is important to the Wall's communities, to discover what they want to see in the future, and to incorporate this into the Hadrian's Wall Partnership (HWP) current and future developments, the HWP being the governance structure of the WHS. A detailed analysis is beyond the scope of this chapter; however, the conclusions of the plan broadly support initiatives by the HWP and investments being developed in the Hadrian's Wall ten-year plan. The public response and insights were collated by Dr Stelios Lekakis and Dr Mina Dragouni (Lekakis and Dragouni 2021) on behalf of the HWP, whose research I am indebted to.

There have been recurring issues throughout the consultations undertaken by the HWP and its predecessors (e.g. Hadrian's Wall Management Plan Committee 2008). Some of these persistent themes and recommendations are expanded upon below.

Visitor information, improved promotion and communication

The need to develop awareness of the WHS and improve engagement was keenly felt, particularly in the urban east (Tyne and Wear) and the Cumbrian coast. Correlating to the areas of the monument that are most physically visible, Northumberland has the strongest WHS association (86% of participants responding that visibility/awareness was good or very good), with Tyne and Wear also high (70%). This was in contrast to Cumbria, where a majority responded that visibility was poor or very poor. 88% of respondents believed digital means were the best way to share WHS status and value, conduct public engagement and promote core WHS communications. Improved signage was important to 76% of stakeholders, mainly across public footpaths, free sites and national paths, followed by roads and cycle routes.

New and improved visitor attractions, experiences and activities

Developing economic and promotional activities, events, and introducing local business schemes were stakeholder priorities. WHS literacy was very high (over 90%), reflecting familiarity with WHS status and recognition of its contribution to conservation. WHS literacy indicates a belief that the WHS has a positive impact, and that World Heritage is a valuable brand, as seen in its incorporation in businesses, products and marketing. I often wonder what Hadrian would make of the many businesses or products (including booze!) which bear his name. Indeed, 89% of participants recognised the Wall as contributing to local and regional economies. It seems intuitive that the Wall benefits the local economy, wellbeing and sense of pride and place. STEAM data (a way of modelling the economic impact of tourism) from 2016 estimated two million visitors with a £2.6 billion contribution to the local economy and a £716 million estimated contribution via WHS visitor expenditure. Recognition that heritage is not just 'nice to have' but is essential to livelihoods is driving some future WHS developments.

Accessibility, transport and navigation

Accessibility, not just to the monument's iconic places but especially in Cumbria and the west, has been repeatedly highlighted, with barriers to participation being geographic distance, available transportation and physical site access. Supported solutions were improvements to infrastructure, connectivity, mobility and accessibility. Investing in public transportation was the primary consideration in making the Wall a great place to live, work and visit, with the second being promotion and events, and improved amenities the third. Creating or improving cycling and walking paths was also important to stakeholders. The importance of sustainable walking tourism is discussed in Chapter 11 by McGlade, Richards and Pickles.

Climate action

Conservation is important to stakeholders, especially regarding the effects on the archaeology from flooding and erosion (particularly in Cumbria and on the west coast). Concerns were expressed regarding the reduction of climate impact on food, land management and biodiversity. Public/ green transportation was important to stakeholders, with sustainable transport (77%) and visitor flow management (53%) viewed as solutions to future sustainability and climate control.

Regarding climate, it must be added that Partnership members each have 'net zero' targets, to cut down on emissions that will damage the environment. Local authority partners have declared a climate emergency, setting clear targets to achieve net zero carbon emissions.

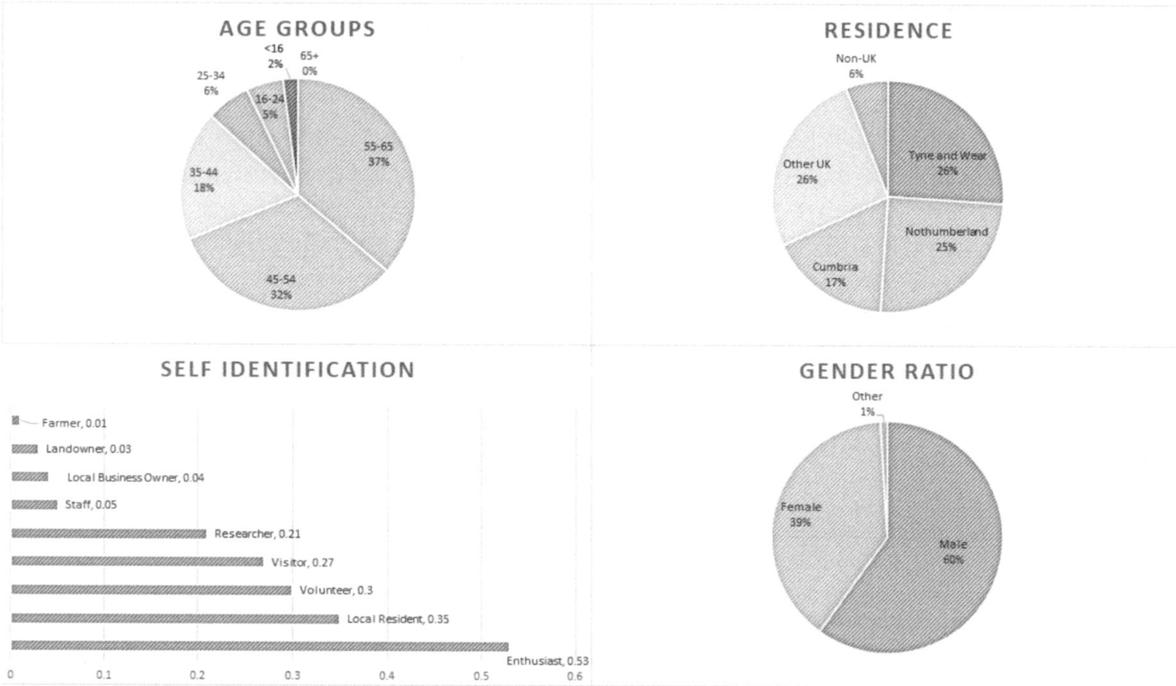

Figure 1: Hadrian's Wall Management Plan 2021-2025 Consultation respondents breakdown by age, gender, location and relationship with Wall, Hadrian's Wall Partnership Board

Consultation notes

There are caveats to the consultation. Some sections were not included due to technical issues. Responses were generally from those already engaged, and reflected local demographics of predominantly white residents (97%). Figure 1 has a further breakdown of the age, gender and location of the respondents, as well as more information on their relationship with the Wall.

What does the new plan hope to do that has not been done in the past?

Previous plans have responded to these themes, with some, such as transport, accessibility and signage, being perennial issues due to the size and geographic nature of the monument. Critically at this time, Hadrian's Wall has a strong Partnership, with large-scale developments in the ten-year investment plan, a substantial injection of capital from the Borderlands Inclusive Growth Deal, and the very public and complementary objectives of the 1900th anniversary festival.

Hadrian's Wall possesses a 'string of pearls' in the sites and attractions, but also cherished services such as the AD122 bus, and cycling and walking routes. Pearls need a necklace to draw them together, and this is being developed in the ten-year investment plan. This concerns the distribution of £30 million from 2022 to 2031/2, with funds drawn from a number of sources, including the Borderlands Inclusive Growth Deal.

The Borderlands Inclusive Growth Deal is an economic development package, and is the first 'bite at the cherry' for the ten-year plan, with an allocation of £18 million to Hadrian's Wall for the purposes of economic regeneration and development. It speaks to the strength of the current partnership model that consensus on areas for focus and investment has been prioritised over competing project bids, with the desire to reduce competition and to collaborate to maximise benefit for all Hadrian's Wall stakeholders.

The themes of the Borderlands Hadrian's Wall investment chime with concerns seen in the MP consultation: transport and navigation, cycling and walking, visitor information, new and improved visitor attractions, new visitor experiences, and activities. Part of the ten-year investment plan is a framework to simplify the complicated Hadrian's Wall offer, with developments that make it easier for the visitor to experience the WHS, and the identification of areas for investment. These include visitor hubs and gateways, with locations selected for capacity and reflected in comments made in the consultation as areas in need of increased visibility, such as the west and urban east. Visitor attractions and visitor stopping points will be developed to respond to investments and to improve visitor offer and amenities. Stopping points would further support goals around understanding and the visitor economy, being themed around the WHS, the diversity of people, and the landscape.

Other project areas of the ten-year investment plan correlate to what stakeholders raised in the consultation as important. These include:

- Signage
- Marketing
- Sustainable transport access/transport and navigation
- Infrastructure at visitor attractions
- Stopping points
- Cycling and walking routes
- Innovation fund for businesses
- Attractions investment programme
- Signature events programme

There is also a desire, as expressed by partners and reinforced in the consultation, for Wall-wide events and festivals. At the Hadrian's Wall Networking Day 2020, the 1900th anniversary of the Wall was eagerly discussed by members of the Wall community. Under the auspices of the WHS Learning and Interpretation group, the collaboration of Wall partners, and the essential work of freelancers, the 1900th anniversary will be celebrated by the Wall community. The festival contributes to the future of Hadrian's Wall with a planned legacy of:

- Improved promotion and national/international publicity
- Promoting the Wall to the staycation market and encouraging the community as brand ambassadors
- Strengthening of the HWP, vital to the success of ten-year investment plan
- Community and partnership skills and networks developed, with a community more engaged.

Because of this, the 2021-2025 MP will address issues raised in ways which have not been the case in previous plans.

Successes, benefits and strengths of the current management system of Hadrian's Wall

Vital to the future of the WHS is management and funding. The current HWP is unconstituted and managed by a mixed public partnership of 19 organisations, along with just under 25% of UK World Heritage Sites according to research by WH:UK (Blandford 2019). These include the Lake District, our fellow frontier the Antonine Wall, and Durham Cathedral, although there is much variation between the management of these sites. The current model is best described as a 'coalition of the willing', with highly engaged partners recognising and harnessing the benefit of being a WHS, which could not exist without their continued support and buy-in. The current structure is majority core funded by the local authority partners, but each contribute in different ways. The Partnership is strengthened by equal benefits in Wall-wide initiatives, and by the representative and flexible delivery groups and subgroups which respond to the needs of the WHS identified in the MP.

WHS in the UK are varied and so a 'one size fits all' approach to management or funding is not necessarily desirable. Hadrian's Wall is an undeniably complex WHS: from the bodies responsible for the management of its heritage assets, to the wide variation in landscape, population density, deprivation indices, access to amenities, opportunity and transport. Around 1.4 million people live within the WHS with the majority concentrated in two cities of Roman foundation, Newcastle and Carlisle. The Wall traverses nine local authority areas, all of whom are Partnership members. Organisations which manage significant heritage assets, landscapes, trails and attractions are also members of the Partnership: Historic England, English Heritage, the National Trust, the Vindolanda Trust, Tullie House Museum and Art Gallery, Northumberland National Park, Hadrian's Wall National Trail Partnership, and Natural England. Essential board support comes from academic institutions (represented by Newcastle University), transport providers, community interest groups, and destination management organisations (represented by Cumbria Tourism), which together form the HWP. The delivery groups are Archaeological Research, Conservation, Planning and Heritage Management, Learning and Interpretation, and Marketing and Transport. Additional delivery groups for projects and stakeholders complement these, such as the Politician's Forum. Figure 2 has an illustrated map, and Figure 3 shows visualisations of the WHS structure and Partnership.

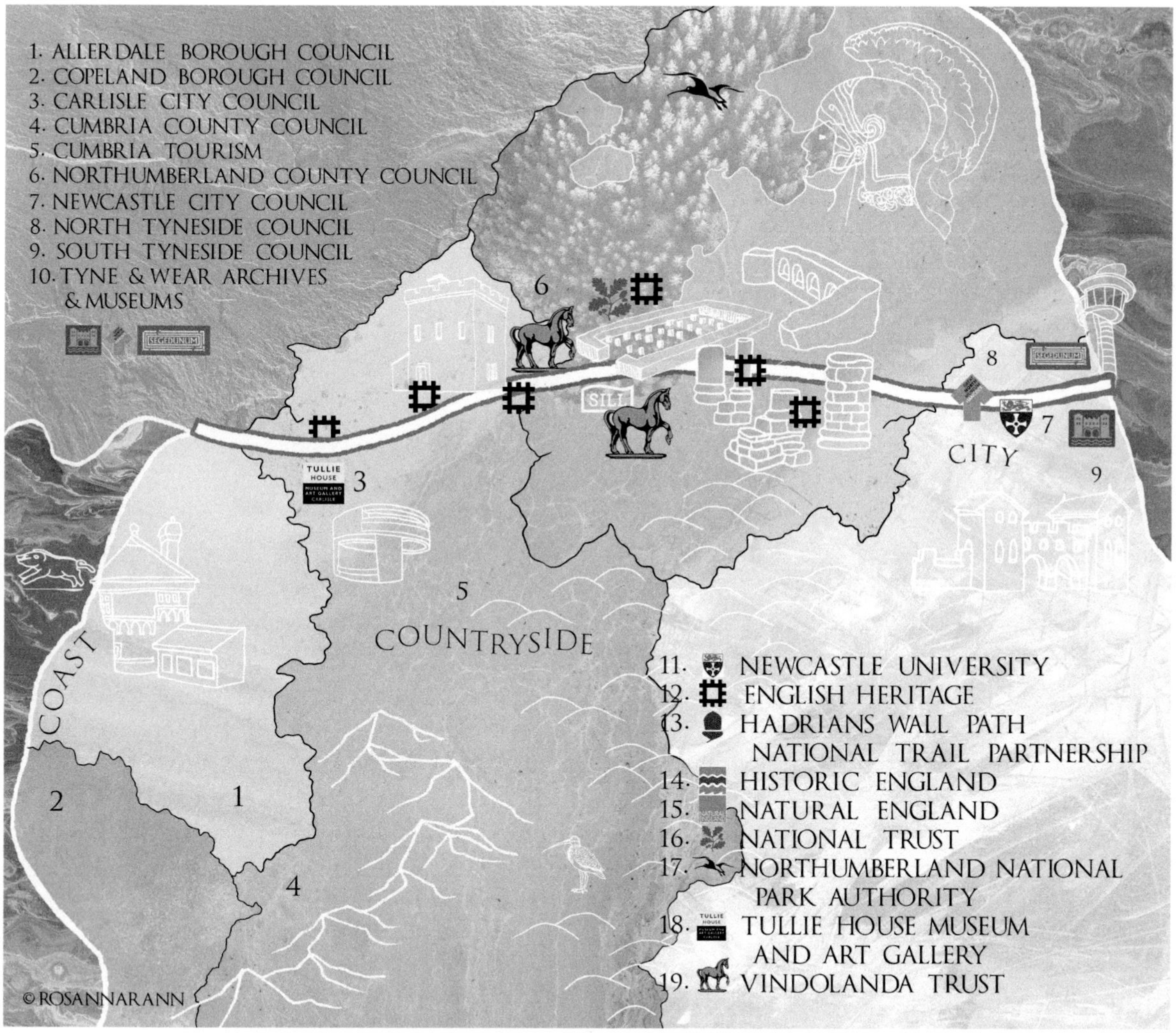

Figure 2: Illustrated map of the local authorities, heritage and environmental organisations, and academic institutions who are part of the Hadrian's Wall Partnership © Rosanna Rann

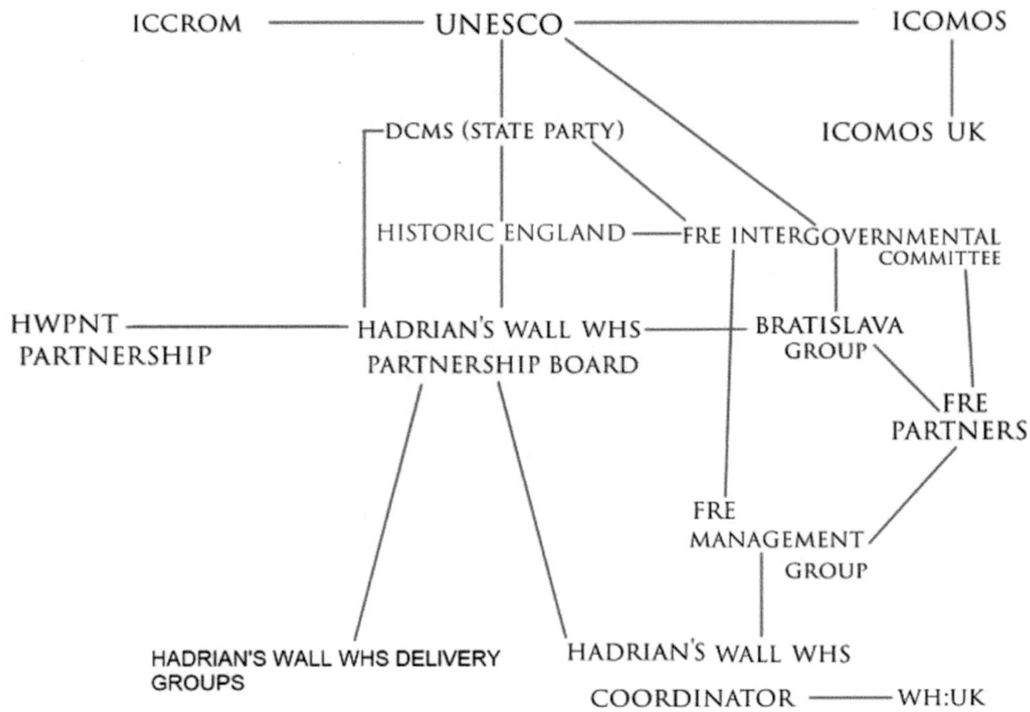

Acronyms
UNESCO: United Nations Educational Scientific Cultural Organisation
ICCROM: International Centre for the Study of the Preservation and Restoration of Cultural Property
ICOMOS: International Council on Monuments and Sites
DCMS: Department of Culture Media and Sport
FRE: Frontiers of the Roman Empire
WHS: World Heritage Site
HWPNT: Hadrian's Wall Path National Trail

Figure 3: Organisational structure of the Frontiers of the Roman Empire World Heritage Property, Hadrian's Wall Partnership Board

Currently the WHS has two dedicated staff, the Management Plan Coordinator (MPC) who is essential to maintaining our WHS status and is supported by core funding, and a Development Officer, supported by a National Lottery Heritage Fund (NHLF) project. This core coordination team undertakes varied duties, including MP development and implementation, liaising with stakeholders, piloting initiatives, WHS administration, outreach and fundraising, to name a few. WHS officers are housed within local authorities, Cultural Services at Northumberland (along with the core funding) and Economic Development at Carlisle, but work on behalf of the Partnership as a whole. WHS staff in this way have access to the advice and technical support needed for WHS management and expertise in operational activities such as finance, human resources, conservation, planning and development, infrastructure and communication. This system works as there is a high level of partner commitment, with hosting partners being directly engaged with the WHS. The particular advantages of the current management system are in its flexibility, partners' vast reserves of experience and knowledge, and in the collaborative nature and approach it has fostered. There is no perception of, or difficulties arising from, an approach that is too 'top down', which can occur with a separate WHS trust.

This structure fulfils the key elements of the English approach to the protection and management of the WHS:

- A stakeholder steering group with support from the key partners, representing major owners, managers and communities
- Effective coordination between the MPC and delivery groups
- An MPC to coordinate production of the MP
- Designation of specific WHS assets (such as National Parks and the Solway Area of Outstanding Natural Beauty (AONB))
- Local authority membership ensures the Wall continues to be a key consideration in planning applications, with planning authorities adopting policies to protect its Outstanding Universal Value (OUV)
- Local authority commitment to the protection, promotion and management of the WHS is demonstrated through core funding and board membership.

Sustainable funding and governance on Hadrian's Wall: the past and the future

Since first being inscribed as a WHS in 1987, the management system for Hadrian's Wall has undergone a number of changes. Current governance was developed after 2014 with the closure of the Hadrian's Wall Trust. The Trust operated with a large, publicly funded budget and, at its peak, with a team of around 14 full and part-time staff. The system was vulnerable to cuts, and after 2014 the work of the Trust continued through HWP organisations, WHS delivery groups, the MPC, the embedding of legacy projects (and so staff and expertise) within partners, and the HWP board. The public perception is that the Wall is one discernible 'thing' run by one organisation, and to this end a trust is logical but not the only option. The HWP presents a unified shop front to the world through a shared website, branding, and a general inbox for the Wall.

Past management structures, such as the Hadrian's Wall Tourism Partnership (HWTP), or Hadrian's Wall Heritage Ltd, have had similar goals: to build trust and cohesion amongst organisations along the WHS in order to bring economic (such as through sustainable tourism), social and environmental benefits, the protection of the WHS, and to improve understanding (through the promotion and development of education, marketing and community initiatives). The structures established to achieve these aims have largely remained and been built upon.

Four of the UK WHS have a dedicated multi-skilled core team of four or more staff. Of these, three are dedicated independent charitable trusts (Edinburgh, New Lanark, and the Jurassic Coast) and the other is local authority-led (Cornish Mining). In terms of costs, a dedicated WHS trust averages £420,000, with 4.5 staff, whereas for reference, a mixed WHS public partnership is £91,000 with an average of two staff. These multi-skilled core WHS teams are better able to increase WHS management resilience, and to support partners to increase fundraising, engagement and promotion.

Unfortunately, WHS status does not confer funding. However, it can be leveraged to do so, and Partnership members in WHS initiatives or individual ventures have successfully done so. Research by WH:UK indicates from 2013/14 to 2017/18, £2.2 million in NLHF funds went to Hadrian's Wall (Blandford 2019). Partnership working has led to over half a million pounds being raised for the 1900th anniversary in 2021. Other funding sources are central and local governments, the European Union, trusts and foundations – which the varied objectives of the MP are able to align. There is further value in the capability of the HWP's varying types of organisation (local authorities, charitable trusts, etc.) to host different funders, specific collaborative WHS projects, and staff.

Though not opposed in principle, there isn't a strong appetite for another Hadrian's Wall Trust. A trust to support a core team would need grants, physical assets and to build non-grant dependent revenue outside public sources. Unless fully publicly funded, independent WHS trusts need membership schemes, donations (whether it be crowd funding or from high-net-worth individuals), intellectual property and product lines, all while at least in part being dependent on public funds.

On the Wall this would all be in competition with our partners. From conversations with other WHS and Hadrian's Wall partners, for the future of the Wall at this time, it would be desirable to develop a structure that is still based upon partner consensus, but able to take a strategic lead for the WHS. This could be with the current Partnership as constituted or unconstituted, but housed within specific partners as a dedicated multi-skilled team, answerable to the HWP board, and so increasing Partnership buy-in, capacity and capability. A dedicated team within the existing, or similar, governance structure, comprising a wide complementary skillset including WHS management, marketing and communication, development and fundraising, administration, learning and engagement, would fulfil the objectives of the MP in a greater way than ever before and truly secure the Wall's future.

Unlike the Wall itself, the future of the WHS is not set in stone. Nevertheless, Hadrian's Wall on the verge of its 1900th anniversary is in a strong position. Appropriately, Kipling's *A Song to Mithras* comes to mind: 'Many roads Thou hast fashioned – all of them lead to Light!'

Bibliography

Blandford, C. (2019) UK World Heritage: Asset for the Future: A Review of the State of UK World Heritage Sites. Telford: World Heritage UK

Brough, D. and Scott, J. 2013. *The Frontiers of the Roman Empire World Heritage Site.* in Stone, P.G. and Brough, D. 2013. *Managing, Using, and Interpreting Hadrian's Wall as World Heritage.* London: Springer.

Hadrian's Wall Management Plan Committee 2008. Frontiers of the Roman Empire World Heritage Site Hadrian's Wall Management Plan 2008-2014. Accessed 27 February 2022 <https://hadrianswallcountry.co.uk/sites/default/files/3__Hadrian%27s_Wall_2008-2014_-_Greyscale_text_%26_appendices%5B1%5D.pdf>

Hadrian's Wall Partnership 2014. Hadrian's Wall Management Plan. Accessed 27 February 2022 < https://hadrianswallcountry.co.uk/hadrians-wall-management-plan>

Lekakis, S. And Dragouni M. (2021) Public Consultation: Hadrian's Wall Management Plan 2021-2025.

Norman, K. and May, S. 2014. Hadrian's Wall World Heritage Site Consultation 2014 Report. London: University College London

Young, C. 2013. The Need for a Management Plan and the 1st and 2nd Plans, in Stone, P.G. and Brough, D. (eds) *Managing, Using, and Interpreting Hadrian's Wall as World Heritage.* London: Springer.

The future of cultural resource management on the Frontiers of the Roman Empire World Heritage property

Rebecca Jones (Historic Environment Scotland)

Ever since the creation of the World Heritage Convention in 1972, the World Heritage list has expanded regularly as more and more sites around the world are inscribed by UNESCO. Part of UNESCO's World Heritage mission is to encourage international cooperation in the conservation of our global heritage.

Yet, in 97% of cases, each site is located in a single country, rather than crossing many: this means that the sites do not necessarily need to draw on international expertise to maintain and conserve their 'properties' (the formal name for World Heritage sites). The Frontiers of the Roman Empire World Heritage project, which has been running for some 20 years, is an ambitious aspiration which has international cooperation at its very heart. Whilst the nomination and development of future Roman Frontiers World Heritage properties have been a major international focus for the partners, the day-to-day management and cooperation of the existing Frontiers of the Roman Empire World Heritage property between the UK (England and Scotland) and Germany continues.

This chapter looks at the current direction of travel for the Frontiers of the Roman Empire World Heritage Site, and the opportunities and challenges for the future.

Introduction

'*Heritage is our legacy from the past, what we live with today, and what we pass on to future generations. Our cultural and natural heritage are both irreplaceable sources of life and inspiration.*

What makes the concept of World Heritage exceptional is its universal application. World Heritage sites belong to all the people of the world, irrespective of the territory on which they are located.' (UNESCO 2022a)

The United Nations Educational Scientific and Cultural Organisation (UNESCO), established in 1945, was founded to advance peace and security by promoting collaboration among nations through education, science and culture.

International discussions around the protection and conservation of the world's important cultural sites began in the 1950s with discussions extending to natural areas in the 1960s (Jones *et al.* 2021). This culminated in the creation and signing of the World Heritage Convention in 1972 (formally called the Convention Concerning the Protection of World Cultural and Natural Heritage – UNESCO 1972). Whilst in 2022 Hadrian's Wall celebrates 1900 years since its titular's emperor's visit in AD 122, so too does UNESCO celebrate 50 years of the World Heritage Convention.

The success of the World Heritage initiative has been notable: as of 2021, there are 1154 sites inscribed on the list, and over 190 countries have ratified the convention. Indeed, UNESCO recognises the huge benefits that come with inscription on the World Heritage list, in that it:

'...brings an increase in public awareness of the site and of its outstanding values, thus also increasing the tourist activities at the site. When these are well planned for and organized respecting sustainable tourism principles, they can bring important funds to the site and to the local economy.' (UNESCO 2022b)

World Heritage across borders

Despite this global ambition to protect the world's outstanding cultural and natural sites, the vast majority of these sites each lie in a single country (referred to as 'state parties' by UNESCO). There are currently only 43 classed as 'transboundary', representing management partnerships between different countries. Of these, many are transboundary because they straddle modern geopolitical

Figure 1: Photo of the Forum in Rome (taken in 2016)

borders, such as the historic centre of Rome and the Holy See, shared between Italy and the Vatican City[1] (Figure 1).

And yet, UNESCO recognises their importance, with Irina Bokova, their former Director-General, stating:

'Transboundary projects truly enhance the founding principles of the World Heritage Convention, which was designed to build peace through cultural cooperation and foster collective responsibility over shared heritage.' (UNESCO 2019)

But getting inscribed on UNESCO's World Heritage list is a long and complicated process, and it is perhaps unsurprising that fewer than 4% have opted to make that journey more difficult by collaborating across national borders.

So, if around 97% of sites on the list are situated in one country alone, they do not necessarily *need* to draw on international expertise to maintain and conserve their properties. This is where the Frontiers of the Roman Empire (FRE) World Heritage project is unique: running for over twenty years, it is an ambitious aspiration which has international cooperation at its very heart. The objective of the FRE is to create a World Heritage Site (WHS) (now sites) which would encompass all the frontiers of the Roman Empire, from northern Europe to north Africa. Such an inscription would aid in meeting what are known as the 'five Cs' (UNESCO 2022b) – UNESCO's strategic objectives to: strengthen the Credibility of the list; ensure effective Conservation; promote effective Capacity-

[1] <https://whc.unesco.org/en/list/91>

building (particularly amongst the partners); increase awareness through Communication; and enhance the role of Communities the length and breadth of the frontiers of the Roman Empire.

The trailblazer: Hadrian's Wall

Following the ratification of the convention, 12 sites were inscribed on the list in 1978. These first inscriptions included some well-known places (Galápagos Islands; Mesa Verde; Lalibela) as well as others which are surprisingly not better known, such as the slave-trading island of Gorée in Senegal. By 1986, when the UK inscribed its first properties on the list, it had grown to 244 sites. 1987 saw a further 41 sites inscribed on the list, including Hadrian's Wall in the UK, the Great Wall of China, the Acropolis in Athens (Greece), Venice (Italy), Kilimanjaro (Tanzania) and the Hawaii Volcanos National Park (USA).

In order to be inscribed, a simpler process in 1987 than today, Hadrian's Wall was able to argue for its exceptional preservation, massive stone wall and impressive array of forts and fortlets. It was inscribed on the list simply as *Hadrian's Wall.*

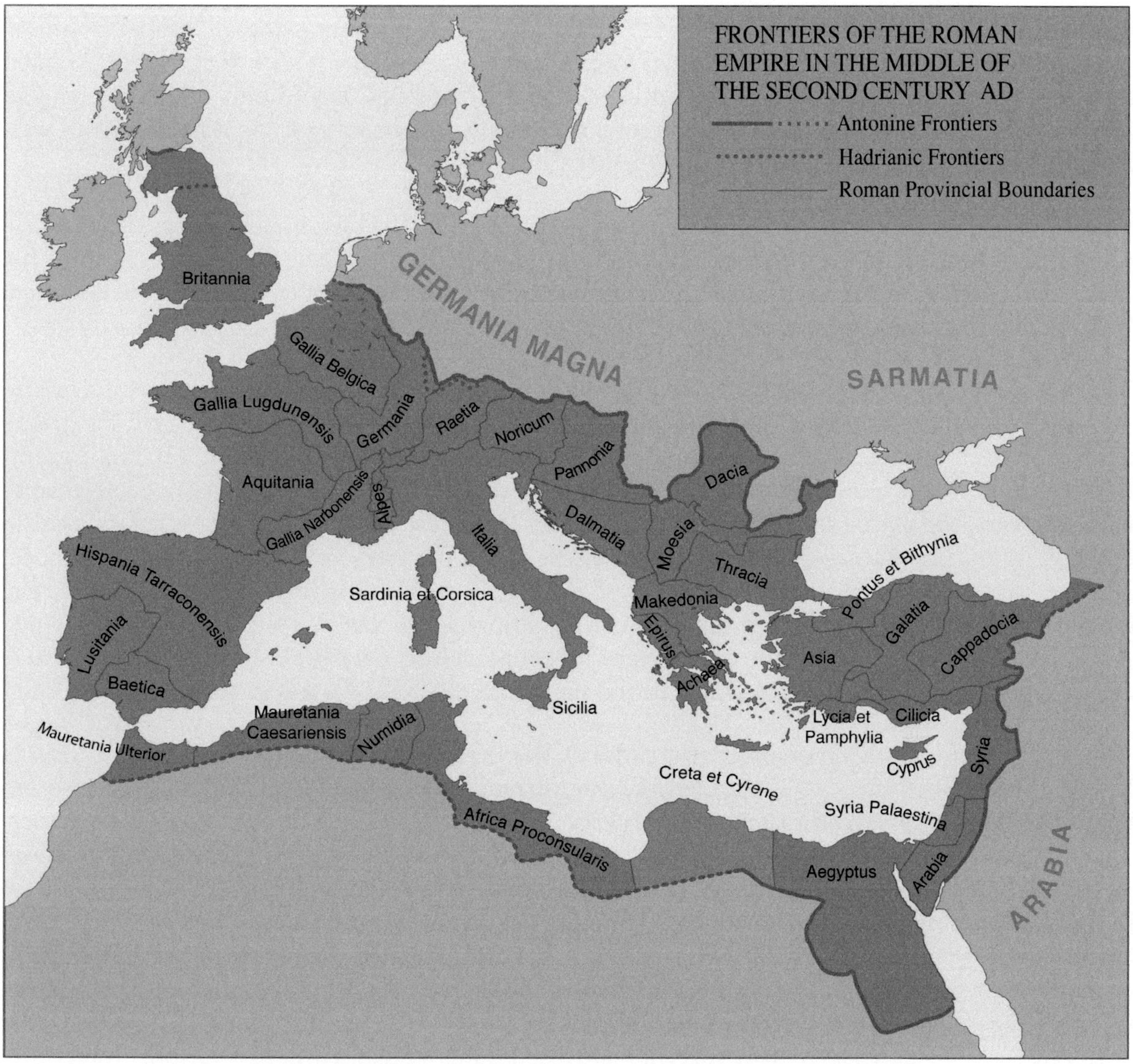

Figure 2: Map of the Roman Empire in the mid-2nd century AD (created as part of the EU Culture 2000-funded Frontiers of the Roman Empire project, 2008)

A decade or so later, conversations started regarding the potential for the Upper German-Raetian *Limes* to be nominated. The word *Limes* (pronounced Lee-mes) is the modern term in common use for Roman frontiers, derived from the Latin for road or boundary/frontier. By the 1990s, UNESCO had introduced its Global Strategy for a representative, balanced and credible list, following recognition that it lacked balance both in terms of site types and geography, with Europe dominating (UNESCO 1994). Yet Roman scholars and cultural heritage specialists began to recognise that if other stretches of the Roman frontier could be nominated, not just Hadrian's Wall, then the implications were potentially huge, with perhaps a dozen countries across Europe seeking to nominate their frontier stretches, before we even look beyond Europe to frontiers in the Middle East and North Africa (Figure 2). Discussions then began to move towards the concept of a multi-national World Heritage property (Breeze and Jilek 2008: 25; Breeze and Jones 2020: 63).

Birth of the Frontiers of the Roman Empire

The early 2000s saw a series of discussions between Roman archaeologists and cultural resource managers in Europe; fortunately for the nascent FRE World Heritage property, these roles were often combined in the same person. The European Association of Archaeologists created a working group on Roman Frontiers, and their annual meetings were instrumental in moving forward the dialogue. With the desire of UNESCO to create a more balanced list and not add endless new sites from Europe, the solution of a single transboundary property encompassing all Roman frontiers was a recognisable goal. The convention of international bureaucracy is such that a single Roman Frontiers World Heritage property, potentially in many countries, would only count as a single site on UNESCO's World Heritage List, thereby not unduly unbalancing it. As Hadrian's Wall was already inscribed, the site was already on the list.

In addition, at a meeting at the World Heritage Centre in 2002, the terminology for multi-country properties was changed from transboundary to transnational, to acknowledge that there could be more than two state parties in the new-style property, and the re-arranging of the World Heritage List to identify transnational sites.

The UK government, as UNESCO state party for Hadrian's Wall, agreed to a change in the inscription name of the Wall to the *Frontiers of the Roman Empire*, enabling its expansion. This gave the green light to continue international dialogue, with European partners fortunate in getting a grant from the European Union (EU)'s Culture 2000 fund to enable a range of cooperation projects and workshops to take place (detailed in Breeze and Jilek 2008; this was the first of several successful EU funding bids by Roman frontiers partners). European partners worked together to produce a definition of the World Heritage property to enable future nominations to be added, and this is known as the Koblenz Declaration, after the city in which it was written in 2004 (Jilek 2008). A specialist advisory group to the embryonic FRE property was created, known as the Bratislava Group, again named after the city where it first met in 2003.

A summary nomination statement was created by the Bratislava Group and accepted by UNESCO in 2005 (Breeze and Young 2008). At the time, the various partners were working towards a 'serial phased transboundary World Heritage' property. In practice, this meant that various countries across Europe were putting the necessary building blocks in place in order to progress with a nomination, including political commitment. The intention was that each country would apply to have its national segment inscribed onto the wider FRE property when it was ready, the partners thereby moving forward at their own pace. This was critical given the complexities inherent in each different country and the putting together of an appropriate nomination dossier, including rigorous site selection and justification, and detailed mapping. The EU-funded FRE project was critical in enabling partners to work together and discuss shared issues of conservation, protection, management, interpretation and presentation (Breeze and Jilek 2008).

Figure 3: Documents prepared for the inscription of the Antonine Wall as part of the Frontiers of the Roman Empire, submitted 2007 and inscribed 2008 © Historic Environment Scotland

As a result of this work, the Upper German-Raetian *Limes* was successfully inscribed in 2005; the Antonine Wall followed in 2008 (Figure 3). The Frontiers of the Roman Empire World Heritage property was properly born.

Game changers

At the same time as the flurry of activity around the preparation for Roman frontiers nominations, other serial transboundary sites were under discussion. The same year that that the Upper German-Raetian *Limes* was inscribed, the Struve Geodetic Arc was also inscribed, comprising 34 sites in ten countries which were original 19th-century station points helping to identify the exact size and shape of planet Earth.[2]

Also at this time, countries across Asia were in discussions around the nomination of various aspects of the Silk Roads. Sub-regional workshops were held in various Central Asian countries exploring the need for a concept paper, strategic approach, selection of sites and political support. This ultimately led to an 'International World Heritage expert meeting on serial nominations and properties' in Ittingen, Switzerland in 2010. Various recommendations at that meeting were recognised by the World Heritage Committee in its meeting in Brazil later that year (UNESCO 2010; Williams 2014).

Although the meeting intended to aid serial discussion, such as those taking place for the Silk Roads, some of the suggestions which emerged were game changers. For example, it transpired that transboundary sites should have all stretches on national tentative lists. These are the list each state party supplies to UNESCO, decennially or more frequently, listing the properties they

[2] <https://whc.unesco.org/en/list/1187/>

are considering for nomination before submitting the nomination to UNESCO for consideration. Such a requirement meant that the proposal to add further stretches of the Roman frontier when the various countries were ready was no longer possible. Given the sheer extent of the Roman frontier and differing political situations in those countries containing frontier remains, the idea of all having, firstly, their sections on their national tentative lists and, secondly, their nominations ready to progress together, was totally unrealistic.

By this point, ten countries across Europe were collaborating on an FRE World Heritage property which would stretch from the north-western frontiers in Britain all the way to the Black Sea (Figure 2). For some partners in Europe, this was an important dimension in gaining political agreement. A new way forward needed to be found.

It was agreed by the European partners that a Thematic Study and Nomination Strategy would need to be created to progress the FRE vision. Joint meetings of the Inter-Governmental Committee (IGC) of the existing World Heritage property and the Bratislava Group (expert advisors) were held, with representatives from ICOMOS (the International Council on Monuments and Sites, advisors to UNESCO). This led to the production of a report, co-authored by three experts with support from the governments in Austria, Germany and the Netherlands. This report was agreed by the partners and then approved by UNESCO in 2017 (Ployer *et al.* 2017; UNESCO 2017).

This enabled the partners to proceed with nominations, with the agreement to divide the FRE into four European properties:

- The existing FRE property comprising the three linear barriers in Europe (Hadrian's Wall, the Upper German-Raetian *Limes*, and the Antonine Wall)
- the Lower German *Limes* (running along the River Rhine in the Netherlands and lower Germany)
- the Danube *Limes* (western section comprising Germany, Austria, Hungary and Slovakia, with a proposed eastern extension to Croatia, Serbia, Bulgaria and Romania)
- the Dacian *Limes* in Romania.

Although the report contained suggestions for the Middle East and North Africa, it was recognised that further discussions would need to take place with representatives from those countries to enable this to progress.

New Frontiers of the Roman Empire World Heritage properties

Several of the countries in the western part of the Danube *Limes* had been making good progress towards nomination, with consideration of site selection and meeting the necessary UNESCO criteria to argue for their Outstanding Universal Value (OUV – the reason for a site's inscription on the list). World Heritage sites are of outstanding value to humanity, regardless of current geopolitical borders.

Yet the significance of modern geopolitical borders cannot be overstated. By signing the World Heritage Convention (UNESCO 1972) and nominating sites, nation states are bound by the convention and its operational guidelines, and are expected to prioritise the conservation and management of World Heritage.

Four European countries in the western Danube were ready to submit their nomination together in 2017 (Germany (Bavaria), Austria, Slovakia and Hungary). This was duly submitted by the four state parties in early 2018 but complications over the Governor's Palace at *Aquincum* (Budapest) in Hungary led to a delay and deferral from the 2019 World Heritage Committee, when it was originally due to be formally considered. After discussion amongst the partners and with ICOMOS, it was resubmitted ready for consideration in 2020, but that World Heritage Committee was postponed due to the COVID-19 pandemic.

In the meantime, colleagues on the Lower German *Limes* in the Netherlands and Germany (Nordrhein-Westfalen) prepared their nomination and submitted it in early 2020 for consideration in 2021.

Due to the postponement of the 2020 World Heritage Committee, UNESCO ran an extended meeting in 2021 aimed at addressing the issues due for discussion in both 2020 and 2021. The Lower German *Limes* was successfully inscribed. The Danube *Limes* faced further complications with the relatively late withdrawal of Hungary from the nomination but, after further discussions within UNESCO's Committee, the remaining three countries in the western sector of the Danube *Limes* (Germany, Austria and Slovakia) were successful in getting the inscription agreed by the Committee.

Thus, as of July 2021, the World Heritage 'cluster', proposed in the nomination strategy (Ployer *et al.* 2017), had finally come into existence.

International cooperation

'*Since wars begin in the minds of men, it is in the minds of men that the defences of peace must be constructed.*' (UNESCO 1945)

The founding principles of UNESCO are to build peace through international cooperation in education, science and culture. Whilst it is a tough sell to suggest that archaeological collaboration on a frontier almost 2,000 years old will build world peace, the soft power that connecting nations does bring through their heritage should not be undervalued. It is those connections that bind us in the past as well as in the present. It was through the determination of some key scholars and heritage managers in the early 21st century that we have now successfully managed to create a tri-partite World Heritage property stretching across five countries in Europe. A further five European countries are actively working on nominations. There were some discussions with Jordan in the mid-2000s and Tunisia placed its Roman frontier on the tentative list in 2012. But since 2019, there has been a series of discussions with various countries in the Middle East and North Africa on developing FRE nominations.

Ironically, the developments of the COVID-19 pandemic, whilst blocking in-person contact, normalised the process of online discussions, enabling an initiative by the Austrian Ambassador to UNESCO to bring together UNESCO Ambassadors in eight countries across the Middle East and North Africa into workshops with European heritage professionals. This is a developing area of cooperation that promises much for the future, together with partners in eastern Europe progressing their nominations.

In many ways, the thread that hangs the three currently inscribed FRE sites together is our colleagues in Germany, who now manage parts of all three. Yet the whole process has been a collaborative effort requiring support at all levels, from those managing the sites daily on the ground, through to support at a governmental level in the partner countries, putting forward the nominations and recognising the support required to maintain them. In some countries, being part of that wider international community has aided archaeologists and cultural heritage managers to be able to sell the concept to their national politicians. Whilst those of us working with the FRE concept were disappointed that we were no longer working towards a single FRE site encompassing the whole Roman frontier, by finding a practical solution, the shared vision has been able to progress, and we are now working out how to manage this cluster in the future.

Given the international cooperation enshrined in UNESCO, and the desire to conserve our global heritage together, it is perhaps slightly ironic that the earlier changes in the rules made that international cooperation harder to achieve for the FRE partners.

It is these barriers that are perhaps one reason why over 96% of sites on the World Heritage list are situated in one country alone. These sites may not need to draw on international expertise to maintain and conserve their properties, yet surely it is the transboundary sites (fewer than 4% on the list) that actively encourage and, indeed, require, international cooperation in their conservation. One of the most ambitious, the Ancient and Primeval Beech Forests of the Carpathians and other reaches of Europe, has sites in 18 countries across Europe[3]. The architectural work of Le Corbusier, an Outstanding Contribution to the Modern Movement, has buildings in seven countries across three continents.[4]

It is these transboundary sites, including the FRE, which are centred in international cooperation. The FRE itself is an ambitious aspiration which is now being realised. With the creation of the two further FRE properties in 2021, the first World Heritage 'cluster' was created. Others are likely to follow, including the Silk Roads, with one inscribed in 2014 (the Routes Network of Chang'an-Tiansham Corridor)[5] but many more on national tentative lists.

'[the Cluster] will enable us to expand from individual sites and properties to an overarching European monument, which may grow to include parts from other continents in the future.' (Ployer *et al.* 2017: 107)

The future

Whilst the pandemic events of 2020-2021 have taught us just how unexpected the future can be, so they have also shone a light on how interconnected our world is. They have also taught us to adopt new ways of working, including online interactions to replace face-to-face meetings. In an international context, our technological connectivity enables closer collaborative working, as partners who perhaps used to meet annually to discuss shared challenges and opportunities are now able to do so more frequently, with meetings only requiring a few hours out of the working day, rather than the expense and time of travelling across Europe. Whilst nothing replaces being able to meet in person, and the informal networking those events present, online working enables more frequent interaction.

It is through this more frequent meeting that we will be able to progress our management structures for the new FRE 'cluster' and enable everything from UNESCO's periodic reporting cycle (a conservation monitoring mechanism) to pushing forward with ideas for funding.

The initial EU's Culture 2000 grant for the partners in the FRE initiative (Breeze and Jilek 2008) enabled connections, networks and partnerships to form, and was the start of several different European funding initiatives enabling multi-country cooperation on our shared vision for the FRE World Heritage property. Despite having to split our WHS into multiple 'properties' on UNESCO's list, we can be confident that we are working together on the single largest cultural World Heritage monument in Europe. This 'togetherness' is supported by the production of a series of multi-language books on Roman frontiers, now nearing its complete encirclement of the empire, thereby emphasising the one-ness of the FRE cluster and the role of Roman frontiers in defining the Roman Empire.[6]

---

[3] <https://whc.unesco.org/en/list/1133>
[4] <https://whc.unesco.org/en/list/1321>
[5] <https://whc.unesco.org/en/list/1442>
[6] Available online at <https://www.univie.ac.at/limes/html/brochure.php>

Yet, challenges as well as opportunities remain: Brexit has reduced opportunities for European funding for the UK partners; cultural heritage managers frequently have to conform to the whim of their political masters, given that World Heritage applications are endorsed by national governments; the COVID-19 pandemic had a huge financial impact on sites which relied heavily on tourism for their income; and the climate emergency will present a very real and present threat to the fragile remains of 1900-year-old monuments.

But, to quote Benjamin Franklin, 'out of adversity comes opportunity'. The move to online working has created more frequent opportunities to collaborate and has opened avenues for working with potential new Roman frontiers partners in the Middle East and North Africa. Using technology to connect now, our heritage is interconnected the length and breadth of the Roman Empire; Roman soldiers and their families and followers moved across large distances and left documentary and archaeological traces. Scholars are therefore required to understand this larger international picture in order to appreciate the remains – sites, artefacts and ecofacts – in their own countries. Research areas have expanded in recent decades from a focus on the interpretation of individual

Figure 4: The new Roman head sculpture – Silvanus – created at Nethercroy through the Rediscovering the Antonine Wall project (2020-2021) and winner in the Outdoor Category of the Association for Heritage Interpretation awards, 2021. © Historic Environment Scotland

Figure 5: Domvs Scientiarvm, reconstructed Roman villa at Viminacium, Serbia (taken in 2018)

sites/frontiers and groups of artefacts through to the purposes of frontiers, frontiers in their landscape settings, identity and ethnicity, women on frontiers, religion, supply, and food and drink. Roman frontiers' specialists meet approximately every three years for a major international congress where new research is presented and discussed. This is known as the *Limes* Congress, or the Congress of Roman Frontier Studies.

To be able to present our spectacular monuments to the public and use them for educational and societal benefit, we must continue to understand them, through research and collaboration, and to care for and conserve them, in line with international best practice and through learning from each other.

To cite an example from Hadrian's Wall's northern neighbour, the Antonine Wall, recent projects have looked at making Roman heritage more relevant and using it for regeneration activities including contemporary Roman-inspired sculpture (Figure 4) and Roman-themed playparks (Jones 2021; Weeks 2020). We are not alone in these ideas, with imaginative ways of interpretation recorded across the Empire, from the use of digital technologies (e.g. Dobat 2020), YouTube presentations (for example, those prepared by the Roman Army EU collective in Spain) through to physical reconstructions, such as the spectacular reconstructed Roman villa and fort at Viminacium in Serbia (Figure 5). For Hadrian's Wall, novel forms of museum interpretation have been discussed in Chapter 5 by Birley and Griffiths. The re-enactors and living history practitioners' point of view was expressed by Brown and Robson in Chapter 12, and the use of digital technologies to aid interpretation, including game design and the 3D printing of collections, were discussed by Stocks and Birley in Chapter 10 and Hackenbroich and Williams in Chapter 4 respectively.

All contributors to this publication love the Wall, and the frontiers of the Roman Empire, with a passion. We are rightly proud of our ambitious FRE World Heritage project, which has now been running for some 20 years and owes its genesis to the original inscription of Hadrian's Wall in 1987. So in this final chapter, and in these final words, the international partners wish all those working on Hadrian's Wall a very happy 1900th birthday. We endeavour to work hard to continue our international cooperation to ensure that our sites can celebrate their second millennia in the future.

Acknowledgements

I am grateful to Marta and Katie for inviting me to write this overview of the FRE as we look to the future. I'd like to thank David Breeze for commenting on an earlier draft of the text, and also to honour the late Sebastian Sommer, who did so much to push forward the vision for the FRE 'cluster'.

Bibliography

Breeze, D.J. and Jilek, S. (eds) 2008. *Frontiers of the Roman Empire: The European Dimension of a World Heritage Site*. Edinburgh: Historic Scotland.

Breeze, D.J. and Jones, R.H. 2020. The Frontiers of the Roman Empire World Heritage Site, in Tončinič, D., Kaič, I., Matijevič, V. and Vuko, M. (eds) *Studia honoraria archaeologica. Zbornik radova u prigodi 65. rođendana prof. dr. sc. Mirjane Sanader*: 63-70. Vienna: Phoibos Verlag.

Breeze, D.J. and Young, C. 2008. Frontiers of the Roman Empire World Heritage Site. Summary Nomination Statement, in Breeze, D.J. and Jilek, S. (eds) 2008. *Frontiers of the Roman Empire: The European Dimension of a World Heritage Site*: 29-35. Edinburgh: Historic Scotland.

Dobat, E. 2020. Connecting museums and sites. Advanced Limes Applications – a Creative Europe project, in Breeze, D.J. and Hanson, W.S. (eds) 2021. *The Antonine Wall. Papers in honour of Professor Lawrence Keppie*: 448-454. Oxford: Archaeopress.

Jilek, S. 2008. The role of the Bratislava Group, in Breeze, D.J. and Jilek, S. (eds) 2008. *Frontiers of the Roman Empire: The European Dimension of a World Heritage Site*: 200-203. Edinburgh: Historic Scotland.

Jones, R.H. 2021. What Divides us also Connects us: Roman Frontiers, World Heritage and Community. *Journal of the Historic Environment Policy and Practice* 12.2: 120-145.

Jones, R.H., Macinnes, L. and Thiel, A. 2021. Frontiers of the Roman Empire: creating a transboundary World Heritage property. *Bericht der Bayerischen Bodendenkmalpflege* 62: 603-610

Ployer, R. Polak, M, Schmidt, R. 2017. *The Frontiers of the Roman Empire: a Thematic Study and Proposal World Heritage Nomination Strategy*. Vienna: Phoibos Verlag

UNESCO 1945. UNESCO Constitution. United Nations Educational, Scientific and Cultural Organization. Accessed 18 November 2021 <http://portal.unesco.org/en/ev.php-URL_ID=15244&URL_DO=DO_TOPIC&URL_SECTION=201.html>

UNESCO 1972. Convention Concerning the Protection of World Cultural and Natural Heritage. UNESCO World Heritage Centre – The World Heritage Convention. Accessed 18 November 2021 <https://whc.unesco.org/en/conventiontext/>

UNESCO 1994. Global Strategy. United Nations Educational, Scientific and Cultural Organization. Accessed 18 November 2021 <https://whc.unesco.org/archive/global94.htm>

UNESCO 2010. World Heritage Committee, Thirty-fourth Session, Item 9B. WHC-10/34. COM/9B. Report on serial nominations and properties. Accessed 18 November 2021 <https://whc.unesco.org/archive/2010/whc10-34Com-9Be.pdf>

UNESCO 2017. World Heritage Committee, Forty-first Session, WHC/17/41.COM 8B.50 Decisions adopted during the 41st session of the World Heritage Committee (Krakow, 2017). Accessed 18 November 2021 <https://whc.unesco.org/archive/2017/whc17-41com-18-en.pdf>

UNESCO 2019. Transboundary cooperation for conservation of World Heritage – a global view. Expert meeting 304 June 2019 Maun, Botswana. Paris: UNESCO

UNESCO 2022a. World Heritage. United Nations Educational, Scientific and Cultural Organization. Accessed 18 November 2021 <https://whc.unesco.org/en/about/>

UNESCO 2022b. The World Heritage Convention: Benefits of Ratification. United Nations Educational, Scientific and Cultural Organization. Accessed 18 November 2021 <https://whc.unesco.org/en/convention/>

Weeks, P. 2020. The Antonine Wall as a World Heritage Site: People, priorities and playparks, in Breeze, D.J. and Hanson, W.S. (eds) 2021. *The Antonine Wall. Papers in honour of Professor Lawrence Keppie*: 455-462. Oxford: Archaeopress

Williams, T. 2014. The Silk Roads: an ICOMOS Thematic Study. France: ICOMOS

Hadrian's Wall: exploring its past to protect its future

Marta Alberti (Vindolanda Trust) and
Katie Mountain (Pre-Construct Archaeology)

This volume is one of several published works exploring Hadrian's Wall as a cultural resource and discussing strategies for its management. Predecessors include the volume by Stone and Brough (2014) on using, managing, and interpreting the Wall. Further studies on interpretation both of the Wall and of the wider Frontiers of the Roman Empire World Heritage property can be seen in Breeze (2019) and Mills (2022). The political complexities of managing the Wall have been the subject of numerous academic papers (for example Bell 2013 and Mason et al. 2003) and practical guidelines, such as the editions of the Hadrian's Wall Management Plans, which have been overseen by the various guises of the Hadrian's Wall Partnership. This volume aims to differ from the others: it looks ahead at the challenges and opportunities faced by Hadrian's Wall, and is firmly rooted in archaeological research, building on the foundations of Hadrian's Wall Research Framework (Symonds and Mason 2009). We have also aimed to keep the tone and language of our writing accessible, rather than targeting specifically Hadrian's Wall heritage professionals.

When approaching the tasks of editing this book, from asking contributors for their input to organising papers thematically, we keenly understood the need for a new and forward-looking perspective. This view was shared by us, the editors, and the authors of the individual papers. Through years of living and working in the shadow of the Wall, we understood how the weight of scholarly work risks creating a bird's-eye view of the monument. We also appreciated how archaeological heritage professionals had often focused (or been pushed to limit their focus) on purely archaeological matters, rather than getting involved in issues of cultural resource management. Such disconnect between archaeological research and heritage management, as well as reliance on the bird's-eye view, often result in the finer and important details being missed, not least the daily struggles at the foundations of our knowledge. This volume, presented to mark Hadrian's Wall 1900th anniversary, challenged the authors and editors to return to those foundations and look at the practical and everyday experiences of working with and facing the future of the Wall.

With this volume we wished to explore the themes that have come to the forefront of Hadrian's Wall cultural resource management over the last 10 years. Such themes will only become more crucial for the future maintenance and protection of the World Heritage Site. They range from the impact of climate change on archaeological remains, to the role of technology and digital resources in reaching new audiences, to the continued importance of a 'Wall tourism' approach that needs to be both sustainable for the environment and fulfilling for the visitor.

To ensure a multivocality that reflects the multi-faceted nature of Hadrian's Wall, the volume approached a range of authors from prominent to early career scholars and practitioners. Significantly, these contributors are drawn from different professions and backgrounds. Academics, excavators, museum curators, living history practitioners, tour guides, walkers, trail managers and business owners all play a daily and vital role in constructing, re-constructing, and maintaining the foundations of knowledge required to manage the past, present, and future of Hadrian's Wall.

Threading the themes

Just like the various tangible remains that compose Hadrian's Wall, the themes that emerge from each contribution are best understood in relation to one another. Their clear identification (**in bold** below) is important so that they can be recognised and addressed in future work.

First, it is clear that **new threats and challenges** (or radicalisation of old ones) have emerged in conserving, managing, and researching both the buried and exposed remains of the Wall. To overcome such issues, **new methods** have emerged over the past 10 years. For example, the combined geoarchaeological approaches to site management and the use of 3D imaging in collection management are increasingly employed to both understand and interpret the archaeology of the Wall. These techniques are frequently being used to support methods such as geophysical survey, which has continued to be employed as the practices and technologies around this have been refined and its theoretical underpinning consolidated.

Second, the **generation of new knowledge through research affects interpretation** of both the Wall's archaeological remains and its impressive collections. Hadrian's Wall studies already benefit from a large set of diverse material culture, and this body of data grows with each passing year, generating a wealth of often contradictory interpretations. For such an ancient monument, the management and interpretation of the Wall suffers from the very modern difficulties around information-related issues. For example, a great deal of the available data from the Wall is difficult to access, lacking an open-access digital format and requiring in-person visits to archives and stores, or a specialist library. The methods surrounding data collection and curation have varied greatly through the years with fluctuations in quantity and quality. Wall curators, archaeologists, and heritage managers face the often daunting challenge to put such a large repository of data to good use, not only by generating new knowledge through research, but also by providing those who wish to research or simply visit the Wall with a coherent, multiple-perspective interpretation. Such interpretation needs to encompass not only individual sites, but their wider relationship with the Northern Frontier and the Frontiers of the Roman Empire.

Third, the successes and challenges of **making information available in digital format** are identified by a number of contributors to this book. Access to data and the format it can be presented in have a direct impact on the understanding (both present and future) of those who interact with the archaeology of the Wall. Compared to 10 years ago, millions more people have access to mobile technology, which offers challenges and opportunities in equal measure to the flow of information from the Wall. Such technological advances open a world of possibilities: people who live thousands of miles away from the Wall can attend an online course dedicated to it, and younger generations who have never visited a Roman site can immerse themselves in one through a mobile or computer game. Over the past decade, Hadrian's Wall has become more global than ever before.

Finally, from the far distances of worldwide audiences we must balance the challenges and opportunities that remain by **listening to local concerns**. These include issues raised by those who maintain and manage the varied natural landscapes along the Wall , as well as challenges faced and posed by the walkers who explore them. This volume includes the vital voices and experiences of re-enactors and business owners who make their living recreating past life on the Wall. Local concerns are imbued by the issue of sustainability, not least with regards to the natural environment, but also in terms of access to knowledge. Authors have highlighted the difficulties in reconciling environmentally sustainable tourism with inclusive tourism, and in popularising a traditionally academic subject whilst respecting the environment surrounding the Wall.

Overall, the main themes of this volume are threaded by inter-connectivity and multiple perspectives. Efforts to 'unify' the Wall, and to place it in the international context of the Frontiers of the Roman Empire World Heritage property, have considered the diverse nature of its sites and collections, as well as the themes the monument shares with the wider frontier network. And yet, perhaps in an attempt to make the Wall more appealing and easier to understand, archaeological heritage professionals can sometimes gloss over complexities in favour of more utilitarian and 'definitive' interpretations. This volume does not avoid the complexities and contradictions where they occur, and does not shy away from the challenges that lie in the future for Hadrian's Wall.

Lessons learned

Because of the multiple perspectives involved in producing this book, the strength of the volume is not limited to a linear or simple set of conclusions. There are, however, some important lessons that we - editors and authors alike - have learned.

The first is that although there is a rich and detailed amount of information about the Wall, its component parts and the lives of the communities who lived (and live) alongside it, we remain some distance from 'resolving' all its uncertainties. Most importantly, archaeology and heritage professionals on the Wall are increasingly comfortable with the reality that simple and single narratives may never be enough to solve any of the issues faced by the future management of the monument.

Our second conclusion is that, despite the vast quantity of evidence, both in the form of architectural remains and material culture, one cannot simply assume that the Wall is 'safe' and that no further action is needed other than studying what we already have. In this volume's opening paper, Breeze uses a summary of past exploration, excavation, and research to argue how valuable a cultural resource the Wall is, how much remains to be learned about it, and how dangerous it is to rest on past glories. New challenges are constantly emerging. The effects of climate change and the related issues of riverine and coastal erosion contribute to challenge the assumption that what is yet to be excavated is implicitly kept safe for generations to come (Birley and O'Meara; Wilmott, this volume). Both professionals and visitors to heritage sites must constantly review their actions in the light of the latest available scientific data. This includes, for example, the careful management and use of the National Trail (Pickles, McGlade and Richards, this volume). The Wall has always attracted visitors, and tourism can be a lifeline to communities and businesses who live and operate along it today. But as tourism can be volatile and susceptible to external pressures, there is a clear need for more sustainable and accessible options, along with collaborative actions from all the institutions, landowners, and visitors. We all have a responsibility to protect the Wall and its environment - a message we keenly wanted to be seen throughout this volume. The future thus might involve looking at innovative ways of displaying sites and finds - an example from the German *Limes* (Pausch, this volume) offers an environmentally conscious alternative to traditional site excavation and consolidation.

Our third conclusion is that interpretation remains a key issue, not only for Hadrian's Wall structures, but also for the collections of artefacts that represent the peoples and cultures of the Wall. The latter must now be recognised, as a matter of priority, as an integral part of the World Heritage property. Hadrian's Wall collections are presented and interpreted the way they are because of the choices that heritage professionals made about what to display and how. These choices were influenced by time, theory, context, and the contemporary ethics of their collection and display - all factors that are different today from what they were 10 years ago. Today's scholars can view some of the Wall's collections through digital means, further opening the Wall to the world and enabling yet more research. Such expansion raises the ethical questions of the ownership of digital information. Curators on the Wall have acquired a new duty, often with little recognition or support: to protect the Wall's physical and digital collections for the future, while making them ever more widely accessible (Hackenbroich and Williams, this volume). Collection accessibility can, however, become a desirable but cumbersome add-on to the already stretched curatorial figures, who must contend with vast backlogs of materials deposited by commercial archaeology units, and strategic defunding of the sector (McIntosh and Price, this volume).

Our fourth and final conclusion is that there is still room for improvement in the way in which all components of the World Heritage property work together. This is on a local level, as well as nationally and internationally. On one hand, we are delighted to have representatives of all the major heritage institutions managing sites along the Wall sharing their plans for visitor engagement and education going forward (Woodward et al., this volume). On the other hand, we learned how re-enactors - who frequently share their passion, skills, and knowledge through interactive displays and events - feel that their contribution to the interpretation of life on the Wall could be improved by better communication with heritage professionals, and by the introduction of standards of accuracy and service (Brown and Robson, this volume).

Visitors to Hadrian's Wall have a great deal of options when it comes to the sites and collections to learn about life in the frontier. There is also a lot of choice about how to access resources: large strides have been taken in the innovative ways we can teach and share knowledge, including the success of online courses (Collins, this volume), as well as family-friendly and fun games (Stocks and Birley, this volume). Each site must, then, carefully pitch the presentation of its evidence at different levels and facets of knowledge (Birley and Griffiths, this volume), complementing rather than competing. Although there are many ways to interpret the Wall, with the numerous stakeholders involved all dealing with differing environments, locations, and facilities, all the strategies can work together to create a meaningful experience for visitors as well as reaching out to new and more diverse audiences and reflecting the key issues of today, and of tomorrow.

Missing perspectives

The editors of this volume have consciously been as inclusive as possible when pulling together perspectives on researching, managing, and protecting the Wall. Nonetheless, many more organisations and individuals than those represented here hold a stake in its future.

For example, developer-funded commercial archaeology projects take place almost daily in the Wall's buffer zone and its surroundings. The data they generate plays an important role in adding to the growing pool of Wall knowledge and can be made available - at a cost to the developer - to the public through the Archaeology Data Service (ADS) website. Printed publications of excavations in the form of papers and monographs require even more time and money, and some discoveries might be bound by confidentiality until the full developer process has been finalised. As a result, in a world where information is more widely available and shared than ever before, data from commercial projects are still woefully underrepresented in academic literature, mirroring a division between two worlds that yet stand to be reconciled (Weekes et al. 2019).

One area where the borders between these two worlds seems more permeable is that of archaeological and historical Societies, whose membership embraces academics, professional archaeologists and other interested parties. Ever since their foundation, the Society of Antiquaries of Newcastle upon Tyne (SANT) and the Cumberland and Westmorland Antiquarian and Archaeological Society (CWASS) have held a special relationship with the Wall. The Newcastle Antiquaries' journal, *Archaeologia Aeliana*, (which celebrates its 200th edition in 2022) and the Transactions of CWASS have long been the place of choice for publication of Hadrian's Wall research and both actively encourage and support papers from commercial, community, and research excavations. Every 10 years, the Societies come together to host the Hadrian's Wall Pilgrimage, a week-long tour of the Wall first held in 1849 by the pioneering Roman Wall scholar and author of the first handbook to the Wall (1851), John Collingwood Bruce. The tour attracts 'Wall pilgrims' from across the world, and to mark each pilgrimage a book is produced with an overview of Wall discoveries made in the previous 10 years (the latest edition by Collins and Symonds 2019). In recent decades, these Pilgrimage handbooks have sought to incorporate the discoveries of developer-funded archaeology, though limited by the formats of the publication.

Another important perspective missing from this volume – and from Hadrian's Wall research and management guidelines - is that of the hundreds of members of the interested public who, every year, offer their time and skill volunteering for/along the Wall (Weekes et al. 2019). The Wall's volunteer population includes, among others, excavators at Vindolanda, Hadrian's Wall condition monitors at various sites managed by Historic England, guides and students seeking to acquire the experience deemed necessary to gain employment in the sector. The debate on whether institution-led heritage volunteering is a cost-cutting manoeuvre and a form of exploitation or a legitimate form of public archaeology continues to keep archaeologists and heritage managers busy. All the while there remains a real and increasing passion for the Wall community to continue to expand and evolve through direct participation.

These missing perspectives present avenues for further study and also merge with this volume's learning points, which can guide us in finding directions for the future.

Directions for the future

This volume opened with Breeze asking, 'What is Hadrian's Wall?'. Through the voices of our contributors, we have explored its nature as a multi-faceted, complex monument, with many stories to tell. Both today and in the future, we have much to gain by including in cultural resource management those voices that have been previously overlooked. Re-enactors, archaeological researchers, curators, Trail managers, walkers and visitors, and those who work directly on the ground, hold crucial opinions and knowledge which can help to navigate the Wall's complexities and sound early alarm bells concerning issues that might arise in the future.

There are clear new pathways of collaboration between the professional institutions, the people living on, and walking along the Wall, and new communities to be reached both locally and worldwide. The way forward for the Wall, we believe, is to be open to such collaborations, especially international ones, rather than to fold into itself. There are undoubtedly challenges in managing a World Heritage property with so many institutions and stakeholders, but Hadrian's Wall also holds unparalleled opportunities for international cooperation, and sound management practices based on constant scientific advances and new research. This is exemplified by its unique role not only as part of a transboundary World Heritage property but one of what is now a network or 'cluster' of Frontiers of the Roman Empire World Heritage properties.

Management frameworks and guidelines are helpful, but cannot simply be applied top-down. This volume is our way of taking a step towards a 'ground-up' approach to managing Hadrian's Wall's cultural resources, which we believe will serve us well in exploring the monument's past to protect and secure its future.

Bibliography

Bell, V. R. 2013. 'The politics of managing a World Heritage Site: the complex case of Hadrian's Wall'. *Leisure Studies*. 32 (2), 115–132

Breeze, D. J. 2019. *Hadrian's Wall: A study in archaeological exploration and interpretation.* Oxford: Archaeopress

Bruce, J. C. 1851. *The Roman Wall,* Edition 1. Newcastle upon Tyne

Collins, R. and Symonds, M. F. A. 2019. *Hadrian's Wall 2009-2019. A Summary of Excavation and Research, prepared for The Fourteenth Pilgrimage of Hadrian's Wall, 20-28 July 2019.* Kendal: Titus Wilson

Stone, P. G. and Brough, D. 2014. *Managing, using, and interpreting Hadrian's Wall as World Heritage.* New York, NY: Springer

Symonds, M. F. A. and Mason, D.J. P. 2009. *Frontiers of Knowledge: a research framework for Hadrian's Wall - part of the Frontiers of the Roman Empire World Heritage Site; Vol. II, Agenda and Strategy.* Durham: Durham County Council

Mason, R., MacLean, M. and De la Torre, M. 2003. *Hadrian's Wall World Heritage Site. English Heritage, A case study.* Los Angeles: Getty Conservation Institute

Mills, N. 2021. *Visitor Experiences and Audiences for the Roman Frontiers: Developing good practice in presenting World Heritage.* London: BAR International Publishing

Weekes, J., Watson, S., Wallace, L., Mazzilli, F., Gardner, A. and Alberti, M. 2019. 'Alienation and Redemption: The Praxis of (Roman) Archaeology in Britain'. *Theoretical Roman Archaeology Journal.* 2(1), 1-17

Hadrian's Wall was first inscribed in the World Heritage Site UNESCO list in 1987. In 2005, the Frontiers of the Roman Empire World Heritage property was created as the Wall was joined by the Upper German Raetian Limes. In 2008, the trans-national Frontiers of the Roman Empire World Heritage property expanded again with the inclusion of the Antonine Wall. Tireless work continues in multiple countries to unite all Frontiers of the Roman Empire under the UNESCO banner. Photo courtesy of Savin Photographs.

Index

Hadrian's Wall is not indexed though its individual elements are